# Using Arabic

This is a guide to Arabic usage for students who have already acquired the basics of the language and wish to extend their knowledge. Focusing mainly on Modern Standard Arabic, it is divided into three clear sections on varieties of Arabic, grammar, and vocabulary. 'Varieties of Arabic' describes the linguistic situation in the Arab world, showing students variations in register through the use of authentic texts. The vocabulary section is designed not only to expand students' knowledge of Arabic words, but also to show them which words are most current, and which are appropriate to different registers. The final chapter provides an overview of Arabic grammar, giving many modern-day examples, and highlighting common errors. Clear, readable and easy to consult, *Using Arabic* will prove an invaluable reference for students seeking to improve their fluency and confidence in Arabic.

Mahdi Alosh is Associate Professor of Arabic in the Department of Near Eastern Languages and Cultures, Ohio State University. His previous publications include *Speak and Read Essential Arabic I (1991), Learner, Text and Context in Foreign Language Acquisition: An Arabic Perspective (1997)*, and *An Introduction to Modern Standard Arabic (2000)*.

# Companion titles to *Using Arabic*

*Further titles in preparation*

# Using Arabic

## A Guide to Contemporary Usage

MAHDI ALOSH

Associate Professor of Arabic, Ohio State University

CAMBRIDGE
UNIVERSITY PRESS

PUBLISHED BY THE PRESS SYNDICATE OF THE UNIVERSITY OF CAMBRIDGE
The Pitt Building, Trumpington Street, Cambridge CB2 1RP, United Kingdom

CAMBRIDGE UNIVERSITY PRESS
The Edinburgh Building, Cambridge, CB2 2RU, UK
40 West 20th Street, New York, NY 10011–4211, USA
477 Williamstown Road, Port Melbourne, VIC 3207, Australia
Ruiz de Alarcón 13, 28014 Madrid, Spain
Dock House, The Waterfront, Cape Town 8001, South Africa

http://www.cambridge.org

First published 2005

Printed in the United Kingdom at the University Press, Cambridge

Typeset by the author in Times

*A catalogue record for this book is available from the British Library*

ISBN 0 521 64832 7 paperback

# Contents

*Contents*

Contents

# Foreword

One of the goals of this book is to provide students of Arabic with knowledge about the components of the language and how they are actually used by Arabic speakers. It also provides information to advanced students and teachers on proper Arabic usage. This book has an unusual design. It is neither a reference grammar, nor a vocabulary list, nor is it a textbook. It is rather a practical guide to help students work their way through aspects of Arabic which pose the greatest difficulty for them.

It differs from textbooks in its scope. Instead of a focus on grammar solely, or on vocabulary, this book approaches Arabic as a complete whole, though with a focus on Modern Standard Arabic. It explains the linguistic situation in the target culture and describes the varieties of Arabic, showing through examples which variety is appropriate for which situation. It also presents a model representing levels of register. The focus, of the book however, is mainly on three important aspects of Arabic: (1) the sociolinguistic variables which determine the most appropriate ways of using the linguistic elements in order to understand and make oneself understood, (2) the building blocks of the language, or its vocabulary, and (3) the structure that holds the words together, or its grammar.

In addition, this book contains both the normative rules of use and a description of how Arabic is actually used by Arabs. This is a radical departure from the vast majority of conventional grammars and textbooks. The section on usage deals with common errors made by learners of Arabic and even by native speakers. The study of errors helps learners of Arabic who wish to approximate Register level 3 (see the section on Register) to gain access to a good selection of these items usually scattered in different books and articles.

This book is written with the assumption that the user has already acquired the basics of Arabic, including the writing system, the sound system, and the essentials of Arabic grammar along with a decent repertoire of high frequency lexical items. The material included herein will only add to what the users have and help them to ascertain the accuracy of their learning.

In the section on Arabic varieties, I have tried to provide a lucid description of the diglossic situation and stayed away from complicated linguistic terminology. The point is to lay out the linguistic situation in a clear, straightforward fashion and let the students make up their minds about the issues and which kind of language they wish to use.

This book contains material rarely found in textbooks, and if found, it would be scattered around. Categories such as names of people; towns; countries; organizations; geographical regions; historical eras; social, national, and religious events; technical terms; loan words; terms of address, brand names; currencies; distance; and weight are hard to find in a single source. Furthermore, idioms and proverbs are also included. Grammatical categories are laid out in the form of flow charts, tables, and graphs to help students grasp the total picture and make it easy for them to understand the details and locate the information they wish to check.

# Abbreviations and acronyms

| | |
|---|---|
| adj. | adjective |
| n. | noun |
| v. | verb |
| prep. | preposition |
| part. | particle |
| m. | masculine |
| f. | feminine |
| adv. | adverb |
| CA | Classical Arabic |
| MSA | Modern Standard Arabic |
| C | Colloquial Arabic |
| dem. | demonstrative |
| rel. | relative |
| p. | perfect, past |
| pr. | imperfect, present |
| ap. | active participle (اسم الفاعِل) |
| pp. | passive participle (اسم المفعول) |
| s.o. | someone |
| s.t. | something |

## Transliteration system

### Vowels

| | | |
|---|---|---|
| ا | ā | as in *dad* and *bar* |
| و | ū | as in *boot* |
| و | ō | as in French *beau* |
| ي | ī | as in *beet* |
| ﹷ | a | as in *but* |
| ﹹ | u | as in *put* |
| ﹻ | i | as in *bit* |
| ﹻ | e | as in *bet* |
| و | o | as in *beau*, but half as long |
| ﹷ | a | typically pronounced as a neutral vowel, between *schwa* and [e] |

### Consonants

| | | |
|---|---|---|
| ث | th | voiceless interdental, as in *thin* |
| ح | ḥ | voiceless, pharyngeal fricative |
| خ | ḵ | voiceless velar fricative, as in Scottish *loch* |
| ذ | ḏ | voiced interdental, as in *this* |
| ش | š | as in *ship* |
| ص | ṣ | emphatic, or pharyngealized /s/, as *sod* |
| ض | ḍ | emphatic, or pharyngealized /d/, as in *dull* |
| ط | ṭ | emphatic, or pharyngealized /t/, as in *Todd* |

| | | |
|---|---|---|
| ظ | D̲ | emphatic, or pharyngealized, interdental /d̲/ |
| ظ | ẓ | emphatic, or pharyngealized form of /z/ |
| ع | c | voiced, pharyngeal fricative |
| غ | ġ | roughly similar to the Parisian /r/ |
| ر | r | similar to the Spanish trilled /r/ |
| ج | j | as in *measure* |
| ج | dj | as in *judge* |
| ق | q | uvular stop, similar to /k/, but further back, as in *cut* |
| ء | ’ | glottal stop (not indicated in initial position when it is followed by a vowel) |

**Stress**

` placed right after the stressed syllable (e.g. *mad`rasa* versus *madrasa`* 'school')

# 1 Varieties of Arabic

## 1.1 What is Arabic?

The word 'Arabic' is an umbrella term that subsumes several varieties[1] of this language, which vary with region and situation. Learners of Arabic and those who wish to learn Arabic should be aware of all aspects of the linguistic situation so that they can make appropriate choices with regard to which variety they need to study and whether a single variety would be adequate for their purposes. Those who have already achieved a certain level of proficiency can benefit from this information in filling the gaps in their linguistic-cultural knowledge of Arabic. In addition, attaining an advanced level may not be possible without the ability to perform appropriately, using more than one variety, i.e., Modern Standard Arabic and one of the other Arabic varieties.

---

[1] The term 'variety' is used here to refer to a type of language that is used with a specific social distribution.

1

This book is focused on Modern Standard Arabic and how to use it correctly and develop it further. The first chapter deals with Arabic as a complete whole, including the colloquial end of the language continuum. With this background, the student of Arabic will have a better understanding of the linguistic situation in its entirety and will be able to assess his competence in relation to what he knows about it.[2]

## 1.2    Arabic diglossia

Arabic is one of a few language systems in the world that are characterized by the coexistence of two distinct varieties of the same language, used side by side in the same speech community, each having a set of specialized functions. Situational and contextual factors influence the choice of elements from either variety in a speech event. This phenomenon is known as diglossia. It was Charles Ferguson who stimulated interest in this linguistic situation and defined it in his classic article 'Diglossia', in *Word* (Ferguson 1959), although he was not the first one to use the term. Arabic diglossia, however, is not a recent linguistic development; it dates back to pre-Islamic times. Several aspects of diglossia were discussed in linguistic and literary treatises in the ninth century and have continued up to this day (Altoma, 1969).

There are basically two varieties: elevated and low. The elevated one may be called Classical Arabic (CA) or Modern Standard Arabic (MSA), the latter being the modern counterpart of CA, a term known and used in the West only. To Arabs, both are known as *al-fuṣḥā* الفـصـحى. They share almost the same syntax and morphology, but they exhibit differences in the areas of style

---

[2]  For convenience, 'he' will be used to refer to both genders.

and the lexicon. CA is the language of a vast body of Arabic literature, scholarly works, religious studies, the exegesis of the *Qur'ān*, the traditions of the Prophet Muhammad, and above all it is the language of the *Qur'ān*, the holy book of the Muslims. MSA is the language of scholarship, technology, school instruction, government offices, modern literature, the media, and almost all formal transactions and situations, including political speeches, and religious sermons in mosques and churches. It is learned mostly in school, but even the least educated person has a measure of comprehension of MSA. The pilot tests conducted for the Arabic adaptation of *Sesame Street* are a case in point. They revealed that listening comprehension scores among three- and four-year-olds of MSA texts were 65.5-91% in Pilot I. The research was conducted in four Arab capital cities (Alosh, 1984).

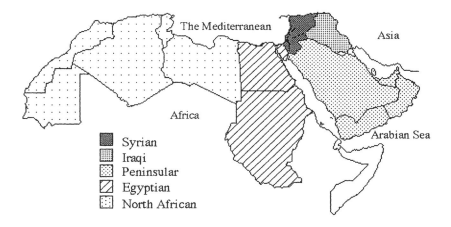

Figure 1. Major dialectal areas in the Arab world

MSA is fairly uniform throughout the Arab world; minimal variation is observed. Its rules are codified in grammar books and its lexicon contained in dictionaries. In this book, the concern is primarily with this variety, namely, MSA.

The other is the low variety known as Colloquial Arabic (C), to which Arabs refer as *al-ʿāmiyya* العامية or *ad-dārija* الدارجة. It is the language that is acquired natively and used for everyday, interpersonal, casual communication in the home and on the street. This variety is characterized by extreme variation throughout the Arab world, as exemplified in the numerous dialects. The map in Figure 1 shows the main five dialectal areas. It should be noted that each area contains multiple dialects. (See Alosh, 1997 for a detailed discussion.)

### 1.2.1 *Defining factors*

There are linguistic and non-linguistic factors that contribute to the existence and maintenance of a diglossic situation. In the case of Arabic the linguistic factors span the entire linguistic system. There are phonological, morphological, syntactic, and lexical features whose choice determines which variety is used. These will be discussed below in detail.

Non-linguistic factors are also involved in the perpetuation of diglossia. The most important factor in Arabic may well be religion. The word of God is believed to have been revealed to the Prophet Muhammad in what is known today as Classical Arabic. About 1.2 billion Muslims venerate Arabic because of its close association with the Qur'ān.

In addition to religion, Arab nationalism is another strong factor in perpetuating the diglossic situation. In the Symposium on the Arabic Language and the Media convened in Damascus in November 1998, the keynote speech of Zuheir Masharqa, Vice President of Syria, and almost all the presentations, associated MSA with Arab unity. Masharqa asserted that it is *the* fundamental principle of Arab nationalism (Masharqa

1998). He entrusted the media with the responsibility of promoting MSA and making it easier for all Arabs to acquire and use. The presentations abounded in repeated calls to preserve the purity of MSA, rid it of the common errors observed in the media, and restrain the use of colloquialisms in the media and advertising. Muhammad Salman (1998), Minister of Information, asserted the importance of the model set by President Assad by his insistence on using solely MSA in public functions. He added that Arabic (i.e. MSA) is a basic ingredient of the make-up of the individual's identity and of internal (i.e. Syrian) and national (i.e. pan-Arab) unity.

An attitudinal survey of faculty members at a Jordanian institution of higher education found enthusiasm toward MSA use and Arabization. The researcher concluded that communication across Arab countries would be difficult without MSA, which enjoys communal support and loyalty (Al-Abed Al-Haq 1998).

Another survey of subjects representing fourteen Arab countries found that they were satisfied with the diglossic situation and that it does not pose a problem (Al-Kahtany 1997). It also revealed a negative attitude toward standardization of a particular regional dialect. Even Syrian subjects rejected Kaye's (1970) proposition that Damascene Arabic be a standard dialect. Dweik (1997) also found no preference of any single variety to replace MSA.

MSA and CA preserve a huge legacy of literature and scholarship. Any proposals for reform or modification are summarily rejected for fear of cutting off the present generation and posterity from this legacy. Salha Sanqar, Minister of Higher Education in Syria, considers MSA the backbone of educational curricula (Sanqar 1998). Shaker Al-Faḥḥām (1998), President of the Arabic Academy, sees CA/MSA as the depository of the nation's literary and intellectual treasures and the link between the past and present. He regards the use of C in some satellite television broadcasts as a great danger, and calls for a firm stand against such practice.

MSA is the official language of more than 250 million Arabs in twenty-two countries which are members of the Arab League, and one of the official languages of the United Nations Organization. Additionally, the attitude of most Arabs toward MSA and C helps to maintain an active, strong role for MSA. The majority of people view MSA/CA with veneration and believe that it is a powerful, beautiful language. Competence in the elevated variety is a source of pride and an indication of a high level of education. Conversely, C is generally regarded with disdain, as the language of the illiterate and vulgar people. Some writers have expressed extreme views against C. Mubarak views it as inferior to or a deformed form of MSA (Mubarak 1970). Other Arab writers have an even harsher characterization of C as a protégé of ignorance and imperialism (Nasif, 1957, p. 49) or as a form unworthy of being called a language (Hussein, 1944, p. 236). These and the preceding factors are counterbalanced by the role of C as the language of daily communication and the code which all Arabs use with facility and with no need for instruction, grammar books, or dictionaries. In fact, many native speakers take great pride in their first language, i.e., their dialect.

### 1.2.2   *A dichotomy or a continuum?*

Several linguists, particularly in the second half of the twentieth century, studied Arabic diglossia and attempted to propose models that can account for the extreme variation in language use. Ferguson characterized the situation as a binary one with a high variety and a low one, but he also mentioned that two or more varieties may be in use (1959). El-Hassan, in 1977, identified and described a variety he named Educated Spoken Arabic (ESA), and Mitchell recognized it and studied it as well (1980). Meiseles (1980) suggested that Oral Literary Arabic existed alongside ESA. Blanc (1960) and Badawi (1973) recognized five distinct levels of Arabic. These views may be represented diagrammatically as follows:

ARABIC

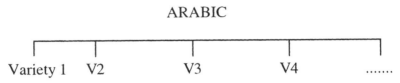

Figure 2. Arabic with a number of distinct varieties

Those varieties, or styles, are described by the above linguists mainly in terms of lexical and grammatical categories, not on the basis of the context of situation in which the language interaction is taking place. Three, four, or even five different levels are too restricted to account for the variability observed. In fact, there may be an infinite number of levels at which speakers are in a constant state of flux influenced by a host of sociocultural and sociolinguistic variables. Close observation of language behaviour among native speakers in a variety of situations does not support the compartmentalization of styles into discrete language varieties. It is quite rare to find a sustained stretch of discourse in one variety, unless it is prepared. Speakers continuously vacillate among different levels, depending on sociolinguistic variables. As Parkinson rightly observes, 'Naming and carefully defining distinct intermediate styles ... has a tendency to reify that style and give it an independent existence which it may not have for native speakers who apparently have no category for thinking and talking about it, and whose behavior simply may not be so consistent as to warrant a named style' (1991:37).

Alternatively, the different models, styles, levels, varieties, or whatever they may be called may fall on a language continuum with a range from MSA to the most local C. This is not a new idea. Meiseles mentions it, but he neither elaborates on it nor relates it to sociolinguistic factors which determine selection of language forms. This dynamic model that I suggest for Arabic may be represented in the following diagram (Alosh 1991 and 1997 for more details).

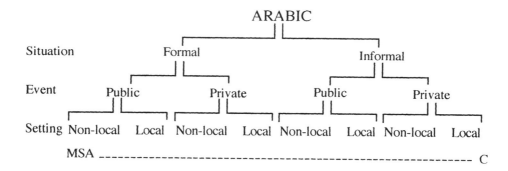

Figure 3. Arabic language continuum

The various combinations of situation, event, and setting, along with other variables, such as gender, age, social status, topic, and so forth, when added to the equation, affects language performance and the distinctions of the MSA/C 'mix' grow finer and finer. No single description can possibly be used alone to characterize an entire language interaction; several may be needed.

In sum, there are certain characteristics which can distinguish MSA from C. They may be summarized in the table below.

| MSA | C |
|---|---|
| Learned primarily by school instruction | Acquired naturally as a mother tongue |
| Used in formal situations | Used for casual, everyday communication |
| Mostly written | Oral use |
| Almost uniform throughout the Arab world | Great variation across dialects at all levels |
| Prestigious and esteemed by its speakers | No prestige associated with its use |
| Complex grammar | Simple grammar (no cases) |
| Official language | Language of the common people (not codified) |
| Closed to borrowing from other languages | Open to loan words |
| A dictionary and grammar are needed in order to learn it | Its use requires no dictionary or grammar |

Table 1. Characteristics of MSA and C

### 1.2.3 *Constraints on use*

There are some supralinguistic, sociocultural, and sociolinguistic factors that constrain language use and make speakers use certain forms rather than others. Among these are the age, gender, place of origin, socioeconomic status, and level of education of the interlocutor, as well as the topic of interaction, the purpose or message, and, most significantly, the situation which determines the formality level.

For example, it is more likely than not, even in C, for a younger speaker to use plural forms to address an older, more respected individual. A student might say to a teacher, 'عنوانكم، عنوان حضرتكم/ سيـادتكمْ' 'your address'. Some speakers are able to modify their speech when talking to an individual from another dialectal area by changing certain sounds they feel are stigmatized or certain lexical items deemed too local.

So, someone who has *garīb* 'near' in his repertoire, might, in an urban setting in Greater Syria or Egypt, use *'arīb* if he is talking to a city dweller. Level of education and profession have a significant impact on the choice of language. You may hear the same language function expressed in two vastly different ways when used by speakers from two different socioeconomic strata or belonging to two different professions. A teacher, for instance, trying to make his way in a very crowded place might say in C pronunciation:

١ـ اسمَحْلي / عفواً / عَدَم المُؤاخَزة !excuse me

whereas a porter or a young apprentice in a manual profession might say, in a similar situation,

٢ـ اوعَ ضَهْرَك! / دير بالك! mind your back/watch out!

The forms used in example 1 are polite expressions influenced by MSA. The first and third instances are pronounced, however, according to C conventions, where the two words اسـمح and لي are merged together, [ḍ] is pronounced [z], and final [a] is [e]. On the other hand, the forms in 2 are entirely in C, in terms of pronunciation and word choice.

Two educated individuals talking privately in a local setting are more likely than not to use C even if they are educated. But if the topic is intellectually set at an elevated level, many MSA terms find their way into their speech naturally. A few selected examples of such terms include the following listed below, pronounced according to MSA rules. Several of them, overheard by the author, were said by adults and school children:

خطة تنمية اقتصادية 'economic development plan'
تضخُّم مالي/اقتصادي 'monetary/economic inflation'

خطاب التنصيب 'inaugural address'

الإصلاح الزراعي 'agrarian reform'

قانون من أينَ لكَ هذا 'corruption law'

الغزو الثقافي 'cultural invasion'

قواعد اللغة 'the grammar of the language'

الفن الانطباعي 'impressionistic art'

رُوّاد الأدب الحديث 'pioneers of modern literature'

هـاتف خَلَوي 'cellular phone'

غرفة الحاسوب 'computer room'

القَنَوات الفضائية 'satellite channels'

الترفيع الآلي (in schools) 'automatic promotion'

ذهنِيَة التخلُّف 'mentality of backwardness'

نقاش عَقيم 'futile discussion'

انسِحاب جُزئي 'partial withdrawal'

تسوية سلمية 'peaceful settlement'

مُفاوَضات السلام 'peace negotiations'

Political speeches tend to be entirely in MSA. Nonetheless, popular leaders such as Jamal Abdul-Nasser of Egypt did slip into C when addressing the masses, perhaps to demonstrate solidarity. Other leaders, such as Hafez al-Assad of Syria, used MSA exclusively to convey a message, that of a pan-Arab orientation. Some people punctuate their speech in private speech events with MSA terms, or even considerable stretches of discourse, to project a particular image: sophisticated, accomplished, highly learned.

## 1.3   Diglossia versus bilingualism

Diglossia should not be confused with bilingualism or multilingualism. In bilingualism, two distinct languages, each with a complete spectrum of discourse levels, are used in the same speech community, whereas in diglossia, one of the two basic varieties of the same language specializes in one set of levels, and the other variety is allocated the other set. According to Ferguson (1959), specialization of function is the hallmark of diglossia. The high (MSA) and low (C) varieties are in complementary distribution; formal situations call for the use of MSA and informal, casual interaction requires C. Figure 4 contains a graphic representation of diglossia and bilingualism or multilingualism.

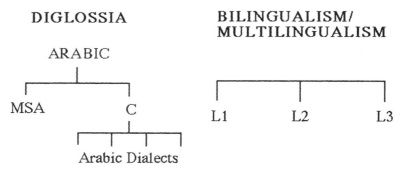

Figure 4. Representations of diglossia and bilingualism

Nor should diglossia be confused with the situation where there is one language and various dialects, such as in English, where every dialect has a complete register for all levels of formality. Figure 5 shows the difference schematically.

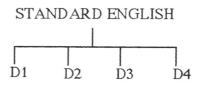

Figure 5. One language with dialects

### 1.3.1 *Language acquisition and learning*

In a bilingual community, the two languages may be acquired natively, as in the case of Spanish and English in some parts of the United States. However, in diglossia, only the low form is acquired natively; the high form is learned through school instruction. To Ferguson, the method of acquisition is an important defining factor of diglossia.

### 1.3.2 *Standardization*

The high form of Arabic (MSA/CA) has long been standardized. The first grammar was compiled by Abul-Aswad Al-Du'ali in the seventh century in Basra in southern Iraq and was refined shortly after by al-Khalil ibn Ahmad. In many old Arabic sources, the cited reason for the need to compile a grammar was the spread of linguistic errors among Arabs after increased contact with non-Arabs.[3] The new science was simply called *al-ᶜarabiyya* (Arabic), and it became known as *al-naḥw* (grammar, literally, 'way/method' ) only after a congratulatory remark made by the Caliph Ali to Al-Du'ali. He said, 'What a method you have followed!' Ali ibn Abi Talib, the fourth Caliph, was the first ruler to commission writing a grammar. Al-Du'ali is also credited with the pointing of Arabic letters, a reform measure that made Arabic orthography more precise and easier to read.

Many dictionaries were compiled over the centuries. In the nineteenth and twentieth centuries, specialized and bilingual dictionaries began to appear.

---

[3] Abu Saᶜd (1990) cites thirty-four major books on linguistic errors authored by outstanding scholars from the second to the tenth centuries of the Islamic calendar only (9th-16th of the common era).

An important step toward the universalization of MSA was the decision to use it in the media. All newspapers, magazines, and most radio and television broadcasts are in MSA. Soap operas and some talk shows are, however, broadcast in C. Interestingly, translated soap operas, such as Mexican productions, are dubbed in MSA, and they have scored huge popular success. In 1978, the decision to adapt *Sesame Street* into MSA had a huge impact on almost all children's television programs. Following the release of *iftaḥ yā simsim* (*Sesame Street*), most animated cartoons were translated into MSA.

### 1.3.3  *Arabization*

In the modern Arabic linguistic renaissance, which started in the nineteenth century, Arabization was perhaps the most important factor in standardizing MSA. Arabization (*at-taʿrīb*) is used in this section in two senses; a traditional, linguistic sense and in a social, modern sense.[4] The traditional meaning pertains to the process of making loan words fit into Arabic morphological patterns. That is, verbs conjugate like Arabic verbs and nouns decline and are pluralized according to Arabic conventions. The modern meaning involves the transfer of knowledge and learning to Arabic. This sense also includes using Arabic (MSA) in all aspects of life, such as education, communication, government offices, and in the intellectual domain. In addition, the effort of coining new words and terms in modern sciences is an important part of this process. Some researchers and editors have also equated Arabization with translation.

---

[4] It is interesting to note that Sibawayhi, an early grammarian, was the first to use the term *taʿrīb* 'Arabization'.

## 1.4    Register

When we learn our first language, we acquire the language system in addition to an implicit knowledge of how to use elements of the system appropriately. Unfortunately, a learner of Arabic as a foreign language might not have the opportunity to acquire such competence in the classroom. Only by learning, exposure, or conscious effort will he be able to do so. This ability is especially needed at an advanced level of proficiency. At such an advanced level, he should be able to appreciate the richness of the language, experience its entire spectrum, and be able to alternate along the language continuum, selecting different forms in order to interact orally with native speakers in authentic situations in an appropriate manner.

Arabic is mistakenly perceived as a homogeneous whole. Nonetheless, with a growing proficiency, the learner needs to be aware not only of the diglossic situation (i.e. C versus MSA) but also of levels of register and how to adjust his speech according to non-linguistic variables.

### 1.4.1    *Register versus diglossia*

Register is concerned with the relationship that exists between interlocutors, such as gender, socioeconomic status, and age. The choice of language elements can be made either from a single variety (e.g. plural forms versus singular to indicate respect) or from the high and low varieties. On the other hand, speech in a diglossic community requires selection of elements (e.g. phonological, lexical, and grammatical forms) from more than one variety; a situation where speakers switch back and forth between C and MSA, depending on such factors as situation (i.e. level of formality), medium (oral or written), message (purpose for choice), and role (e.g. chairman of the board or school principal in a meeting with subordinates). It should be noted that both C and MSA can have at least two levels of register each.

Samples from C are obtained either from an attested corpus I compiled for another study (Alosh 1997) or from Syrian Arabic with which I am familiar. C samples can easily be substituted with forms from the different Arabic dialects.

### 1.4.2   *Levels of register*

Register levels are not to be confused with the varieties of Arabic discussed above under Arabic diglossia. They may be arbitrarily divided into three: R1, R2, and R3. The lowest level, R1, is informal and casual. Although C forms may be used, MSA forms may also be used, but they are perceived by speakers as C. R2 is probably the level at which the language used is similar to the Arabic used in the spoken media. It is standard, educated speech, but pausal pronunciation may be utilized, where case and mood markers are dropped. R3 is the highest register level. It is very careful speech, official and formal, whether extemporaneous or prepared. It adheres strictly to the pronunciation and grammatical conventions of MSA and is characterized by low frequency word choice. Examples of it include political speeches, sermons, proceedings at a court of law, news broadcasts, and talk among Arabic specialists in a public, highly formal situation. Four main factors determine the level of register, namely, age, gender, status, and origin. Figure 6 depicts the relationship between Arabic varieties and register levels. It also shows the overlap between C and MSA at the R2 level.

Register     **R1**         **R2**         **R3**

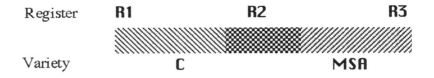

Variety           **C**          **MSA**

Figure 5. Relationship between register levels and varieties

In speech, register is marked at all linguistic levels, including the phonology, morphology, syntax, and lexicon. The lowest register level (R1) has many C forms and R2 represents a modified version of MSA, where all rules are observed except for inflectional endings and, in many cases, numbers. Language behaviour at the R3 level is exclusively in MSA. It must be noted that all linguistic levels are closely interrelated when choice is made in order to interact in a given speech event. The phonology, lexicon, and grammar may all be involved as the speaker proceeds along the three register levels, as this attested example demonstrates (Alosh 1997):

R2                    مجلسُ الإدارة بيُوافق عليها بعدَ إجراء تعديلات

*maglisu l-idāra bi-yuwāfiq ʿalayhā baʿda ijrā' taʿdīlāt.*

'the board of directors approves them after making modifications.'

This sentence is elicited from an Egyptian subject in a semi-formal situation, hence the designation of this sample as R2. Note the C/MSA overlap in the use of /g/ and /j/ in the same sample. It also contains C markers (e.g. the indicative b-prefix) and MSA markers (e.g. the inflectional endings in *maglisu* and *baʿda*). This sentence may hypothetically be rendered as follows at the R3 level:

R3                    يوافقُ عليها مجلسُ الإدارةِ بعد إجراء تعديلاتٍ.

*yuwāfiqu ʿalayhā majlisu l-idārati baʿda ijrāʾi taʿdīlātin.*

As we proceed to R3, C markers are lost, additional inflectional endings are used, and word order is involved.

### 1.4.3 *Diglossia-related variation*

At the phonological level, certain sounds in MSA in certain speech communities have cognates, or reflexes, that are used exclusively in C. For example, in most urban areas, excluding the peninsula, /q/ is pronounced /ʾ/. In rural Palestine, parts of Baghdad, southern Iraq, parts of southern Egypt, and Jewish dialects of Tlemcen and Oran in Algeria /q/ is pronounced /k/ (Sawaie, 1993).

Some lexical items are typically C, other typically MSA. At the morphological level, the future, the indicative, and the progressive aspects are marked by prefixes which are not used in MSA. Negation and the passive voice are also differently handled by the two varieties. Table 2 represents some phonological reflexes as well as morphological, syntactic, and lexical oppositions which characterize the C and MSA varieties.

|  | C | MSA |
|---|---|---|
| **Phonology** | /k/ in rural Palestinian | /q/ |
|  | /ʾ/ in some urban speech | /q/ |
|  | /tš/ in rural Palestinian, Gulf | /k/ |
|  | /z/ in many urban dialects | /ḏ/ |
|  | /d/ in many urban dialects | /ḍ/ |
|  | /s/ in many urban dialects | /ṯ/ |
|  | /t/ in many urban dialects | /ṯ/ |
|  | /q/ in Gulf Arabic | /ġ/ |

|  |  |  |
|---|---|---|
| **Morphology** | /y/ in Gulf Arabic | /j/ |
|  | /-e/ feminine marker | /-a/ |
|  | *b-* indicative marker | 0 |
|  | *ḥa-/raḥa-* future marker | *sa-* or *sawfa* |
|  | *ᶜam-* progressive marker | 0 |
|  | *-š* negative suffix | 0 |
|  | *-o* (bayto) possessive pro. | (*bayt*)-*uhu, -ahu, -ihi* |
|  | *-on* (bayton) possessive pro. | (*bayt*)-*uhum, -ahum, -ihim* |
|  |  | ('their house,' m., f.) |
|  | *-ēn* number marker | (*bayt*)-*ayn* |
|  | *illi* | *allatī, alladī, alladāni,* |
|  |  | *alladayni, allatāni, allatayni,* |
|  |  | *alladīna, allātī, allawātī* |
| **Syntax** | 0 case endings | *-a, -u, -i, -ayni, -āni, -un, -an,* |
|  |  | *-in, ūna, -īna* |
|  | *mū, miš* | *laysa+-an, ġayr +-in* |
|  | *mā* + present | *lā* + present verb |
|  | *mā*+past verb | *mā* + past verb |
|  | *mā*+past verb | *lam* + jussive |
|  | passive verbs: rare | verbs have passive forms |
|  | *šū* 'what' e.g. *šū ismak?* | *mā,* e.g. *mā-smuk?* (Egyptian, *ismak ēh?*) *What's your name?* |
|  | numbers are invariable. | numbers vary with number, gender, and case, e.g. *ḵamsatu kutubin* (m.) *ḵamsu sayyārātin* (f.) |
| **Lexicon** | word order: subject/verb | verb/subject |
|  | *rāḥ* 'to go' | *dahaba* |
|  | *šāf* 'to see' | *ra'ā* |
|  | *kamān* 'also, too' | *ayḍan* |
|  | *aywa/ēwa* 'yes' | *naᶜam, balā, ajal* |

| | |
|---|---|
| *bass* 'only' | *faqaṭ* |
| *kwayyes* 'good' | *jayyid, malīḥ, ḥasan* |
| *šway* 'little' | *qalīl* (min), *qalīlan* |
| *ᶜalašān* 'because (of)' | *li'anna* |
| *ᶜāyez / ᶜāwez* 'need, want' | *urīdu, aḥtāju* |
| *lissa* 'not yet' | *lam ... baᶜdu* |
| *wēn/fēn* 'where' | *ayna* |

Table 1. Diglossia-related oppositions

### 1.4.4   *Register-related lexical variation*

The identification and description of levels of register is a highly impressionistic, imprecise process. It depends largely on the knowledge on the part of the speaker of known linguistic features of C and MSA, and under which circumstances they may be selected. The speaker's knowledge of these distinctions is a function of his competence in MSA. The more education he has in MSA, the finer the distinctions among register levels are, particularly between R2 and R3. A less educated speaker might, hypothetically, vary his speech across register levels in this manner:

| R1 | R2 | R3 |
|---|---|---|
| *bākol ḥummoṣ* | *ākul ḥummoṣ* | |

'I eat hummus (dip made from chick peas)'

whereas a highly educated speaker might produce an utterance that observes inflectional endings and pronunciation fully.

| R1 | R2 | R3 |
|---|---|---|
| *bākol hommoṣ* | *ākul ḥummoṣ* | *ākulu ḥimmaṣan* |

Apparently, additional knowledge concerning the proper pronunciation of the word and the appropriate mood marker for the verb in MSA contributes to a better defined distinction between levels.

1.4.4.1 Age-related: As in all languages, there are certain words reserved for use with infants, toddlers, and young children. Obviously, these words are used in C only, that is, R1, although some of them are acceptable standard items. Some examples of baby talk common in Greater Syria and perhaps in other Arabic speech communities include the following:

*nēnne* 'food'     نِينّه

*mbū* 'water, want to drink'     مبو

*kək* 'dirty'     كَخْ

*daḥ* 'new, good'     دَح

*baḥ* 'all gone'     بَح

*tiš* 'go out'     تِش

*dādā* terms of address for brother and sister     دادا

*dādde* said when training/cajoling a toddler to walk     دادّه

*bābā* 'daddy'     بابا

*māmā* 'mom'     ماما

*aḥ* 'want to go to the bathroom'     أح

*oḥ* 'hot'     أح

*buʾ* 'fall down'     بُؤ

*yeᶜ* 'disgusting, repulsive'     يِع

*wāwā* 'injured, hurt, sick, this is painful'     واوا

*nūnū* 'small; potty, toilet, want to go to the bathroom'     نونو

*bubbūᶜ* 'baby'     بُبّو

*deddēᶜ* 'punishment; spanking'     ددّيه

*ḥāʾ* 'donkey or horse;' "Go!" to a donkey or horse'     حاء

*ʿaw* 'doggy'        عَوْ

*bibī`b* 'car'        بيب

*kūku* 'bird'        كوكو

1.4.4.2 Gender-related: Differences in usage between the two sexes may be phonological and lexical. Some women, for example, tend to de-pharyngealize emphatic sounds (e.g. *fakat* 'only' for *faqaṭ*. In addition, certain expressions are typically either feminine (e.g. *yaʿlē`* يعليه 'he's awful; I hate him' and *arīḍa* أريضة 'expressing consternation, displeasure') or masculine (e.g., *ʿarṣ* عـــرص 'pimp; person of low moral character; with no scruples') though it is observed some typically masculine forms are also used by some women.

Cursing, invocation of harm to come upon someone; vulgarisms; profanities; obscenities; and expletives are features of the lowest register level in C. Some males use sexually explicit vulgarisms and other curse words with religious overtones (i.e. cursing the other person's religion, which is severely frowned upon). Women usually use invocations, some of which contain grotesque descriptions of horrible, deadly diseases afflicting their opponent (e.g. *yibʿatlo ḥemma* يبـعـتلو حمّى 'may he be struck with fever'; *yibʿatlo dā' is-sill* يبـعـتلو داء السلّ 'may he be struck with tuberculosis'). Even terms of endearment may have such grotesque expressions in Syria and Lebanon (e.g. تقبرني 'may you bury me' = I love you).

1.4.4.3 Status-related: A high level of education is a factor that enables speakers to perform appropriately at all register levels. Nevertheless, some speakers would refrain from using vulgarisms regardless of the situation. Alternatively, some people may punctuate their speech with MSA words and phrases, including set phrases, such as the following:

سِيّان 'alike, the same'

سَلِمَت يَداك 'May your hands be safe = Thank you'

الحَمدُ لله الذي لايُحمَدُ على مكروه سواه

'Thank God, the only one who is thanked for adversity.'

هداك الله 'May God guide you to the true faith.'

لا يُحتَمَل 'unbearable'

غَيْر شَرعي 'illegal'

(أكل، طعام) يُؤكَل 'delicious, elaborate (food, dish)'

الشيءُ بالشيءِ يُذكَر 'incidentally, in relation to the preceding'

1.4.4.4 Origin-related: The speech patterns of most people give them away in terms of their place of origin. Few people can mislead their interlocutor as to where they come from. This factor may affect register, but it is not a crucial one. It pertains to how certain sounds typical of a particular speech community are perceived in another speech community. They may be perceived as either prestige or stigmatized forms. In the latter situation, a speaker may be prompted to avoid using such sounds in a speech community whose majority does not use them. Phonological features, both segmental and supra-segmental, mark speech regionally. An elongated ultimate or penultimate vowel, for example, characterizes Damascene local speech (e.g. *hātā* 'give it to me,' *ketbōn* 'their books'), a stress on the final syllable distinguishes Cairene Arabic (e.g. *arbaʿa* as opposed to *arˋbaʿa* 'four'), the /ē/ vowel in lieu of /ā/ indicates Lebanese and other speech (e.g. *bēb* for *bāb* 'door'), and so forth.

1.4.4.5 The general lexicon: The lexicon is probably the least complex category for making clear distinctions among the three levels of register. As noted above, knowledge of MSA is crucial in maintaining performance at the R3 level. Note that most items listed under R1, though used by the common people in casual, informal situations and are perceived as part of the C repertoire, are in fact proper standard Arabic. Stylistically, however, they still belong on a lower register level because of the way they are perceived. These may be considered items shared between C and MSA.

An interesting observation concerning the lexicon is the use of a disproportionate amount of quadriliteral verbs in C. I have identified over 100 items, excluding those that are formed by duplication, such as كشكش، كركر، فسفس and derived quadriliteral verbs. Below is a sample of the verbs selected.

| | |
|---|---|
| زَحْلَط | 'to slide' |
| لَغْمَط | 'to smear' |
| طَرْبَش | 'to smash' |
| قَلْعَط | 'to soil, stain' |
| لَحْمَس | 'to caress' |

The following list of items illustrates register variation. Some of the items listed under R1 may be dialect forms, but the majority of them are either Standard forms or derived from a Standard form. They are normally used in colloquial speech. The distribution under R1, R2, and R3 is based on my own perception and judgement. Other native speakers might not agree with me.

| R1 | R2 | R3 | Meaning |
|---|---|---|---|
| اختشى | استَحى | خَجِلَ | to be ashamed |
| شَلَع | استَفْرَغ | تَقَيَّأ | to throw up |

| | | | |
|---|---|---|---|
| التَمَّ (القوم) | اجتَمَعَ | تَكَوَّفَ | to congregate |
| التَهى (عن) | انشَغَلَ | انصَرَفَ (إلى) | to be busy |
| الحَقني | أدركني | أغثني | Help me! |
| امبارح | البارِح | أَمسِ | yesterday |
| انبَسَطَ | فَرِحَ | سُرَّ | to be happy |
| انفَلَقَ | انْشَقَّ | تَصَدَّعَ | to split, crack |
| امَّحَقَ | اختَفى | زالَ | to perish |
| أواعي | ثياب | أمتعة | clothes |
| أهْوَج | مُتَسَرِّع | طائش | reckless |
| بَتْع | قُوَّة | شدَّة | vigour, power |
| بَحْبَحَ | زادَ | وَسَّعَ | to provide |
| بَحَّ | رَشَّ | نَفَثَ | to spray |
| بَراني | خارجي | ظاهري | external |
| بَغَضَ | كَرِهَ | مَقَتَ | to loathe |
| بزاء | بُصاق | لُعاب | saliva, spit |
| بسّ | قطّ | هرّ | cat |
| بَطَّال | رديء | فاسد | bad, corrupt |
| بناية | عمارة | مَبنى | building |
| بَهْدَلَ | حَقَّرَ | أهانَ | to humiliate |
| تَبَعها | لَها | مُلكُها | her property |
| تَبَهْوَرَ | تَعاظَمَ | تَفاخَرَ | to boast |
| تَرَك | أقلَع/امتَنَع | كَفَّ | to refrain |
| تَعافى | شُفِيَ | بَرِئَ | to recover |
| جاوَبَ | أجابَ | رَدَّ | to answer |
| ضَمّة | جُرْزة | حزمة | bunch |
| جَفِس | غليظ الطبع | ثقيل الروح | unpleasant |

| | | | |
|---|---|---|---|
| جَلَّلَ | غَطّى | ألبَسَ | to cover |
| جُوّاني | داخلي | باطني | internal |
| حُرمة | زوجة | إمرأة | wife/woman |
| حَنَش | حَيّة | ثُعبان | snake |
| خَبّا (الفتاة) | سَتَرَ | حَجَّبَ | to veil |
| خَرَيَش | أفسَدَ | شَوَّشَ | scribble, muddle |
| خَرْمَش | خَمَش | خَدَش | to scratch |
| خَمَّج | أنْتَنَ | فَسَدَ | to become bad |
| دَلّال | سمسار | وَسيط | middleman |
| خَيِّر | كَريم | مِعْطاء | generous |
| دَهْوَرَ | أوقَعَ | غَرَّرَ | deceive |
| رَتا | أصلَحَ | رَفَأ | to mend, repair |
| رَشَق | شاطر | بارِع | skillful |
| رَمَحَ | رَفَسَ | رَكَلَ | to kick |
| زاحَ | أبْعَدَ | نَحّى | to push aside |
| زَنْقة | ضيّق | عُسْر | predicament |
| زَوَّقَ | حَسَّنَ | زَخْرَفَ | to embellish |
| سايب | مَتْروك | مُهْمَل | neglected |
| سَعْر | عَدوى | وَباء | epidemic |
| سَكَّرَ | سَدَّ | أغْلَقَ، صَكَّ | to close |
| شافَ | رأى | أبْصَرَ | to see |
| شُبّاك | كُوّة | نافذة | window |
| شبوبيّة | شَباب | فُتُوَّة | youth |
| شَحَّ | قَلَّ | نَدَرَ | to dwindle |
| شَحَدَ | استَجْدى | تَسَوَّلَ | to ask for alms |
| شَخَّ | بالَ | قَضى حاجتَه | to urinate |

|  | | | |
|---|---|---|---|
| to cancel | أبطَلَ | ألغى | شطَبَ |
| to braid | عَقَصَ | ضَفَرَ | شكّلَ (الشَعر) |
| to squander | أتلفَ | فقَدَ | ضيّع |
| nature, temper | جِبلّة | طبيعة | طينة |
| to loathe | مَلَّ | كَرِهَ | عافَ |
| destitute | مُعْدَم | فقير | عَدْمان |
| companionship | مُخالَطة | مُصاحَبة | مُعاشَرة |
| dregs, sediment | ثُفالة | راسب | عَكَر |
| chewing gum | لُبان | علّك | علكة |
| to construct | شيّدَ | بنى | عَمّرَ |
| empty | شاغر | خالٍ | فاضٍ |
| to make a hole | خرَقَ | ثقَبَ | فخَتَ |
| to split | صدَعَ | شقَّ | فلَقَ |
| sophisticated | مُحنّك | مُجرّب | قارح |
| pure, genuine | مَحْض | أصيل | قُحّ |
| prostitute | بَغيّ | مومس | قَحبة |
| to be stingy | قتّرَ | ضيّقَ | قرّطَ |
| to loathe | اشمأزَّ | كَرِهَ | قزّ |
| to sew | رتَقَ | خاطَ | قطَبَ |
| to set out to do | طفِقَ | أخَذَ | قعَدَ (يفعل) |
| to record | أثبَتَ | سجّلَ | قيّدَ |
| stove | مَوْقِد | تَنّور | كانون |
| to settle down | استقَرَّ | هدأ | كَنَّ |
| to make a turn | انعطفَ | انحرفَ | كَوّعَ |
| to throw | طرَحَ | رمى | لَحَشَ |
| degradation | تَحْقير | إهانة | بَهْدَلة |

| | | | Meaning |
|---|---|---|---|
| مَحْل | قَحْط، جَفاف | جَدْب | drought |
| مَرْطَبان | زُجاجة | قارورة | bottle, jar |
| مَرْعوب | خائف | مَذعور | terrified |
| مَزْبوط | مَضْبوط | صَحيح | correct |
| مَعَسَ | هَرَسَ | سَحَقَ | to mash, pound |
| مْنوب | أبَداً | إطلاقاً | never, ever |
| مَهول | عَظيم | مُدْهِش | amazing |
| مينا | مَرْسى | مَرْفأ | sea port |
| نَدَهَ | صاحَ | نادى | to shout |
| نَطَّ | قَفَزَ | وَثَبَ | to jump |
| نَقْد | مَهْر | صَداق | dower |
| هَيِّن | سَهْل | يَسير | easy |
| وخَم | وَسَخ | قَذارة | dirtiness |
| وَرَّ | رَمى | قَذَفَ | to throw away |

## 1.4.5 Register-related phonology

Phonological register variation involves the acoustic quality of sounds, including vowel length, place of articulation, and epenthesis (adding an additional sound).

| | R1 | R2 | R3 | Meaning |
|---|---|---|---|---|
| **Consonants** | *maʿūl* | *maʿqūl* | *maʿqūl* | reasonable |
| | *kadīm/adīm* | *qadīm/adīm* | *qadīm* | old |
| | *garīb/arīb* | *qarīb* | *qarīb* | close, nearby |
| | *bəġdir* | *aqdir* | *aqdir* | I can |
| | *tlāte* | *salāsa* | *ṯalāṯa* | three |
| | *dahab* | *zahab* | *ḏahab* | gold |
| | *lazīz* | *ladīd* | *laḏīḏ* | delicious |

|          |            |              |            |                  |
|----------|------------|--------------|------------|------------------|
|          | *ṭūm*      |              | *ṭūm*      | *ṭūm*            | garlic |
|          | *ẓarīf*    |              | *ḏarīf*    | *ḏarīf*          | nice, charming |
|          | *sānawiyye*|              | *ṯānawiyye*| *ṯānawiyya*      | high school |
|          | *miyye*    |              | *mi'a*     | *mi'a*           | hundred |
|          | *mīt …*    |              | *mi'et …*  | *mi'atu …*       | a hundred … |
| **Vowels** | *hōn(e)*  |              | *hunā*     | *hunā*           | here |
|          | *bētō*     |              | *baytuh*   | *baytuhu*        | his house |
|          | *štarēta*  |              | *ištaraythā*| *ištaraytuhā*   | I bought it |
|          | *bḵīl*     |              | *baḵīl*    | *baḵīl*          | stingy |
|          | *mkālame*  |              | *mukālame* | *mukālama*       | phone call |
|          | *waḥde*    |              | *wāḥide*   | *wāḥida*         | one (f.) |
| **Words** | *ḥommoṣ*  | حُمُّص / حمّص | *ḥimmaṣ*   | chick peas |
| **sometimes** | *baṭṭīḵ* | بَطّيخ / بطّيخ | *biṭṭīḵ* | water melon |
| **pronounced** | *barṭīl* | بَرْطيل / برطيل | *birṭīl* | bribe, kickback |
| **incorrectly** | *nafṭ* | نَفْط / نفْط | *nifṭ* | oil, petroleum |
| **by native** | *ma°dan* | مَعْدَن / مَعْدن | *ma°din* | metal |
| **speakers** | *fuṭūr* | فُطور / فَطور | *faṭūr* | breakfast |
|          | *manṭiqa*  | مَنْطقة / مِنْطَقة | *minṭaqa* | area, zone |
|          | *ma°raḍ*   | مَعْرَض / مَعْرِض | *ma°riḍ* | exhibition |
|          | *matḥaf*   | مَتْحَف / مُتْحَف | *mutḥaf* | museum |
|          | *ḥunjara*  | حُنْجُرة / حَنْجَرة | *ḥanjara* | larynx, throat |
|          | *ar-rabāṭ* | الرَباط / الرباط | *ar-ribāṭ* | Rabat |
|          | *ḵilsatan* | خلسَةً / خُلسَةً | *ḵulsatan* | furtively |
|          | *masāḥa*   | مَساحَة / مِساحة | *misāḥa* | area |

### 1.4.6 *Register-related grammar*

Morphological and syntactic features which are likely to vary according to register level are included in this section. The material included is only an illustrative sample, not exhaustive by any means. Furthermore, grammarians disagree sometimes on what is and is not acceptable usage in MSA. I have tried to list those items that enjoy unanimity.

|  | R1 | R2 | R3 | Meaning |
|---|---|---|---|---|
| **Indicative** | *be-trīd* | *turīd* | *tawaddu* | you wish |
|  | بِتريد | تُريد | تَوَدُّ |  |
|  | *b-šāṭir* | *ušāṭir* | *ušāṭiru* | I share with |
|  | بْشاطِر | أُشاطِر | أُشاطِرُ |  |
|  | *b-yiʔədrū* | *yaqdirūn* | *yastaṭīʿūna* | they can |
|  | بْيِئدروا | يَقدرون | يَسْتَطيعونَ |  |
|  | *b-rajjeʿā* | *aruddhā* | *arudduhā* | I return it |
|  | بْرَجِّعا | أرُدْها | أرُدُّها |  |
| **Progressive** | *ʿam tākol* | *ta'kul* | *ta'kulu* | she is eating |
|  | عَم تاكُل | تَأكُلْ | تَأكُلُ |  |
|  | *ʿammāl tākol* | *ta'kul* | *ta'kulu* | she is eating |
|  | عَمّال تاكُل | تَأكُلْ | تَأكُلُ |  |
| **Future** | *raha-/ḥa-iji* | *sa-ātī/sa-aḥḍur* | *sawfa-aḥḍuru* | I'll come |
|  | رَحْإجيَ/حَإجي | سآتي/سَأحضُر | سَوفَ أحْضُرُ |  |
| **Negative** | *mū ktābi* | *laysa kitābi* | *laysa kitābi* |  |
|  | مو كتابي | لَيسَ كِتابي | لَيسَ كِتابي | not my book |
|  | *mū mabṣūṭ* | *ġayr masrūr* | *laysa masrūran* |  |
|  | مو مبسوط | غَير مَسرور | لَيسَ مَسروراً | unhappy |

| | | |
|---|---|---|
| *mū šarwe* | *laysat ṣafqa jayyida* | *laysat ṣafqatan jayyida* |
| مو شَرْوة | لَيسَت صَفقةً جَيِّدة | لَيسَت صَفقة جَيِّدة |

it's not a good bargain

| | |
|---|---|
| *lā teṭlaʿī bi-l-bard* | *lā takrujī bi-l-bard* |
| لا تِطلَعي بِالبَرْد | لا تَخرُجي بِالبَرْد |

Don't go out in the cold!

| | | |
|---|---|---|
| *mā ʿajabā* | *mā aʿjabahā* | *lam yuʿjibhā* |
| ما عَجَبَها | ما أعْجَبَها | لم يعْجِبْها |

She did not like it.

| | | |
|---|---|---|
| *mā b-yinfaʿ* | *lā yanfaʿ* | *lā fā'idata minhu* |
| ما بْيِنْفَع | لا يَنْفَع | لا فائِدَةَ مِنْهُ |

It's no good.

**Interrogative**

| | | |
|---|---|---|
| *šū b-tu'ṣod?* | *māḏā taqṣid?* | *māḏā taʿnī?* |
| شو بْتُؤْصُدْ؟ | ماذا تَقْصِد؟ | ماذا تَعْني؟ |

What do you mean?

| | |
|---|---|
| *lēš met'akker?* | *limāḏā anta muta'akkir?* |
| ليش مِتأخِّر؟ | لِماذا أنتَ مُتَأخِّر؟ |

Why are you late?

| | | |
|---|---|---|
| *ēmtā weṣel?* | *matā waṣal?* | *matā waṣala?* |
| إمتى وصِل؟ | مَتى وَصَل؟ | مَتى وَصَلَ؟ |

When did he arrive?

| | | |
|---|---|---|
| *wēn rāḥet?* | *ilā ayna ḏahabat?* | *ilā ayna maḍat?* |
| وين راحِت؟ | إلى أينَ ذَهَبَتْ؟ | إلى أينَ مَضَتْ؟ |

Where did she go?

**Passive**

| | |
|---|---|
| *b-tettākal mešwiyye* | *tu'kalu mašwiyyatan* |
| بْتِتّاكَل مِشوِيِّة | تُؤْكَلُ مَشْوِيَّةً |

It's eaten grilled.

nsaḥbet šahātto        suḥibat ruḳṣatuh

انْسَحْبِت شَهاتّو       سُحِبَتْ رُخْصَتُه

His licence was suspended/revoked.

b-tetḳālaf iza ṣaffēt hōn      tuḳālaf in waqafta hunā

بْتتخالَفْ إزا صَفَّيت هون     تُخالَفُ إنْ وقفتَ هُنا

You'll be given a ticket if you park here.

**Case Marking**

bəškor l-jamᶜiyye   aškur l-jamᶜiyya   aškuru l-jamᶜiyyata

بِشْكُر الجَمعِيَّة    أشْكُر الجَمعِيَّة    أشْكُرُ الجَمْعِيَّةَ

I thank the association.

men ktīr        min katīr        min katīrin

مِنْ كتير       مِنْ كَثير       مِنْ كَثيرٍ    of many

bel-wāqeᶜ      fil-wāqiᶜ      fil-wāqiᶜi

بالواقع       في الواقع      في الواقع    in fact

b-'addir juhūkon   uqaddir juhūdkum   uqaddiru juhūdakum

بْأدِّر جُهودكُن     أقَدِّر جُهودكُم    أُقَدِّرُ جُهودكُم

I appreciate your effort

b-el-wilāyāt      fi-l-wilāyāt      fī-l-wilāyāti

بالوِلايات      في الوِلايات    في الوِلايات

in the [United] States

b-el-mujtamaᶜ    fi-l-mujtamaᶜ    fī-l-mujtamaᶜi

بالمُجْتَمَع     في المُجْتَمَع    في المُجْتَمَع    in society

**Agreement: Dual[6]**

sayyārtēn kbār   sayyāratān(i) kabīratān(i) [5]   two big cars

سَيّارتين كْبار   سَيّارتان كَبيرتان   سَيّارتانِ كَبيرتانِ    f.

---

[5] Inflectional endings in parentheses are characteristic of R3.

[6] In R1, adjectives formed according to the ten most common patterns as well as basic colours have plural agreement with the dual noun. Attributive adjectives (*nisba*) are invariable; they show no number or gender concord in R1.

| | | | |
|---|---|---|---|
| *sayyārtēn ḥəmr* | *sayyāratān(i) ḥamrāwān(i)* | | two red cars |
| سَيّارتين حمر | سَيّارتان حَمْراوان | سَيّارتانِ حَمْراوانِ | f. |
| *sayyārtēn mṣadyīn* | *sayyāratān(i) ṣadi'atān(i)* | | |
| سَيّارتين مْصَديين | | سَيّارتانِ صَدِئتانِ | f. |
| | | | two grey cars |
| *sayyārtēn bennī* | *sayyāratān(i) bunniyyatān(i)* | | |
| سَيّارتين بنّي | سَيّارَتان بُنّيتان | سَيّارَتانِ بُنّيَتانِ | f. |
| | | | two brown cars |
| *šebbākēn kbār* | *šubbākān(i) kabīrān(i)* | | |
| شبّاكين كْبار | شُبّاكان كَبيران | شُبّاكانِ كَبيرانِ | m. |
| | | | two large windows |
| *šebbākēn bīḍ* | *šubbākān(i) abyaḍān(i)* | | |
| شبّاكين بيْض | شُبّاكان أَبْيَضان | شُبّاكانِ أَبْيَضانِ | m. |
| | | | two white windows |

| | | | | |
|---|---|---|---|---|
| **Plural** | *sayyārāt bennī* | *sayyārāt(un) bunniyya(tun)* | | |
| | سَيّارات بنّي | سَيّارات بُنّيَّة | سَيّاراتٌ بُنّيَّةٌ | f. |
| | | | | brown cars |
| | *sayyārāt ḥemr* | *sayyārāt ḥamrā'* | *sayyārātun ḥamrā'u* | |
| | سَيّارات حُمر | سَيّارات حَمْراء | سَيّاراتٌ حَمْراءٌ | f. |
| | | | | red cars |
| | *sayyārāt mṣaḍye* | *sayyārāt(un) ṣadi'a(tun)* | | |
| | سَيّارات مْصَدْيه | سَيّارات صَدِئة | سَيّاراتٌ صَدِئةٌ | f. |
| | | | | rusty cars |
| | *šababīk ġālye* | *šabābīk(un) ġāliya(tun)* | | |
| | شَبابيك غاليه | شَبابيك غاليَة | شَبابيكٌ غاليَةٌ | m. |
| | | | | expensive windows |

**Numbers** The C variety enjoys a simplified number system compared with

MSA. Note that in the singular the number *follows* the counted noun, from three and above the number precedes. In the dual, the noun takes the dual suffix. This rule goes for both C and MSA.

| | | | |
|---|---|---|---|
| *lēra[7] waḥde* | *layra(tun) wāḥida(tun)* | | one lira |
| ليرة وَحْده | لَيْرَة واحدَة | لَيْرَةٌ واحدةٌ | f. |
| *lērtēn* | *layratān(i)* | | two liras |
| ليرْتين | لَيْرَتان | لَيْرَتان | f. |
| *tlet lērāt* | *talāt(u) layrāt(tin)* | three liras | |
| تْلتْ ليرات | ثَلاث لَيْرات | ثَلاثُ لَيْرات | f. |
| *idaᶜšar lēra* | *iḥdā ᶜašrata layra(tan)* | | eleven liras |
| إدَعْشَرْ ليرة | إحْدى عَشْرَة لَيْرَة | إحْدى عَشْرَةَ لَيْرَةً | f. |
| *tlet-ṭaᶜšar lēra* | *talāta ᶜašrata layra(tan)* | | thirteen liras |
| تْلطْعْشَر ليرة | ثَلاث عَشْرَة لَيْرَة | ثَلاثَ عَشْرَةَ لَيْرَةً | f. |
| *ᶜešrīn lēra* | *ᶜišrūn(a) layra(tan)* | | twenty liras |
| عشْرين ليرة | عشْرون لَيْرَة | عشْرونَ لَيْرَةً | f. |
| *mīt lēra* | *mi'at(u) layra(tin)* | | one hundred liras |
| ميتْ ليرة | مئَة لَيْرَة | مئَةُ لَيْرَةٍ | f. |
| *alf lēra* | *alf(u) layra(tin)* | | one thousand liras |
| ألْفْ ليرة | ألْفْ لَيْرَة | ألْفُ لَيْرَةٍ | f. |
| *bēt wāḥed* | *bayt(un) wāḥid(un)* | | one house |
| بيتْ واحد | بَيْتْ واحد | بَيْتٌ واحدٌ | m. |
| *bētēn* | *baytān(i)* | | two houses |
| بيتيْن | بَيْتان | بَيْتان | m. |
| *tlet byūt* | *talātat(u) buyūt(in)* | | three houses |
| تْلتْ بْيوت | ثَلاثَة بُيوت | ثَلاثَةُ بُيوتٍ | m. |
| *idaᶜšar bēt* | *aḥada ᶜašara baytan* | | eleven houses |

---

[7] The lira (pound) is the unit of Syrian currency.

34

| Colloquial | (translit) | MSA (translit) | MSA (Arabic) | English | |
|---|---|---|---|---|---|
| إدَعْشَر بيت | tlet-ṭaʕšar bēt | ṯalāṯta ʕašara baytan | أَحَدَ عَشَرَ بَيْتاً | thirteen houses | m. |
| ثْلطَعْشَر بيت | ʕešrīn bēt | ʕišrūn(a) bayt(an) | ثَلاثَةَ عَشَرَ بَيْتاً | twenty houses | m. |
| عشْرين بيت | mīt bēt | mi'at(u) bayt(in) | عشْرون بيت / عشْرونَ بَيْتاً | one hundred houses | m. |
| ميْت بيت | alf bēt | alf(u) bayt(in) | مئة بيت / مِئَةُ بَيْتٍ | one thousand houses | m. |
| أَلْف بيت | | | ألْف بيت / أَلْفُ بَيْتٍ | | m. |

**Word Order**

C is less stringent in word order than MSA. Certain particles and expressions can occupy any position in the sentence. (See 3.8.)

R1   *betlā'īhā bas bə-ššām.*    بِتْلائيها بَسْ بالشام.

R1   *bas betlā'īhā bə-ˇššām.*    بَسْ بِتْلائيها بالشام.

R1   *betlā'īhā bə-ˇššām bas.*    بِتْلائيها بالشام بَسْ.

R2/3   *tajiduhā b-iššāmi faqaṭ.*    تَجِدُها بالشام فَقَط.

You find it in Damascus only.

R1   *raġad lessa mā weṣlet.*    رَغَدْ لِسَّة ما وِصْلِتْ.

R1   *raġad mā weṣlet lessa.*    رَغَدْ ما وِصْلِتْ لِسَّة.

R1   *lessa raġad mā weṣlet.*    لِسَّة رَغَدْ ما وِصْلِتْ.

R2/3   *lam taṣil raġad baʕd(u).*    لَم تَصِل رَغَدَ بَعْدَ.

Raghad has not arrived yet.

R1   *kamān mīn jāye?*    كَمان مين جايه؟

    *mīn kamān jāye?*    مين كَمان جايه؟

    *mīn jāye kamān?*    مين جايه كَمان؟

R2/3   *man qādimun ayḍan?*    مَنْ قادِمٌ أَيْضاً؟

Who else is coming?

R1   *mīn ttaṣal mbāreḥ?*    مين اتَّصَل مْبارِح؟

|          | *mbāreḥ mīn ttaṣal?* | مْبارِح مِيْن اتَّصَلَ؟ |
|          | *mīn mbāreḥ ttaṣal?* | مِيْن مْبارِح اتَّصَلَ؟ |
| **R2/3** | *mani ttaṣala al-bāriḥ(a)?* | مَنِ اتَّصَلَ البارِح (البارحة) ؟ |
|          | Who called yesterday? | |

| **R1**   | *šū ṣār baʿdēn?* | شو صار بَعْدِيْن؟ |
|          | *šū baʿdēn ṣār?* | شو بَعْدِيْن صار؟ |
|          | *baʿdēn šū ṣār?* | بَعْدِيْن شو صار؟ |
| **R2/3** | *māḏā ḥadata baʿda ḏālik?* | ماذا حَدَثَ بَعْدَ ذلك؟ |
|          | What happened then? | |

| **R1** | *l-ḥukūme mā btaʿṭī hēk maʿāšāt.* | الحُكومِه ما بتَعطي هيْك مَعاشات. |

| **R2** | *lā tuʿṭī al-ḥukūma(tu) rawātib ka-hāḏih.* | لا تُعْطي الحُكومة رَواتِب كَهذه. |

| **R3** | *lā tuʿṭī al-ḥukūmatu rawātiba ka-hāḏihi.* | لا تُعْطي الحُكومةُ رَواتِبَ كَهذه. |
|        | The government does not pay such salaries. | |

| **R1**   | *māzen bi-sū' b-serʿa.* | مازِن بِسوءْ بْسرعة. |
| **R2/3** | *yasūq(u) māzin(u) bi-surʿa(tin).* | يَسوقُ مازِنُ بِسُرْعةٍ. |
|          | Mazin drives fast. | |

## Word order and change of focus

| **R1**   | *ʿaṭīnī **kamān** war'a.* | عَطيني كَمان وَرْءَة. |
| **R2/3** | *aʿṭinī waraqatan ukrā.* | أعْطِني وَرَقةً أُخْرى. |
|          | Give me another piece of paper. | |

| **R1**   | ***kamān** ʿaṭīnī war'a.* | كَمان عَطيني وَرْءَة. |
| **R2/3** | *aʿṭinī waraqatan anā ayḍan.* | أعْطِني وَرَقةً أنا أيْضاً. |
|          | Give me a piece of paper, too. | |

|        |                              |                              |
|--------|------------------------------|------------------------------|
| R1     | *ʿaṭīnī warʾa **kamān**.*     | عَطيني وَرْءَة كَمان.          |
| R2/3   | *aʿṭinī waraqatan ukrā.*      | أَعْطِني وَرَقَةً أُخْرى.      |

Give me another piece of paper.

**Ellipsis** The MSA particle *an* is consistently dropped in C, and *inna* optionally dropped.

|        |                                      |                              |
|--------|--------------------------------------|------------------------------|
| R1     | *beddō yente'el men bētō.*            | بدّو يِنْتِئِل مِن بيْتو.      |
| R2/3   | *yawaddu **an** yantaqil(a) min baytih(i).* | يَوَدُّ أَنْ يَنتقِلَ مِنْ بَيْتِه. |

He wants to move out of his house.

|        |                                  |                              |
|--------|----------------------------------|------------------------------|
| R1     | *lāzem t'addem ṭalab.*            | لازِمْ تْأَدِّمْ طَلَب.        |
| R2/3   | *yajibu **an** tuqaddima ṭalaban.* | يَجِبُ/لَزِمَ أَنْ تُقَدِّمَ طَلَباً. |

You have to submit an application.

**Demonstratives** The C demonstratives are similar to their MSA counterparts. The only difference is the absence of dual forms from C.

| C |  |  | MSA |  |
|---|---|---|---|---|
| s., m. | *hādā* (this) | هادا | *hādā* | هذا |
| s., f. | *hay* | هَيْ | *hādihi* | هذه |
| d., m., nom. | | هَدول | *hādāni* | هذان |
| d., f., nom. | | هَدول | *hātāni* | هاتان |
| d., m., acc./gen. | | هَدول | *hādayni* | هذيْن |
| d., f., acc./gen. | | هَدول | *hātayni* | هاتيْن |
| pl., m., f. | *hadōl* | هَدول | *hā'ulā'i* | هؤلاء |
| s., m. | *hadāk* | هَداك | *dālika* | ذلكَ |
| s., f. | *hadīk* (that) | هَديك | *tilka* | تلكَ |
| pl., m., f. | *hadōl* | هَدول | *ūlā'ika* | أولائكَ |

**Relatives** C is most parsimonious in this category; it has only one form for the nine MSA forms.

| | | | | |
|---|---|---|---|---|
| m., s. | *(i)lli* | اللي | *al-laḏī* | الَّذي |
| f., s. | | = | *al-latī* | الَّتي |
| m., d., nom. | | = | *al-laḏāni* | اللَذان |
| f., d., nom. | | = | *al-latāni* | اللَتان |
| m., d., acc./gen. | | = | *al-laḏayni* | اللَذَيْن |
| f., d., acc./gen. | | = | *al-latayni* | اللَتَيْن |
| m., pl. | | = | *al-laḏīna* | الَّذينَ |
| f., pl. | | = | *al-lātī* | اللاتي |
| f., pl. | | = | *al-lawātī* | اللَواتي |

**Imperative** There is much similarity in the affirmative and negative forms of the imperative. Dual imperatives do not exist in C.

| | | | | |
|---|---|---|---|---|
| m., s. | *ktōb* | كْتوب | *uktub* | اُكْتُبْ |
| f., s. | *ktebī* | كْتِبي | *uktubī* | اُكْتبي |
| m., d. | – | | *uktubā* | اُكتُبا |
| f., d. | – | | *uktubā* | اُكتُبا |
| m., p. | *ktubū* | كْتُبو | *uktubū* | اُكْتُبوا |
| f., p. | *ktubū* | كْتُبو | *uktubna* | اُكْتُبنَ |

| **Possessive** | *tabaʿī* | تَبَعي | *lī* | لي |
|---|---|---|---|---|
| | *tabaʿ sālem* | تَبَعْ سالِم | *li-sālim* | لسالِم |
| | *elō* | إلو | *lahu* | لَهُ |
| | *el(h)ā* | إلها / إلا | *lahā* | لها |

**Redundancy** This refers to the addition of an element that is not required. Both register levels may be considered MSA. Therefore, they are designated R2 and R3. R2 is viewed lower because it represents a deviation from the standard rules of language and style.

**R2**     *kullamā zādat sāʿātu-l-ʿamal kullamā zāda-l-kaṭa'.*

كُلَّما زادت ساعات العمل كُلَّما زادَ الخَطأ.

**R3**    *kullamā zādat sāʿātu-l-ʿamal zāda-l-ḳaṭaʾ.*

كُلَّما زادت ساعات العمل زادَ الخَطأ.

The longer the hours worked, the more mistakes made.

**R2**    *bi-qadri mā taʿmal bi-qadri mā taksab.*

بقَدْرِ ما تَعمَل بقَدْرِ ما تَكسَب.

**R3**    *bi-qadri mā taʿmal taksab.*

بقَدْرِ ما تَعمَل تَكسَب.

You earn as much as you work.

**R2**    *ʿamila ka-ṭabīb.*

عَمِلَ كَطَبيب.

**R3**    *ʿamila ṭabīban.*

عَمِلَ طَبيباً.

He worked as a doctor.

**R2**    *iftutiḥa l-muʾtamaru wa-lladī yadūmu ṯalāṯata ayyām.*

افتُتِحَ المُؤتَمَرُ والذي يَدومُ ثَلاثَةَ أَيّام.

**R3**    *iftutiḥa l-muʾtamaru alladī yadūmu ṯalāṯata ayyām.*

افتُتِحَ المُؤتَمَرُ الذي يَدومُ ثَلاثَةَ أَيّام.

The conference, which lasts for three days, was opened.

**R2**    *ḍarbu aš-šurṭati li-iṯnayni min-al-mutaDāhirīn.*

ضَرْبُ الشُرْطَة لاثْنَيْنِ مِنَ المُتَظاهِرين.

**R3**    *ḍarbu aš-šurṭati iṯnayni min-al-mutaDāhirīn.*

ضَرْبُ الشُرْطَة اثْنَيْنِ مِنَ المُتَظاهِرين.

The police beating two of the demonstrators.

**R2**    *taʿawwada ʿalā al-mašyi.*

تَعَوَّدَ على المَشْي.

**R3**    *taʿawwada l-mašya.*

تَعَوَّدَ المَشْيَ.

He got used to walking.

## 1.5    Representative texts

The selected texts below illustrate register variation. They are arranged in ascending order from R1 to R3.

1.5.1   **R1**. An excerpt from a diary which contained a description of daily events in Damascus by a semi-literate barber written over a twenty-one-year period (1741-1762).

سنة ١١٥٦

وفي أوائل شهر صَفَر الخير ، جاء خبر عن الحج الشريف بأنّه غرق في الحَسا قريباً من القَطرانة،[8] وذهب على ما قيل مقدار نصف الحاج من خيل وجمال وبغال ونساء ورجال وأموال وأحمال، وقد غرق لأحد التجار سبعةَ عَشرَ حمْل، كل حمل لا يُقام بثمن فاستعانوا بحضرة سليمان باشاالعَظم والي الشام وأمير الحاج، وقالوا: نحن نهب لك مالنا وخذه أنت ولا تتركه للعرب, فحالاً نهض وأخذ معه جماعة وذهب نحو مرحلة، وقد خاطر هو وجماعته، ثم غاب يوماً وليلة بعد ما جدّوا في طلبه، وإذا هو قادم ومعه الأحمال، لم تنقص ولا ذرة ثم ناداهم وسلّمهم إلى أصحابهم، ولم يدنّس حجه بشيء

وفي تلك الأيام زاد الغلاء في بلاد الشام، فبلغنا أنّ رطل الخبز في طرابلس بعشرة مصاري،[9] وفي غزة والرملة بخمس وعشرين مصرية، وفي الشام ليس واقف على سعر، وقد زاد الغلاء والبلاء والقَهر.

حوادثُ دمَشقَ اليومية

للشيَخ أحمد البُدَيري الحلّاق

**Vocabulary**    familiar        جاء، خبر، ذهب، حمْل، ثَمَن، ترك، خاطر، مَصاري

جماعة، واقف، مِصرية

---

[8] Two stations at which pilgrims stopped on their way to Mecca. They are in southern present-day Jordan.

[9] Singular مِصرية. A silver coin which the Ottoman government authorized Egypt to mint in Cairo. Syrians still call money مَصاري.

| | |
|---|---|
| **Grammar** | short, simple sentences; many conjunctions; |
| | is not up to the level of standard grammar; |
| | compound sentences exist       بأنّه غرق، وإذا هو، بلغنا أنّ |
| | correct number-noun agreement[10]     سبعةَ عشرَ حمل، |
| | خمس وعشرين مصرية |
| | deviations in case        سبعةَ عشرَ حمل، ليس واقف |
| | deviations in agreement        سلّمهم، أصحابِهم |
| | basically colloquial structures     ذهب ... مقدارِ نصف الحاج |
| | فحالاً نهض، خاطر هو وجماعته، |
| | ليس واقف على سعر |

**Style**     Al-Budayri's style is casual, highly personal, and very close to colloquial usage. Because the discourse is more like a narrative, action verbs and enumeration occur in close succession.

1.5.2    **R2**. This excerpt is from *al-Majalla*, a magazine that enjoys a wide circulation throughout the Arab world. It is published in London by a Saudi Arabian group. This particular writer, Awni Basheer (a non-Saudi), includes a large number of colloquialisms in his column, sometimes for particular effects he wants to accomplish. The dialect he mostly uses is Egyptian, although he might not necessarily be an Egyptian. The magazine is of the serious type and appeals to the mid- and upper-strata of intellectuals and business people, which makes such a practice seem out of place. This does not mean that Basheer's column is devoid of intellectual substance. He does address serious issues that interest the majority of the magazine's audience in his unique style. The text is basically written in good MSA, free from structural errors.

---

[10] This may be due to the corrections the first editor liberally made.

The C phrases are dispersed through the text without affecting the overall structure.

يا وابور قلّي رايِح على فين؟

هل تصاب بقشعريرة حين تقرأ الصُحُف؟ هل تشدّ شعرَك وتتأزّم وتنفلق حين تسمع الأخبار؟ إذا كنت لا تفعل شيئاً من هذا القبيل فهنيئاً لك. لأنك ستعيش طويلاً وتعمّر بإذن الله كونك بايعها. أما إذا لم تكن بايعها فمن المؤكّد أنك تتمزق حين ترى وتسمع وتعيش حالنا وما يدور حولنا وبيننا.

قبل بضعة شهور وبعد فحص شامل قال لي الطبيب «حالك مش عاجبني». قلت له ولا أنا عاجبني يا حكيم، ولهذا أتيت إليك أريد علاجاً لحالي. فقال، لا فُضّ فوه، مع الأسف لا يوجد أيّ علاج لحالتك. قلت له، وَلوْ يا حكيم! كل هذا التقدم والعلم والتكنولوجيا ولا علاج، ما القصة؟ الحمد لله لستُ مصاباً بالإيدز ولا بالسرطان، ولكنني أموت كل يوم قليلاً قليلاً.

قال وليته ما قال «هذه حقيقة، وإذا لم تلحق حالك ستذوي خلال أربع أو خمس سنوات على أبعد تقدير.»

استوقفتني في حديثه كلمة «تذوي» فسألته عنها فشرح لا شرح الله له صدراً بقوله، بعد أربع سنوات إن لم تمت فستصبح مُعاقاً لا تستطيع المشي أبداً، وستتنفّس بصعوبة إلى أن يأتي أجلك، وصدّقني عندئذ ستتمنى لو أنه يأتي بأسرع ما يمكن.

أعرف أن الحياة عزيزة لكنني لم أكن أعرف مقدار معزتها، لقد هدّ حيلي ابن الذينَ، سألته ما العمل؟ قال بادئ ذي بدء، عليك التوقف عن التدخين، قلت أخففه بدلاً من خمسين سيجارة أدخن عشرين أو عشراً، قال لا ينفع، قلت فخمس لِفافات إذن؟ قال ولا واحدة، يجب أن تمتنع عن التدخين نهائياً.

عوني بشير

المجلة: ٤-٨٣٤/ ٢ تشرين الأول (اكتوبر) ١٩٩٦

| | | |
|---|---|---|
| **Vocabulary** | standard, sophisticated | قُشعريرة، تتأزم، تعمِّر، فحص شامل، |
| | | مُصاب، تقدُّم، ليتَهُ، تذوي، استوقفتني، أجلك، تَوَقُّف |
| | classical phrases | لا فُضَّ فوه، لا شرح اللهُ له صدراً |
| | set phrases | هذا القبيل، هنيئاً لك، بادئَ ذي بَدْء |
| | colloquialisms | وابور، قلّي، رايح، فين، تنفَلق، بايعْها، |
| | | مش عاجبني، وَلَوْ، تلحق حالك، هَدَّ حيلي، ابنُ الَّذينَ |
| | | السَرَطان، مُعاق، لفافة |
| | modern terminology | |
| | loan words | التكنولوجيا، الإيدز، سيجارة |
| **Grammar** | mostly accurate MSA structures; modern usage | |
| | prepositional phrase with a verbal function | عليكَ التوقُّفَ |
| | number-noun agreement | بضعة شهور، أربع أو خمس سنوات، |
| | | خمس لفافات |
| | case[11] | لا تفعلَ شيئاً، أريد علاجاً، مُصاباً، أموت قليلاً قليلاً، |
| | | تصبح مُعاقاً، أبداً، صدراً، عندئذٍ، بَدَلاً من خمسين، |
| | | أدخن عشرين أو عَشراً |
| | negative | لا تفعلُ، لم تَكُنْ، ولا أنا عاجبني، لا يوجدُ، لا علاجَ، |
| | | لستُ مُصاباً، ولا بالسَرَطان، لم تلحقْ، لا شَرَحَ، |
| | | لم تَمُتْ، لا تستطيعُ، لم أكُنْ، لا ينفعُ، ولا واحدةً |
| | relative clauses | ما يدورُ، ما يمكن |
| | ellipsis | ابن الذينَ (فعلوا)، ولا أنا عاجبني (حالي)، لا علاجَ (الحالتي)، |
| | | عشرين (سيجارة)، عشراً (من اللفائف)، لا ينفع (ما تقترح) |

---

[11] Only words with suffixed endings are listed because short vowels denoting case are not provided in the original text.

conditional clauses

إذا كنت لا تفعل شيئاً من هذا القبيل فهنيئاً لك

إذا لم تكُنْ بايعها فمن المؤكّد....، إذا لم تلحق حالك ستذوي،

إنْ لم تُمتْ فستصبح ... ، لو أنّه يأتي،

demonstratives

هذا القبيل، لهذا، هذا التقدّم،

adverbs

حين، طويلاً، قليلاً قليلاً، أبداً، عندئذٍ، نهائيّاً

comparative/superlative degree

أبعد تقدير

interrogative

هل تصاب، ماالقصة، ما العمل

nominal sentences

لأنّك ستعيش طويلاً، كونك بايعها ،

أنّك تتمزّق، لَسْتُ مُصاباً، لكنّني أموت، هذه حقيقة،

أنّه يأتي، أعرف أنّ الحياة عزيزة، لكنّني لم أكنْ أعرف

subjunctive

أنْ يأتيَ، أنْ تمتنعَ

**Style**
Basheer may have resorted to punctuate his article with C elements in order to sound witty and funny. His writing is more conversational than expository. He uses personal information to establish a close relationship with the audience. The tone is clearly informal.

1.5.3  **R2.** This is part of an interview with Omar Abu-Risheh, a Syrian poet. Note that an awkward structure occurs in the reporter's first question, not in Abu Risheh's response.

عمر أبو ريشة

\* أخذتْ منكَ المرأةُ مساحة كبيرة من شعرك.

- المرأة جمال والجمال له جلاله ولذلك فكَلّ ما كتبت عن المرأة لم أجرح فيه عاطفتَها وحافظت عليها. ذلك أني أرى أن الجمال بجب ألا يُهانَ، ومهما قاسيت منها ومن ظلمها لم أجرحْها. سرت على هذا الشعار طيلةَ عمري منذ أن كنتُ في الثالثةِ والعشرين. اسمعْ ما قلتُ في صباي:

فإنْ أبصَرتني ابتَسمي            وحَيِّيني بِتَحْنانِ

وسـيري سَيْرَ حالمةٍ              وقولي كانَ يَهواني

\* حَدِّثْني عن جمال المرأة، وعن رقَّتها وعُذوبتها، ألَم تتوقَّف، عفواً، عن غَدرها ؟

- قـال: المجـرم هو الرجل، ولهـذا السـبب لـم أسِئْ لـها أو أضْطَرّ إلى إهانتِه. للمرأة أخطاء ولها عِنادُها ، ولكنّه عِنادٌ جميل، يمكن أنْ تذيبَه بكلمةٍ

\* نزار قبّاني احتفى أيضاً بالمرأة.

- لقـد نصـحتُ نزار ، وهو صديق، ألا «يكشف» المرأةَ بهذا الشكل، وقلت له إنها مخلوق رقيق لا يحتمل هذه القسوة. فإذا به يقول لي «يا عـمرك إنك لا ترى مـخالب المرأة». ومع ذلك فان نزار عنصر طيب وآدمي.. ورائج كشاعر. وبالمناسبة لم أبحث طوال عمري عن الرَواج. وفي كل مرة يبلغني تكريم هيئة أو جامعة، فإنني أشعر بالخجل. تأكّد أنّ «القيمـة» لا تضيع مطلقاً مهمـا كانت تخاصم الرَواج. أنا لست شاعراً رائجاً ولكنّي أعتزّ بقيمتي كشاعر. أنا لم أنشر كلَّ قصائدي وأنا معك أنّ قَدَرَ الشـعر أنْ يُنشَر. قد يفاجئك قـولي أنّي أترك هذه القصائد لأحفادي

مجلة «سيّدتي» ١٠ آب (أغسطس) ١٩٨٦

| | | |
|---|---|---|
| **Vocabulary** | literary, poetic, sophisticated | جَمال، جَلال، عاطفة، تَحْنان، رَقيق، يَهْوى، رقَّة، عُذوبة |
| | modern terminology | رَواج، رائج |
| | loan words | بك (*bēk*, Turkish term of address) |
| **Grammar** | accurate structures; modern usage; several compound sentences | |
| | case | في الثالثة والعشرين |
| | negative | لم أجرح/أجرحْها/أبحثْ، ألاَّ يُهانَ/يَكشفَ، ألم تتوقف لا يَحتمل/تَرى/ تضيع، لستُ شاعراً |
| | interrogative | هل ، ألم تتوقّف |

45

| imperative | قولي، اِسمعْ، حدِّثني |
| redundancy | أخذت (منكَ) المرأة مساحة كبيرة من شعرك |
| relative clauses | كلّ ما كتبت، ما قلت |
| ellipsis | الثالثة والعشرين (من عمري)، صديق (لي) |
| | بهذا الشكل (الذي رسمه)، تكريم هيئة (لي) |
| conditional clauses | مَهْما قاسيت |
| demonstratives | لهذا السبب، بهذا الشكل، هذه القسوة |
| | مع ذلك، هذه القصائد |
| subjunctive | أنْ يُهانَ/تُذيبَهُ |
| passive | يُهان، أُضطرّ، يُنْشَر |

**Style**   This text is a transcript of an interview, which explains its informal tone. Although some parts sound learned, it is also conversational. The poet, in this excerpt (and elsewhere in the interview), tries to communicate freely and stay away from lofty, elaborate expressions.

1.5.4   **R2.** Below is an excerpt from an extemporaneous speech by the late President Hafez al-Asad of Syria on the occasion of the sixth conference of Arab-American Societies and Associations which was convened in Damascus on October 1st, 1983. Asad was known for sticking to MSA in public speeches.

كلمة الرئيس حافظ الأسد في حفل التكريم الذي أقامه لأعضاء المؤتمر السادس لاتحاد الجمعيات والمؤسسات العربية الأمريكية

... أعود لأقول إننا نرغب من قلوبنا في أنْ تذكروا وطنكم الأم دائماً وأنْ تذكِّروا أولادكم بالوطن الأم دائماً، وتعملوا جهدكم كي لاتضيع اللغةُ العربية. أنتم تعرفون أنّ في الكثير من بُلدان العالم توجد أقليّات قومية، وبعض هذه الأقليّاتِ ليس لها وطن آخر غير

الوطن الثاني -إن صحّ هذاالقَوْل- الذي تعيش فيه. أعني أنَّ بعض هذه الأقليَّات انتقل وطنها الأم إلى شعبٍ آخَر، وبعض هذه الأقليَّات أيضاً من شعوبٍ قليلة العدد، ومع ذلك تحافظُ على لغاتها حيةً بين أبنائها، ويتحدثون في بيوتهم بلغتِهم وعندما لا توجد لديهم مدارس -وأنا أعرف بعض الأقليات العرقية التي لا توجد لديها مدارس- تحافظ على اللغة عن طريق التعليم العائلي وحتى في سورية لدينا نماذجُ صغيرةٌ من هذه الحالات. بالأحرى أنتم، إنَّكم من أمةٍ كبيرة، ووطنكم الأم موجود وهو بخير، وعددكم بالملايين، ويمكن التعاون – ويجب التعاون- بينكم وبين الوطن الأم، وخاصة في هذا الموضوع، وطبعاً في كل المواضيع، ولكن أخَصِّص وأقول خاصةً في هذا الموضوع من كتاب «خُطب وكلمـات وتصريحات السيد الرئيس حافظ الأسد». منشورات دار البعث ١٩٨٣.

| | | |
|---|---|---|
| **Vocabulary** | modern; slightly political; familiar | |
| | language and culture | وطن، لغة، أولاد، أقليَّات، شعب، أبناء |
| | | تعليم، أمّة |
| | collocation | الوطن الأم، اعمَلوا جُهدكُم |
| | set phrases | إن صحّ هذا القول، بالأحرى |
| **Grammar** | accurate MSA structures; modern usage; compound sentences | |
| | prepositional phrase | مع ذلك |
| | specific prepositions following verbs | رغب في، حافظ على |
| | | ذكَّر بـ، انتقل إلى، تحدَّث بـ |
| | demonstratives | هذه الأقليَّات، هذا الموضوع |
| | subjunctive | لأقولَ، أنْ تَذكُروا، أنْ تُذكِّروا، أنْ تُحافظوا |
| **Style** | Given the situation (luncheon or dinner), the text is semi-formal. It has political overtones, but it sounds communicative and contains no lofty or highly refined language. He addresses the audience directly, making specific references to their background and situation. | |

1.5.5 **R3**. Najīb Maḥfūẓ, a Nobel laureate, is an Egyptian novelist and writer. The following excerpt is from a column he wrote for a magazine of wide circulation on the difference between legitimate armed struggle and terrorism.

الفرق بين الكفاح المسلّح والإرهاب

سُئلتُ عن الحدِّ الفاصل بين الكفاح المُسلّح والإرهاب على ضوء حرب المقاومة التي خاضها الشعب المصري عبرَ تاريخه ضدّ الغُزاة والطُغاة، فقلت: إنّ الكفاحَ المسلّحَ يكون مشروعاً عندما لا يكون بإمكانك أنْ تقابلَ عدوَّك الذي يحتلُّ بلدك ومواجهته بمثل قوّته، أي حين لا تملك جيشاً يحارب، ولا يبقى أمامك سوى المقاومة الذاتية إذا أردت عدم الاستسلام أو الفَناء.

ومن هنا تبدأ في استغلال كلِّ الإمكانات المُتاحة، كالجبال مثلما فعلت الجزائر أو الغابات كما فعلت «الماوماو»، فتتكوّن بها العصابات المكافحة بهدف محاربة العدو. وهذا تعتبره الحكومات المُسَيْطرة خُروجاً على القانون، بينما هو كفاحٌ مُسلّحٌ مَشروع، لأنّه الوسيلة الوحيدة المتاحة للرجل الضعيف في مُواجهة الرجل القويّ وإذا لم توجد جبال أو غابات فالجَمعيّاتُ السرّية -كالتي نشأت في مصر عام ١٩١٩- تقوم بُمهمّة إطلاق النيران على الإنجليز. وهذا كلُّه سلوكٌ مشروع. فمتى يكون هذا الكفاحُ المشروع إرهاباً؟ إذا أُسيءَ استعماله، بمعنى أن نضعَ قُنْبُلةً في محطة المترو بلندن بدلاً من إطلاق النار على المسلحين الذين يحتلون أرضنا فتقتل القنبلة نساءً وأطفالاً أبرياء، وتثير الرأي العام الإنساني حول قضيتك.

مجلة «المجلة» ٢٢ (٤٢٤) في ٢٩ شباط (فبراير) ١٩٨٨.

| **Vocabulary** | literary, transparent | |
| --- | --- | --- |
| | modern terminology | كفاح مُسلّح، إرهاب |
| | political terms | كفاح مُسلّح، إرهاب، حرب المُقاوَمة، غُزاة، عَدُوّ، جيش محارب، استسلام، فَناء، عصابات مُكافحة |

حكومات مُسَيطِرة، قانون، مشروع، جمعيّات سرّيّة

إطلاق النيران، قنبلة، الرأي العام، قضيّة

|            | loan words | متْرو |
|---|---|---|

**Grammar**  accurate MSA structures; modern usage; compound sentences

| verbs with specific prepositions | بدأ في، أطلق النار على |
|---|---|
| passive | سُئلتُ، أُسيءَ |
| relative clauses | التي خاضها، الذي يحتلّ، الّذين يحتلّون |
| ellipsis | المُتاحة (لك)، يحارب (العدو) |
| conditional clauses | إذا أردتَ، إذا لم توجد، إذا أُسيءَ |
| negative | لا تكون، لاتملك، لا يبقى، لم توجد |
| nominal sentences | إنّ الكفاحَ، لأنه الوسيلةُ، هو كِفاح مسلّح |
|  | هذا سلوك، أنت في حاجة |

**Style**  The manner of writing is formal, but is communicative, attempting to engage the reader. The text has political overtones, arguing for and against the use of violence.

1.5.6  **R3**. This text is from Ibn ḵaldūn's renowned *Introduction*, the first part of his book *al-ᶜibar*. He was a noted historian who was considered the father of sociology (1332-1406). He completed this work toward the end of 1377.

الباب الثالث، الفصلُ الحادي عَشَر، صفحة ١٦٦

في أنّ مِن طبيعةِ المُلكِ التَرَف

وذلكَ أنَّ الأُمَّةَ إذا تَغَلَّبَتْ، مَلَكَت ما بأيدي أهل المُلك قبْلَها كَثُرَ

رياشُها ونعمتُها فتكثُرُ عوائدُهُم ويتجاوَزونَ ضَروراتِ العَيْشِ وخُشونتَهِ

إلى نَوافلِه ورقّتِه وزينتِه ويذهبونَ إلى اتِّباعِ مَنْ قبْلَهُم في عَوائدهم

وأحوالِهم وتصيرُ لتلكَ النَوافلِ عوائدُ ضَروريَّةٌ في تَحصيلِها ويَنْزِعونَ

مَعَ ذلكَ إلى رقّةِ الأحوالِ في المَطاعمِ والمَلابِسِ والفُرُشِ والآنيَة

ويَتَفاخَرونَ في ذلكَ ويُفاخِرونَ فيه غَيْرَهُم مِنَ الأُمَمِ في أكْلِ الطَّيِّبِ

49

وَلُبْسِ الأَنيقِ ورُكوبِ الفارِه وُيُناغي خَلَفُهُمْ في ذلكَ سَلَفَهُمْ إلى آخِرِ
الدَوْلَةِ وعلى قَدَرِ مُلْكِهِم يَكونُ حَظُّهُمْ في ذلكَ وتَرَفُهُمْ فيه إلى أَنْ
يَبْلُغوا في ذلكَ الغايَةَ الَّتي للدَوْلَةِ إلى أَنْ تَبْلُغَها بِحَسَبِ قُوَّتِها وعَوائِدِ
مَنْ قَبْلَها سُنَّةُ الله في خَلْقِه واللهُ تَعالى أَعْلَم
مُقَدِّمَةُ ابْنِ خَلْدون – دمشق: دار الفكر، بدون تاريخ

| | |
|---|---|
| **Vocabulary** | literary, sophisticated, learned, specialized |
| | set phrases      سُنَّةُ الله في خلقه؛ واللهُ تَعالى أَعْلم |
| | terminology    أهل المُلك؛ ضرورات العَيش؛ عَوائد؛ أمّة؛ دَولة؛ خَلَف؛ سَلَف |
| **Grammar** | accurate structures; classical usage; no punctuation; fully-vowelled text; complex sentences |
| | deviant usage    «قَدَر» بدل «قَدْر» |
| | relative clauses    ما بأيدي؛ مَنْ قبلَهم؛ الَّتي للدولة |
| | conditional clauses    إذا تغلّبت |
| | demonstratives    تلكَ النَوافل؛ في ذلكَ؛ مِنْ ذلكَ |
| | verbal nouns    مُلْك، تَرَف، ضَرورة، خُشونة، نافلة، رِقّة، زينة، اتّباع، تحصيل، لُبْس، رُكوب، قُوَّة، سُنَّة |
| | idiom    رقّة الحال[12] |
| **Style** | This text is written in a formal, scholarly fashion. It contains features of classical Arabic. The style is high flown, e.g., |

كَثُرَ رياشُها ونعمتُها
يتَجاوزونَ ضَرورات العَيْش وخُشونته إلى نَوافله ورِقّته
يَنْزعونَ مَعَ ذلكَ إلى رِقّة الأحوال في المَطاعِم والمَلابِسِ والفُرُشِ والآنِيَة
ويُناغي خَلَفُهُمْ في ذلكَ سَلَفَهُمْ

1.5.7    **R3**. The excerpt below is representative of the literature in the heyday of modern literary revival of Arabic during the first half of the twentieth century. Ahmad Hassan

---

[12] In modern usage, this phrase refers to poverty rather than wealth.

al-Zayyat, editor of the prestigious literary magazine *al-risāla* eulogizes a fellow man of letters, Mustafā Sādiq al-Rāfiʿī.

أُمَّةٌ وحده [13]

يا الله!! أفي لحظة عابرة من صباح يوم الإثنين الماضي يلفظ الرافعي نفسه في طوايا الغيب كومضة البرق لفها الليل، وقطرة الندى شربتها الشمس، وورقة الشجر أطاحها الخريف؛ ثم لا يبقى من هذا القلب الجياش، وهذا الشعور المرهف، وذلك الذهن الولود، إلا كما يبقى من النور في العين، ومن السرور في الحس، ومن الحلم في الذاكرة!!!

كان الرافعي يكره موت العافية فمات به: أرسل إليّ قبل موته المفاجئ يشكو فيه بعض الوهن في أعصابه، وأثر الركود في قريحته، ويقترح عليّ نظاماً جديداً للعمل يجد فيه الراحة حتى يخرج إلى المعاش فيقصر جهده على الأدب، ثم يسرد في إيجاز عزائمه ونواياه، ويعد المستقبل البعيد بالإنتاج الخصب والثمر المختلف؛ ويقول: «إن بنيتي الوثيقة وقلبي القوي سيتغلبان على هذا الضعف الطارئ فأصمد إلى حملة التطهير التي أريدها.»

كتب الرافعي إليّ هذا الكتاب في صباح الأحد، وتولى القدر عني الجواب في صباح الإثنين: قضى الصديق العامل الآمل الليلة الفاصلة بين ذينك اليومين على خير ما يقضيها الرخي الآمن على صحته وغبطته: صلى العشاء في عيادة ولده الدكتور محمد؛ ثم أقبل على بعض أصحابه هناك فجلا عنهم صدأ الفتور بحديثه الفكه ومزحه المهذب؛ ثم خرج فقضى واجب العزاء لبعض الجيرة؛ ثم ذهب وحده إلى متنزه المدينة فاستراض فيه طويلا بالمشي والتأمل؛ ثم رجع بعد موهن

---

[13] The text is not vowelled in the original, expecting the educated reader to provide the missing information. See Appendix 1 for a fully vowelled version.

من الليل إلى داره فأكل بعض الأكل ثم أوى إلى مضجعه.

مجلة «الرسالة» العدد ٢٠٢ في ١٧ مايو (أيّار) ١٩٣٧

| | |
|---|---|
| **Vocabulary** | literary, sophisticated, low frequency |
| | classical         مَوْهِن، ذَيْنكَ |
| | modern terminology     مَعاش، عِيادة، مُتَنَزَّه، اسْتَراضَ |
| | loan words                دُكتور |
| **Grammar** | accurate MSA structures; exemplary prose; no passive verbs |

imagery     طوايا الغيب؛ ومضة البرق لفها الليل؛ قطرة الندى شربتها؛
الشمس؛ ورقة الشجر أطاحها الخريف؛ القلب الجياش؛
الشعور المرهف؛ الذهن الولود؛ ما يبقى من النور في العين/
من السرور في الحس/من الحلم في الذاكرة؛ جلا صدأ الفتور

exclamation     أفي لحظةٍ!

ellipsis     و(ك)قطرة؛ و(ك)ورقة؛ و(من) هذا الشعور؛
و(من) ذلك الذهن؛ و(يشكو) أثر؛ (زمناً) طويلاً

Connective devices     و، ف، ثم

**Style**     The text has a high-flown style, elegant, literary, and poetic. There are several personal touches in reference to the deceased. Verbs alternate between past and present to convey the writer's feelings and the life and accomplishments of the deceased, e.g.,

يلفظ الرافعي نفسه في طوايا الغيب كومضة البرق لفها الليل، وقطرة
الندى شربتها الشمس، وورقة الشجرِ أطاحها الخريف؛

تولى القدر عني الجواب

جلا عنهم صدأ الفتور بحديثه الفكه

رجع بعد موهن من الليل إلى داره فأكل بعض الأكل ثم أوى إلى مضجعه

# 2 Vocabulary

## 2.1 Vocabulary study

Vocabulary is not a neglected subject in Arabic. Arab linguists, both ancient and modern, paid a great deal of attention to vocabulary research and lexicography. However, the focus has primarily been on the native speaker. Today, much attention is being paid to the needs of speakers of other languages learning Arabic. While we know that lexical competence is a critical component of overall proficiency, there is still no single vocabulary list on which to draw for textbook writing. This is partly due to differing conceptual frameworks for teaching Arabic and the lack of generally acceptable answers to the questions listed in the following sections. This part of the book samples lexical items relevant to each question and topic in an attempt to provide students of Arabic with lexical items that can aid their comprehension of texts, old and contemporary, and boost their ability to speak and write more effectively. This knowledge is seldom found in textbooks.

### 2.1.1 *What is a word?*

In English and Arabic alike, there is no clear answer to what constitutes a word. Can 'intention' and 'intentionally' be counted as one or two different words? Is 'toothbrush' one word? The same thing can be argued concerning Arabic. Is the word كَهْرَطيسيّ 'electromagnetic' one word? How about مَعْجون أَسْنان 'toothpaste' which refers to a single item? Is it two items or one? Are فَهِمَ، مَفهوم، استفهام 'to understand, understood, seeking information' three different words or one? It is even more difficult to make a distinction when the meanings are similar as in طُلاَّب and طَلَبة 'students'.

Sometimes the load of semantic information a word has can confuse learners. One Arabic word may translate into a multiword sentence in English (e.g. سَاعَدتُهُ 'I helped him'). Fortunately, this book is not about finding answers to these questions, but rather to present such items in a meaningful manner.

### 2.1.2 *How many words should a learner know?*

There exist some estimates of the number of words a native speaker of English knows, in addition to several frequency counts of the spoken and written languages. In Arabic, there are several frequency lists, but most of them are based on written texts (Abdo 1979). There is one on the spoken Arabic of children intended to guide the development of school textbooks for children and a corpus of Educated Spoken Arabic at the University of Leeds, which is used for sociolinguistic research (El-Hassan 1977). The statistics for Abdo's list tell us that the most frequent 500 words have 56.5% coverage, the first 1000 words have 67%, and the first 2000 words have 78.5% coverage.

### 2.1.3  *Are words learned as discrete items or in sequences?*

Ellis (1997) maintains that vocabulary is initially learned in sequences of words rather than as discrete items. Each chunk is assigned a single meaning, or function. After a sequence is acquired, it may then be analysed into its component parts. This view lends support to the importance of learning language in meaningful chunks, such as idioms, phrasal verbs, similes, phrasal metaphors, and collocations. A beginning student should learn the greeting السَّلامُ عَلَيكُم long before he learns سَلام 'peace' and the prepositional phrase عَلَيكُم. The phrase is basically learned as one unit signifying a greeting. Beginners learn to ask أينَ الحَمّام؟ 'Where's the bathroom?' perhaps with no knowledge of the structure of nominal sentences and that this particular structure atypically has the predicate before the subject.

### 2.1.4  *Can native-like language use be achieved?*

It is argued that native speakers are fluent because they have a vast store of memorized prefabricated phrases, and they do not always have to use grammatical rules in order to put words together (Schmitt and McCarthy 1997). If native-like speaking is speaking idiomatically as Ellis claims (1997), then learning sequences becomes a priority in vocabulary development. This book presents lists of idioms, collocations, phrasal verbs, similes, proverbs, and metaphors, and indicates the context of use for each.

In addition, combinations of words that are related semantically are listed to familiarize users of this book with a wide spectrum of words generally not covered in conventional textbooks.

## 2.2 Word information

### 2.2.1 *Characteristics of words*

For a successful, permanent learning of a word, a set of word characteristics must be known to the learner. These include the following:

1. Pronunciation and spelling. Full vowelling in Arabic is crucial for how a word is pronounced.
2. Root, derivational patterns, and verb conjugation.
3. Part of speech and grammatical function.
4. Denotative and connotative meaning. Sometimes these overlap, but in many cases they are different.
5. Related words (e.g., synonyms, antonyms).
6. Collocations (words which co-occur frequently).

### 2.2.2 *Phonetic information in Arabic words and pronunciation*

Phonetic information contained in an Arabic word includes the three short vowels, the *shadda* which indicates the doubling of a consonant, and *tanwīn* that indicates case and indefinite status, in addition to other less important diacritical marks. This information is under-represented in Arabic words in the majority of publications, including the news media, fiction, and scholarly research, although the writing system is equipped to provide this information through the use of diacritics. This failure to provide full phonetic information, much of which is also inflectional, causes ambiguity that requires readers to do a great deal of guessing from context, which native speakers have generally mastered. The problem is further exacerbated by a frequent failure to dot the final *yā'*, a practice that confuses it with *alif maqṣūra*. The lack of phonetic information leads to pronunciation errors on the part of educated people and even by radio and television announcers. The following examples illustrate the sources that lead to some of the common deviations.

| Vowelled | Unvowelled | Meaning |
|---|---|---|
| تُوُفِّيَ | توفى | to die |
| عَلِيّ | على | proper noun |
| وَفِيّ | وفى | faithful |
| حُمِلَ | حمل | he was carried |

One of the common errors, which is a direct consequence of this practice, that native speakers make is the use of the colloquial تَوَفَّى instead of the Standard form تُوُفِّيَ, which may be avoided by providing either a *damma* over the first letter or dotting the final *yā'*. This is, nevertheless, not an intractable problem. Providing the appropriate diacritical marks can readily disambiguate such forms. Below are some common pronunciation errors. Common errors are not generally in the realm of C forms, but rather they are MSA forms which do not conform to the rules. From a register perspective, common errors may rank as R2 although they are MSA forms.

| Meaning | Correct pronunciation (R3) | Error (R2) |
|---|---|---|
| buttock | أَلْيَة | إِلْيَة |
| on behalf (of) | بالأَصالة عَن | بالإِصالة عَن |
| incense | بَخور | بَخُور |
| clover | بِرْسيم | بَرْسيم |
| bribe | بِرْطيل | بَرْطيل |
| barrel | بِرْميل | بَرْميل |
| indigestion | تُخَمَة | تُخْمَة |
| memento, souvenir | تَذْكار | تِذْكار |

| | | |
|---|---|---|
| ticket, reminder | تَذْكَرَة | تَذْكَرَة |
| barracks | ثُكَنَة | ثَكَنَة |
| seriousness | جِدُّ | جَدُّ |
| blood clot | جَلْطَة | جَلْطَة |
| edge | حافَة | حافَّة |
| motion | حَراك | حراك |
| chameleon | حِرْباء | حَرْباء |
| soup | حَساء | حساء |
| according to | حَسَبَ | حَسْب |
| breast, between arms | حِضْن | حُضْن |
| arena, race track, dance floor | حَلَبَة | حَلَبَة |
| yellowish grain used as tonic | حُلْبَة | حلْبَة |
| to dream | حَلَمَ | حَلَمَ |
| throat | حَنْجَرَة | حُنْجَرَة |
| abscess | خُراج | خُراج |
| nose, elephant's trunk | خُرْطوم | خَرْطوم |
| vegetables | خُضَر | خُضار |
| courtship, engagement | خِطْبَة | خُطْبَة |
| plan | خُطَّة | خطَّة |
| to preside over, to head | رَأَسَ | رئَسَ |
| line of people, convoy | رَتَل | رَتَل |
| number | رَقْم | رَقْم |
| moisture | بِلَّة | (زادَ الطينَ) بَلَّة |
| customer | زَبون | زُبون |
| arsenic | زِرْنيخ | زَرْنيخ |
| thyme | سَعْتَر | زَعْتَر |

58

| wedding | زَفاف | زَفاف |
| door bolt, door knocker | سُقّاطة | سُقّاطة |
| load, charge | شُحْنة | شُحْنة |
| anus | شَرَج | شَرَج |
| police | شُرْطة | شُرْطة |
| chess | شِطْرَنْج | شِطْرَنْج |
| health | صِحَّة | صِحَّة |
| temple | صَدْغ | صَدْغ |
| whistle | صُفّارة | صُفّارة |
| steel; rigid; lower back | صُلْب | صُلْب |
| valve | صِمام | صَمّام |
| Zionist | صِهْيونيّ | صُهْيونيّ |
| association, relation | عَلاقة | عُلاقة |
| addition, increase | علاوَة | عَلاوَة |
| force, by force | عَنْوَة | عُنْوَة |
| opening | فَتْحة | فَتْحة |
| outstanding, celebrity | فَطْحَل | فَطْحَل |
| cauliflower | قُنَّبيط | قَرْنَبيط |
| shivering, shudder | قُشَعْريرة | قَشْعَريرة |
| lock | قُفْل | قِفْل |
| daughter/sister-in-law | كَنَّة | كَنَّة |
| gums | لِثَة | لِثَّة |
| to lick, to devour | لَحِسَ | لَحَسَ |
| to lick | لَعَقَ | لَعَقَ |
| cigarette | لِفافة | لُفافة |
| accent | لُكْنة | لَكْنة |

| deceased | مُتَوَفَّى | مُتَوَفِّي |
|---|---|---|
| narcotics | مُخَدَّرات | مُخَدِّرات |
| coral | مَرْجان | مُرْجان |
| chaste, virtuous | مَصون | مُصان |
| straits | مَضايق | مَضائق |
| metal, mineral, origin | مَعْدِن | مَعْدَن |
| fair, exhibition | مَعْرِض | مَعْرَض |
| from everywhere | حَدَب | (من كلِّ) حَدْبٍ |
| climate | مُناخ | مَناخ |
| task | مُهِمَّة | مَهَمَّة |
| grammarian, grammatical | نَحْوِيّ | نَحْوِي |
| bran, waste, refuse | نُخالة | نخالة |
| sawdust | نُشارَة | نشارَة |
| to be exhausted, depleted | نَفِدَ | نَفَذَ |
| thick stick, club | هِراوَة | هُراوَة |
| tremor; vivacity | هِزَّة | هَزَّة |
| forbearance, leniency | هَوادَة | هُوادَة |
| personality, identity, ID card | هُوِيَّة | هَوِيَّة |

## 2.3 Conceptual organization of words

### 2.3.1 *One word in English, multiple words in Arabic*

Different languages assign meanings to words differently. For example, there are two words for *uncle* in Arabic. The word *cousin* has eight different Arabic equivalents, depending on the gender of the referent and which parental side. The English words for *cousin* and *uncle* are structurally unrelated, whereas, in Arabic, they are related to 'uncle' عَمّ.

| English word | Arabic equivalent |
| --- | --- |
| uncle (paternal) | عَمّ |
| _____ (maternal) | خال |
| aunt (paternal) | عَمّة |
| _____ (maternal) | خالة |
| cousin (father's brother's son) | ابْنُ عَمّ |
| _____ (father's brother's daughter) | ابْنَةُ عَمّ |
| _____ (mother's brother's son) | ابْنُ خال |
| _____ (mother's brother's daughter) | ابْنَةُ خال |
| _____ (father's sister's son) | ابْنُ عَمّة |
| _____ (father's sister's daughter) | ابْنَةُ عَمّة |
| _____ (mother's sister's son) | ابْنُ خالة |
| _____ (mother's sister's daughter) | ابْنَةُ خالة |
| brother-in-law (sister's husband) | صِهْر |
| _____ (husband's brother) | سِلْف |

### 2.3.2 *One word in Arabic, two or more in English*

In contrast to those in the preceding section, there are words in Arabic whose meaning subsumes two or more equivalents in English. The different equivalents are separated by slashes.

| | |
| --- | --- |
| Finger/toe | إصْبَع |
| daughter-in-law/sister-in-law | كَنّة |
| brother-in-law (sister's husband) | صِهْر |
| son-in-law (daughter's husband) | |
| shade/shadow | ظِلّ |
| long/tall | طَويل |
| mountain path/canyon/gulf | شِعْب |

| | |
|---|---|
| tip, point, apex | طَرَف |
| edge, border, limit | (طَرَف المائدة) |
| area, region | (زُرنا الأطرافَ النائية.) |
| party, side | (كان طَرَفاً في النزاع.) |
| limb, extremity | (تعاني من برودة الأطراف.) |
| term (in mathematics and logic) | (طَرَفا المُعادلة) |
| touch, trace, tinge | (في الطعام طَرَفُ حَلاوة.) |
| generous, bountiful, hospitable/ | كريم |
| noble, respectable, decent/precious, valuable | |
| immigrant / emigrant | مُهاجِر |

### 2.3.3  *One word in English, multiple equivalents in Arabic*

The English verb *to wear* collocates with several objects, denoting different meanings. Some of the Arabic equivalents are expressed by different verbs.

| | |
|---|---|
| *to wear* a coat | ارتَدى معْطَفاً |
| _____ spectacles | وَضَعَ/لَبِسَ نَظّارة |
| _____ shoes | لَبِسَ حذاءً |
| _____ perfume | تَعَطَّرَ |
| _____ a hat | اعتَمَرَ قُبَّعَةً |
| _____ a smile | ابْتَسَمَ |
| _____ a beard | رَبّى لحْيَة |
| _____ one's hair in a certain manner | صَفَّفَتْ شَعْرَها ... |
| _____ a flag (ship) | تَرفَعُ عَلَماً |
| _____ a medal | تَقَلَّدَ وساماً |
| _____ one's shirt to tatters | بَلِيَ/خَلِقَ القميص |

| | |
|---|---|
| _____ one's patience | اسْتَنْفَدَ صَبْرَه |
| _____ thin (one's hope) | تَضاءَلَ، نَفدَ |
| _____ well | يَتَحَمَّل، يَدُوم |
| _____ slowly (time) | انقَضى بِبُطْء |
| _____ s.o. out | أَنْهَكَ، أَرْهَقَ |
| *interest* | حصة، سهم |
| *interest* | الولوع، الاهتمام بشيء |
| *interest* | خير، صلاح، منفعة ذاتية |
| *interest* | مصلحة |
| *interest* | فائدة مصرفية، ربا |
| *interest* | أصحاب النفوذ |
| *interest* | شوق، عناية، اهتمام |
| *interest* | أهمية، تأثير |
| *net* | شبكة |
| *net* | شَرَك |
| *net* | كرة تصيب الشبكة في كرة المضرِب |
| *net* | مقدار صاف |
| *net* | جوهر، لُبّ، زبدة |
| *net* | صافٍ |
| *net* | نهائيّ |

### 2.3.4    *English words with multiple equivalents in Arabic*

There are many English words that have more than one typical equivalent in Arabic. Here are some of them with their Arabic equivalents. The different meanings are separated with a slash.

| | |
|---|---|
| abuse | أَساءَ استعْمالَ (السُلْطَة)/أهانَ |
| accomplishment | إتْمام، إنْجاز/ مَأْثُرة |

| | |
|---|---|
| to apply | طَبَّقَ/ تَقَدَّمَ بِطَلَب |
| ball | كُرَة/ حَفْلَةُ رَقْص |
| bank | مَصرِف/ ضَفَّة |
| bar | مَشْرَب/ قَضيب/ مِهْنَةُ المُحاماة/فاصِلٌ موسيقيّ/ما عَدا |
| change | تَحَوُّل/غِيار (من الثِياب)/قِطَعُ النُقود الصَغيرَة |
| character | شَخْصِيَّة/صِفَة |
| cold | بارِد /بَرْدان |
| comfortable | مُرْتاح/مُريح |
| constitution | دُسْتور/تَرْكيب |
| to cry | صَرَخَ/بَكى |
| cure | شِفاء/مُعالَجة/دَواء/تَمْليح أو تَقْديد الأغذِيَة/مَنْصِب ديني |
| decent | مُحْتَشَم/مُرْض/لائِق |
| figure | جِسْم/عَدَد |
| fork | شَوْكَة/شُعْبَة |
| honest | صادِق/صَحيح/مُتَواضِع/فاضِل/غير مَغْشوش |
| invalid | مَريض/باطِل |
| lush | مورِق، أخْضَر، خَصِب/مُزْدَهِر، مُرْبِح/لَذيذ، مُشَةً/غَنيٌّ بِـ شَرابٌ مُسْكِر/سِكِّير |
| office | مَكْتَب/مَنْصِب |
| to order | أصْدَرَ أمْراً/طَلَبَ خِدْمَةً أو سِلْعَة |
| organ | آلَةٌ موسيقِيَّة/عُضْوٌ من الجِسم/أداةٌ |
| to realize | حَقَّقَ/فَهِمَ |
| relations | عَلاقات/أقارِب |
| sentence | جُمْلَة/حُكْمٌ |
| square | مَيْدان/مُرَبَّع/كوس (أداة هَندسِيّة)/مُتْقَن/مُنْصِف/عَريض |

مُشْبِع/مُواجِه/مُباشَرَةً

| | |
|---|---|
| stable | إسْطَبْلُ/ثابِت |
| to succeed | نَجَحَ/ وَلِيَ، تَبِعَ/وَرِثَ |
| traffic | سَيْر، مُرور/تجارة |
| trunk | جِذْع/خُرْطوم/صُنْدوق |

### 2.3.5  *Arabic words with multiple meanings*

Arabic words with multiple meanings are treated in this book
as polysemes (see 2.4.14). A polysemous item is a word that
has more than one meaning. Words which change their
meanings based on the direct object or preposition that follows
them are not included with polysemes. These are listed in
sections 2.4.10 and 2.4.11. A selection of Arabic polysemes
is found in section 2.4.14.

## 2.4   Semantic processing of words

Students may resort to several learning strategies in order to
acquire vocabulary, including rote learning, flashcards, and textual
context. It seems that instruction and learning have ignored to
some extent the importance of forming semantic associations
among words to enhance the acquisition, storage, and retrieval of
lexical items. In the following sections are some ways which aid
deep-level semantic processing of words by organizing and ma-
nipulating words in different ways (Sökmen 1997).

### 2.4.1 *Semantic maps*

Semantic maps contain words that cluster together because
of some semantic features they have in common, not on the
basis of any morphological or structural criteria. Words related
to مَطعَم 'restaurant' may cluster in no specific order as in the

chart for 'restaurant,' or they may be ordered according to grammatical classes as in the semantic map for أَنْف 'nose'. There are nouns, a verbal noun, a verb, an adjective, and three idioms associated with the latter.

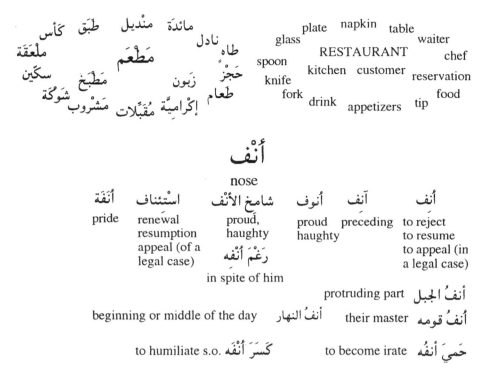

Semantic mapping may be used as a pedagogical/learning tool to review and reinforce learned vocabulary. In a class setting it works as a brainstorming, collaborative activity in which all students participate. After the words are listed, they may be sorted or classified according to some scheme. Not all students who contribute the words, however, are likely to agree on all the associations, because every student has a different cognitive structure and experience. The words associated with each item are listed in no particular order.

| | | | |
|---|---|---|---|
| *healthcare* | | العناية الصحية | |
| dispensary, infirmary | مُستَوصف | hospital | مُستشفى |
| medicine | دواء | clinic | عِيادة |
| syringe | إبرة/حُقنة | treatment | عِلاج |
| tranquillizer | مُهدِّئ | pain killer | مُسكِّن |
| vitamins | فيتامينات | antibiotic | مُضادّ حَيَويّ |
| nurse | مُمَرِّض | physician | طبيب |
| test | تحليل | examination | فحص |
| illness, disease | مَرَض | x-ray | أشعّة |
| exercise | رياضة | old age | شَيخوخة |
| rehabilitation | تأهيل | nutrition | تغذية |
| massage | تدليك | surgery | عملية جراحية |
| preventive medicine | الطب الوقائي | physical therapy | علاج طبيعي |
| cane, walking stick | عُكّاز | immunization | تلقيح |
| ambulance | سيارة إسعاف | wheelchair | كرسي الـمُقعَدين |

| | | | |
|---|---|---|---|
| *honour* | | الشَرَف | |
| respect, esteem | احْترام | high standing | رفْعَة |
| tribute | تَكْريم | appreciation | تَقْدير |
| righteousness | اسْتِقامَة | truthfulness, sincerity | صدْق |
| glory | مَجْد | valour, generosity | مُروءَة |
| high regard | حَسَب | high rank, nobility | عُلا |
| illustrious, eminent | شَريف | (respectable) lineage | نَسَب |
| pride | أنَفَة | Prophet's lineage | سُلالَةُ النَبيّ |
| tribe | قَبيلة | family | أُسْرَة |

| | | | |
|---|---|---|---|
| mistake, error | خَطَأ | lapse, mistake | زَلَل |
| rape | اغْتِصاب | defeat | هَزيمَة |
| flaw, shame | عَيْب | disgrace, shame | عار |
| (in war, especially of women) | | captivity | سَبْيٌ |
| wife | زَوْجَة | adultery, fornication | زِنى |
| sister | أُخْت | daughter | ابْنَة |
| | | mother | أُم |

cousin (paternal uncle's daughter) ابْنَة عَم

cousin (maternal uncle's daughter) ابْنَة خال

---

*transportation*  المُواصَلات

| | | | |
|---|---|---|---|
| bus, coach | حافِلَة | airplane | طائِرَة |
| train | قِطار | car, automobile | سَيّارَة |
| motorcycle | دَرّاجَةٌ نارِيَّة | bicycle | دَرّاجَة |
| ship | سَفينَة | ferryboat | مُعَدِّية |
| camel | جَمَل | boat | قارِب |
| donkey, ass | حِمار | horse | حِصان |
| carriage, wagon | عَرَبَة | mule | بَغْل |
| pontoon, floating house | عَوّامة | caravan | قافِلَة |

---

*family*  الأُسْرَة

| | | | |
|---|---|---|---|
| wife | زَوْجَة | husband | زَوْج |
| mother | أُم | father | أَب |
| sister | أُخْت | brother/half brother | أَخ |
| wet nurse, foster m. | أُم بالرَضاعة | foster b./s. | أَخ/أُخت بالرَضاعة |

68

| | | | |
|---|---|---|---|
| male offspring | صِبْيان | children | أَوْلاد |
| aunt | امْرَأَةُ الخال | female offspring | بَنات |
| grandmother | جَدَّة | grandfather | جَدّ |
| aunt | عَمَّة | uncle | عَمّ |
| aunt | خالة | uncle | خال |
| son-/brother-in-law | صِهْر | aunt | إمْرَأَةُ العَم |
| full brother | شَقيق | sister-/daughter-in-law | كَنَّة |
| daughter | ابْنَة | son | ابْن |
| granddaughter | حَفيدة | grandson | حَفيد |
| cousin | ابْنَة العَم | cousin | ابْن العَم |
| cousin | ابْنَة الخال | cousin | ابْن الخال |
| cousin | ابْنَة الخالة | cousin | ابْن الخالة |
| cousin | ابْنَة العَمَّة | cousin | ابْن العَمَّة |
| brother-in-law (sister-in-law's husband) | | | عَديل |

| | |
|---|---|
| *marriage* | الزَواج |

| | | | |
|---|---|---|---|
| fiancé | خَطيب | engagement | خِطْبَة |
| husband | زَوْج | fiancée | خَطيبَة |
| wife | زَوْجَة | marriage contract | كتاب |
| divorce | طَلاق | marriage | زَواج |
| matrimonial authority | عِصْمَة | alimony | نَفَقَة |
| dowry | صَداق | dowry | مَهْر |
| bride/groom | عَروس | wedding | عُرْس |
| gift, present | هَدِيَّة | wedding | زِفاف |
| guest | مَدْعُوّ | wedding gift | نُقوط |

69

dowry payment made up front مُقَدَّم

balance of dowry to be paid in case of divorce مُؤَخَّر

*school* المدرسة

The items below are arranged arbitrarily into groups: people, objects, school subjects, places, and actions.

## People

| | | | |
|---|---|---|---|
| teacher | مُدَرِّس | teacher | مُعَلِّم |
| pupil, student | تِلْميذ | professor | أُسْتاذ |
| custodian, janitor | فَرّاش | student | طالِب |
| principal | ناظِر | principal | مُدير |
| assistant principal | وَكيل | secretary | أمين سِرّ |

## Objects

| | | | |
|---|---|---|---|
| notebook | دَفْتَر | book | كتاب |
| drawing tools | أدَوات رَسْم | pen, pencil | قَلَم |

## School subjects

| | | | |
|---|---|---|---|
| art | فُنون | music | موسيقى |
| sport | رياضَة | hand work | أشْغال |
| games | ألعاب | mathematics | رياضِيّات |
| algebra | جَبْر | arithmetic | حِساب |
| integral calculus | تَكامُل | differential equations | تَفاضُل |
| physics | فيزْياء | chemistry | كيمياء |
| biology | أحْياء | geology | جيولوجيا |
| history | تاريخ | geography | جُغْرافيا |
| logic | مَنْطِق | philosophy | فَلْسَفَة |

| | | | |
|---|---|---|---|
| sociology | علم الاجتماع | psychology | عِلمُ النَفْس |
| literature | أَدَب | civic education | تَرْبِيَة اجْتِماعِيَّة |
| story | قِصَّة | poetry | شِعْر |
| drama | مَسْرَح | novel | رِوايَة |
| trigonometry | حِساب المُثَلَّثات | literary texts | نصوص أدبية |
| rote learning | مَحفوظات | literary criticism | نَقْد أُدَبي |
| foreign language | لُغَة أجْنَبِيَّة | grammar | قَواعد |
| lesson | دَرْس | religious education | تَرْبِيَة دينيَّة |

Places

| | | | |
|---|---|---|---|
| playground | مَلْعَب | classroom | غُرْفَةُ الصَفّ |
| cafeteria | مَقْصَف | gymnasium | صالة مُغْلَقَة |
| administrations | إدارَة | toilets, restrooms | مَراحيض |

Actions

| | | | |
|---|---|---|---|
| game, match | مُباراة | school hours | دَوام |
| class period | حِصَّة | tardiness | تَأَخُّر |
| activity | نَشاط | truancy | غِياب |
| dismissal | فَصْل | discipline | انْضِباط |
| punishment | عِقاب | expulsion | طَرْد |

### 2.4.2 *Categorization*

Another form of deep-level semantic processing is categorization. It involves the classification of words on the basis of the category to which they belong. Categories may be arbitrarily selected. They can be structural and/or semantic. The following is an excerpt from a column by Mohamed al-Rumayhi, a well-known columnist and editor. Vocabulary items are culled from the text and assigned to categories.

وتَدورُ قصَّةُ الفيلم حوْلَ هذه التَناقُضات الكَبيرة والفَجَّة الَّتي وُجِدَتْ في لُبنان، وربَّما لا يَزالُ بَعضُها موجوداً. فهذا الشابُّ البَيروتيُّ الصَغيرُ والَّذي يَبْدو أنَّ والدَهُ مُثَقَّفٌ وأُمَّهُ تَتَعاطى المُحاماة، هو نِتاجُ التَناقُض في التَربِيَة بَيْنَ المَدْرَسة والبَيْت والشارع البَيْروتيِّ. ففي الوَقْتِ الَّذي تُقِرُّ فيه المَدْرَسةُ أنْ يُنادي هذا الشابُّ بالتَحِيَّة في الصَباح بالفَرَنسِيَّة وبنَشيد فَرَنسيٍّ، يَخْرُجُ من الصُفوف ويَلتَقِطُ مُكَبِّر الصَوت ويَبْدأ بنَشيد وطنيٍّ عَرَبيٍّ «كُلُّنا للوَطَن». الواضِحُ أنَّ البَحْثَ عنِ الهُوِيَّةَ أوَّلُ ما يُقَرِّرُهُ المُخْرِجُ على المُشاهدين من دون أنْ يَحْسِمَه.

في مُقَدِّمات الفيلم تَأخُذُنا أصواتُ أزيزِ الطائِرات الإسرائِيليَّة على رُؤوس المُشاة والمُشاهدينَ وهُم شاخِصوا الأبصارِ إلى السَماء، ويُراهِنُ الشبابُ على أيٍّ منْ أنواع الطائرات الحَربِيَّة هي الَّتي تلكَ في السَماءِ، وكأنَّ الأمْرَ مَقْضِيٌّ ولا رادَّ لَهُ.

ثُمَّ نُشاهدُ الاعتداءَ على الحافِلة الَّتي كانَتْ تَحمِلُ مَجموعَةً من الفلسطينيِّينَ منْ تَلِّ الزَعتَر. وقُتِلَ أبْرِياءُ فيها، مِمَّا أشْعَلَ سِلسِلَةَ الصِدامات في بَيْروتَ الَّتي قادَتْ بدَوْرِها إلى حَرْب. وقَدْ قامَ بهذاالاعتداءِ أفرادٌ مُلَثَّمونَ غَيْرُ مَعروفي الهُوِيَّة بمَلابِسَ عَسْكَرِيَّة. يَبْدأ الاشتباكُ بَيْنَ فَريقَيْن في بَيْروتَ، وتَنقَسِمُ المَدينةُ إلى شَرقِيَّةٍ وغَرْبِيَّة، وتَتَوقَّفُ الدِراسةُ ويَنْتَشِرُ الطُلّابُ في الشَوارع بَيْنَ مَسيرات احتِجاجٍ ومُظاهَرات وبَيْنَ تَسَكُّعٍ عَبَثيٍّ، وتَتَفَكَّكُ العَلاقاتُ الأسَرِيَّة، ويَكثُرُ العَوَزُ والفاقَةُ، ويَتَّجِهُ البَعْضُ كَمَخْرَجٍ إلى الحِجاب والجامِع، ويَنْعَكِسُ كُلُّ ذلكَ على تلكَ الأُسْرَة الصَغيرة الَّتي تَتَقاذَفُها رَغبَةُ الأُمِّ في الخُروج منَ المَحْرَقَة الكَبيرة، ورَغْبَةُ الأب في ألاَّ يَتْرُكَ مَكانَهُ ومَنْزِلَهُ مُسْتَنْكِراً نَظرَةَ الآخَرينَ في البِلاد المُسْتَقبِلَة للمُهاجِرينَ منْ لُبْنان.

بِتَصَرُّف «المَجَلَّة» ٣-٩ تِشرين الأوَّل (أكتوبر) ١٩٩٩

## Conflict

| war | حَرْب | attack, aggression | اعْتِداء |
|---|---|---|---|
| clashes | صدامات | killing | قَتْل |
| military | عَسْكَرِيَّة | close-quarters fighting | اشْتِباك |

## Family

| mother | أُم | father | أَب |
|---|---|---|---|
| wife | زَوْجَة | father, parent | والِد |

## Adjectives

| blunt, rude | فَجَّة | tragic, distressing | مُفْجِع |
|---|---|---|---|
| big, huge | كَبيرة | small | صَغيرة |
| strange, unfamiliar | غَريبة | burning, blazing | مُلْتَهِبَة |
| | | buried, hidden | دَفينة |

## Feminine nouns

| states, countries | دُوَل | war | حَرْب |
|---|---|---|---|
| identity | هُوِيَّة | sky | سَماء |
| poverty, neediness | فاقة | study, school | دراسة |
| march | مَسيرات | desire | رَغْبَة |
| relations | عَلاقات | demonstrations | مُظاهَرات |
| introductory parts | مُقَدِّمات | attributes | صِفات |
| | | story | قِصَّة |

## Masculine nouns

| megaphone | مُكَبِّرُ الصَوْت | film, movie | فيلم |
|---|---|---|---|
| homeland, country | وَطَن | anthem | نَشيد |
| buzzing | أزيز | attack | اعْتِداء |

73

| | | | |
|---|---|---|---|
| necessity, want | عَوَز | hand-to-hand combat | اشْتِباك |
| veil | حِجاب | escape, way out | مَخْرَج |
| going out, leaving | خُروج | protest | احْتِجاج |
| dialogues | حِوارات | loitering, hanging around | تَسَكُّع |
| emigrant | مُهاجِر | the world | العالَم |

### Derived relative (*nisba*) adjectives (اسم النسبة)

| | | | |
|---|---|---|---|
| narrative | رِوائيّ | documentary | وَثائِقيّ |
| of Beirut | بَيْروتيّ | French | فَرَنْسيّ |
| warlike | حَرْبيَّة | Arab | عَرَبيّ |
| military | عَسْكَريّ | Palestinian | فِلَسْطينيّ |
| western | غَرْبيَّة | eastern | شَرْقيَّة |
| Lebanese | لُبْنانيّ | of families | أُسَريّ |
| outside | خارِجيّ | absurd, frivolous | عَبَثيّ |

### Places

| | | | |
|---|---|---|---|
| street | شارع | home, house | بَيْت |
| a quarter in Beirut | تَلُّ الزَعْتَر | Beirut | بَيْروت |
| mosque | جامِع | town, city | مَدينة |
| Lebanon | لُبْنان | house, residence | مَنْزِل |
| camp | مُخَيَّم | school | مَدْرَسَة |
| place | مَكان | incinerator | مَحْرَقَة |

### Profession or calling

| | | | |
|---|---|---|---|
| cultured, intellectual | مُثَقَّف | legal practice, the bar | مُحاماة |
| (film) director | مُخْرِج | students | طُلّاب |

<u>People</u>

| | | | |
|---|---|---|---|
| teenager | مُراهِق | character, person | شَخْصِيَّة |
| passersby | مارَّة | young man | شابّ |
| spectator | مُشاهِد | pedestrians | مُشاة |
| innocent people | أَبْرِياء | youth | شَباب |
| individuals | أَفْراد | women | نِساء |
| | | masked individuals | مُلَثَّمون |

<u>Means of transportation</u>

| | | | |
|---|---|---|---|
| bus, coach | حافِلة | aircraft | طائِرَة |

### 2.4.3 *Matching*

Matching is another tool used to process words at a deep semantic level. Words that collocate may be matched together, such as nouns with appropriate adjectives, synonyms, antonyms, verbs with the proper preposition, and so forth. Words from the above passage are used to create different matching lists: nouns that generally collocate, nouns which go together, and verbs with appropriate prepositions. The answers to the following exercises are in the Answer Key in Appendix 2.

Match nouns from the two lines that generally collocate together. There is an extra item in the second line.

مَسيرَةٌ – مُخْرِجٌ – مَلابِسُ – تَلُّ – نَشيدٌ – شاخِصٌ – مُكَبِّرٌ

الزَعْتَرِ – النَظَرِ – الصَوْتِ – احتِجاج – مَحْرَقَة – وَطَنيّ – عَسْكَرِيَّة – الفيلم

Match verbs with the appropriate preposition. One preposition may be used with more than one verb.

راهَنَ – دارَ – اتَّجَهَ – قامَ – اعْتَدى – انْقَسَمَ – انْعَكَسَ

حَوْلَ – عَنْ – بِ – عَلى – إلى

Match nouns which go together.

أُمّ – طالب – صدامات – حجاب – شابّ – شَرْقِيّ – عَوَز

فاقَة – مُراهِق – غَرْبِيّ – مَسيرَة – مَدْرَسَة – اشْتِباكات – أُسْرَة – جامِع

### 2.4.4 *Word analysis*

Selected words are analysed with regard to how they are spelled and pronounced, their morphological structure and inflections, common derivations,[1] their grammatical function in the sentence in which they occur, the different denotative and connotative meanings they have, and associations with other words (e.g. collocates, synonyms, antonyms, homonyms). A sentence and a phrase are selected from the text above. The words under consideration are underlined.

والِدُهُ مُثَقَّفٌ.

1. The word مُثَقَّفٌ is a passive participle (اسم مـفـعـول) derived from Form II of the root ثقف. It shows a double *ḍamma* on its end, indicating an indefinite status for the noun and a nominative case.

2. The Form I verb has two pronunciations: ثَقِفَ, which means 'to find', and ثَقُفَ, meaning 'to be skilful, clever'. The word in question is derived from ثَقَّفَ 'to set right' and 'to educate', among other meanings. So, the word مُثَقَّفٌ means 'educated, cultured'. The verbal noun derived from ثَقَّفَ is تَثْقيف 'cultivation of the mind, education'. From ثَقَفَ we can derive ثَقافَة 'culture, refinement, education' and ثَقافيّ 'cultural, intellectual'. It is a relative adjective. Form III yields a meaning unrelated to education. ثاقَفَ 'to fence

---

[1] See Derivation 3.4 in the chapter on grammar.

(with s.o.)', and its verbal noun is مُثـاقَفَة 'fencing'. Form V yields تَثَقَّفَ 'to acquire education, learning, refinement'. The verbal noun for it is تَثَقُّف 'culturedness, refinement', and the active participle is مُتَثَقِّف 'self-educated, cultured'.

3. This word is the predicate, or comment, of the sentence. Having no particles or defective verbs introducing this nominal sentence, both the subject and predicate are nominative (اسم مرفوع).

4. Related words: مُتَعَلِّم، مُتَنَوِّر، مُتَأَدِّب، مُطَّلِع، عارِف، عَليم.

## مِنَ المَحْرَقَة

A. The preposition مِنْ. This preposition is normally pronounced مِنْ, but when followed by a word beginning with the definite article الـ, it is pronounced مِنَ. It makes the following noun genitive (مَــجْـــرور). This preposition has eight usages, or meanings.[2] Of these eight, the meaning of incipience applies here.

B. The noun المَحْرَقَة.

1. This is a noun of place derived from Form I verb of the root حــرق. It is definite and feminine as indicated by the article الـ and the feminine marker ة. Its inflectional suffix is *kasra*, denoting the genitive case.

2. Several derivations can be obtained from the Form I verb حَرَقَ 'to burn'. The verbal noun is حَرْق 'burn, incineration'. The plural is حُروق. Add a feminine marker to get a slightly different meaning; حَــرْقَـــة signifies 'burning, a stinging sensation', and especially 'heartburn'. A meaning similar to the preceding one is found also in حَرَقان. The word حَريق means 'conflagration', and the passive participle yields مَحْروق 'burned'. Its plural مَحْروقات, however, means *fuel,*

---

2   See Prepositions 3.11 in the chapter on grammar.

and it is used in this sense in the plural only. Form IV أَحْرَقَ yields the active participle مُحْرِق used in the term قُنْبُلَة مُحْرِقَة 'incendiary bomb'. The verbal noun is إِحْراق. Form VIII اِحْتَرَقَ 'to burn, to be aflame' has اِحْتِراق 'combustion' as a verbal noun, which is used in phrases such as غُرْفَةُ الاحْتِراق 'combustion chamber' and قابِل للاحْتِراق 'flammable, combustible'.

3. This is a prepositional phrase which comprises a preposition مِنْ which governs a noun المَحْـرَقَـة. The noun is, therefore, in the genitive case as indicated by the *kasra* suffix.

4. Related words: مَوْقِد 'oven', نار 'fire', حَرارَة 'heat'.

### 2.4.5 *Lexical ordering*

Associations among lexical items help in learning, retaining, and retrieving words by arranging them according to specific criteria based on semantic, not structural knowledge. This entails the examination of various features of each word to see how it fits in relation to other words. The strings of words below are scrambled. Try to put them in order according to the criterion listed before each set. You can check the Answer Key in Appendix 2 to verify your work.

Whole-part relationship:

جِنزير، بُرْغي، سَرْج، مِقْوَد، دَراجَة، مِصْباح، عَزَقَة، دَواسَة، دولاب

chain, screw, seat, handlebar, bicycle, lamp, nut, pedal, wheel

مِلح، بَهارات، طَبْخة، خُضَر، سَمْن، لَحْم، أرُز

salt, spices, dish, vegetables, shortening, meat, rice

Status:   عَميد، مُعيد، طالِب، أسْتاذ، وكيل، مُحاضِر

dean, graduate student, student, professor, provost, lecturer

قائد، ضابِط، رَئيس، جُندي

commander, officer, president, soldier

Degree of disagreement:

اخْتِلاف، مُقاطَعَة، بَحْث، شِجار، حِوار، تَنازُع، مُناقَشَة

disagreement, parting company/boycott, discussion, quarrel, dialogue, dispute, argument

Role in a process:

صانِع، مُسْتَهْلِك، مُصَمِّم، مُخْتَرِع

manufacturer, consumer, designer, inventor

مُصَوِّر، مُمَثِّل، كاتِب، مُخْرِج، مُنْتِج

cameraman, actor, writer, (film) director, producer

Degree of responsibility:

شُرْطِي، وَزيرُ الداخِلِيَّة، رَئيسُ الجُمْهورِيَّة

police officer, President, interior minister

بائِع، مُدَقِّقُ حِسابات، مُحاسِب

salesman, auditor, accountant

Analogy:

| | |
|---|---|
| desert, sea, ship, camel | صَحْراء، بَحْر، سَفينة، جَمَل |
| air, machine, man, electricity | هَواء، آلة، إنْسان، كَهْرَباء |

General-specific:

| | |
|---|---|
| school, math, education | مَدْرَسَة، الرِياضِيّات، تَعْليم |

Degree of liking:

أحَبَّ، سَرَّ، عَشِقَ، مالَ إلى، أعْجَبَ

please, like, make happy, love, lean toward

Degree of dislike:

أَعْرَضَ عَنْ، أَبْغَضَ، كَرِهَ، انْزَعَجَ مِنْ، نَفَرَ مِنْ

to shun, to loathe, to hate, to be annoyed, to have an aversion to

### 2.4.6 *Pictorial schemata*

Graphs, maps, and flow charts can enhance meaning differentiation of words significantly. Examine the scrambled sequences and see how they look when put in a logical order.

Scale: غائمٌ جُزْئِيَّاً، صَحْوٌ، عاصِفَةٌ رَعْدِيَّة، ماطِر، غائِم، مُتَلَبِّدٌ بالغُيُوم

partially cloudy, clear, thunderstorm, rainy, cloudy, overcast

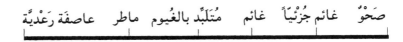

مَلَل، سَعادَة، حُزْن، اكْتِئاب، فَرَح، رِضىً، سُرُور

boredom, happiness, sadness, depression, joy, contentment, pleasure

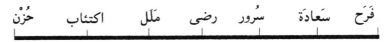

Tree diagram:

a. Health

الجِسْمِيَّة، دَواء، العَقْلِيَّة، مُعالَجَة، مُعالَجَةٌ نَفْسِيَّة، عاداتُ حَسَنَة، أَشِعَّة، الصِحَّة، رِياضة، وِقايَة، جِراحَة

physical, medicine, mental, treatment, psychological treatment, good habits, radiation, health, exercise, prevention, surgery

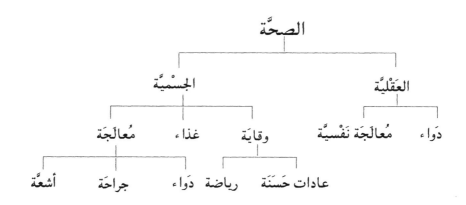

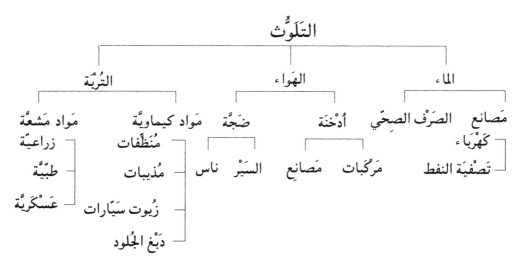

b. Pollution

مَصانِع، تَصْفِيَةُ النفط، الهَواء، عَسْكَرِيَّة، مَرْكَبات، التُرْبَة، مَوادُ مَشِعَّة،
الصَرْفُ الصحّي، مُنَظِّفات، كَهْرَبا ء، مَوادُ كيماوِيَّة، طِبِّيَّة، التَلَوُّث، أَدْخِنَة،
السَيْر، زراعِيَّة، مُذيبات، ناس، ضَجَّة، زُيوتُ سَيّارات، دَبْغُ الجُلود

factories, oil refining, air, military, vehicles, soil, radio-active
material, sewage, detergents, chemicals, medical, pollution,
fumes, traffic, agrarian, solvents, people, noise, automotive
oils, leather tanning

### 2.4.7 *Collocation*

This is the phenomenon where some words generally co-occur with other words, resulting in a phrase that may or may not have a meaning deriving from the meanings of the individual words forming the phrase. It is a characteristic of authentic native usage. Learning collocations may contribute to the mastery of lexis. The examples below are culled from authentic written material, spoken Arabic, and dictionaries.

| | |
|---|---|
| to express a wish or desire | أبْدى رَغْبَةً |
| to make a decision | اتَّخَذَ قَراراً |
| to destroy everything, wreak havoc | أتى على الأخضَر واليابِس |
| old and worn out (also an idiom) | أكَلَ الدَهرُ عَلَيْه وشَرَب |
| worthy of mentioning | حَرِيٌّ بالذكر |
| to take an oath | حَلَفَ يَميناً |
| to bring matters to an end | طَوى البِساط |
| to have mercy upon him | تغمّده برحمته |
| worthy of mention | جَديرُ بالذكر |
| (lit. May God reward you.) thank you | جَزاكَ اللهُ خَيْراً |
| to take s.o. into account | حَسَبَ حِسابَه |

Many collocations are, however, noun-based. Some are noun phrases as those below, and others are adverbials with a descriptive function as in the next subsection.

| | |
|---|---|
| an Arab | ابْنُ عَرَب |
| human being | ابْنُ آدَم |
| his countryman, of the same ethnic group | ابْنُ جِلْدَته |
| bastard, malicious, spiteful | ابْنُ حَرام |
| a fifty-year-old man | ابْنُ خَمْسين |

| | |
|---|---|
| native, citizen, compatriot | ابنُ البَلَد |
| wayfarer, traveller, tramp | ابنُ السبيل |
| robber, thief | ابنُ الليل/الطريق |
| retroactive force or effect | أثَرٌ رَجْعيّ |
| legal procedure | إجراء قانوني |
| census | إحْصاءُ السُكّان |
| chatting, give and take | أخْذٌ ورَدّ/أخْذٌ وعَطاء |
| hollow of the sole of the foot | أخْمَصُ القَدَم |
| wasteland | أرْضٌ بور |
| personal statute | الأحْوالُ الشَخْصيَّة |
| the strong sex, males | الجِنْس الخَشِن |
| the fair sex | الجِنْس اللَطيف |
| Little Bear, Ursa Minor (astronomy) | الدُبُّ الأصْغَر |
| Great Bear, Ursa Major (astronomy) | الدُبُّ الأكْبَر |
| the true religion (i.e. Islam) | الدين الحَنيف |
| public opinion | الرأيُ العام |
| greeting; hello | السلامُ عَلَيْكُم |
| diplomatic corps | السِلكُ السياسي |
| the current month | الشَهْرُ الجاري |
| early morning | الصَباحُ الباكِر |
| the right path | الصِراطُ المُسْتَقيم |
| the entire world | العالَمُ أجْمَع |
| naked eye | العَيْنُ المُجَرَّدَة |
| everything one owns | الغالي والرَخيص |
| divine decree and fate | القَضاءُ والقَدَر |

| | |
|---|---|
| the Qur'ān | الكِتابُ المُبِين |
| colloquial, popular language | اللُغَةُ الدارِجَة |
| the official political circles | المَحافِلُ الرَسْمِيَّة |
| Red Crescent (equivalent of the Red Cross) | الهِلالُ الأحمَر |
| the fertile crescent (parts of Syria and Iraq) | الهِلالُ الخَصِيب |
| loud laments | الوَيْل والثُبور |
| receiver (of alms) | اليَدُ السُفْلى |
| influential, powerful | اليَدُ الطولى |
| work force, labour | اليَدُ العامِلة |
| giver (of alms) | اليَدُ العُلْيا |
| by day and by night | آناءَ اللَيْل وأطْرافَ النَهار |
| the day before yesterday | أوَّلُ البارِحَة |
| a good sign | بادِرَةُ خَيْر |
| prosperity, affluence | بَحْبوحَةُ العَيْش |
| patent | بَراءَةُ اختِراع |
| airmail | بَريدٌ جَوِيّ |
| auspicious sign | بِشارَةُ خَيْر |
| fingerprint | بَصْمَةُ الإصْبَع |
| good performance | بَلاءٌ حَسَن |
| freezing of assets | تَجْمِيدُ الأمْوال |
| compulsory military conscription | تَجْنِيدٌ إجْباري |
| that which caps s.t., crowning touch | ثالِثةُ الأثافي |
| disagreeable (person) | ثَقيلُ الظِلّ |
| sex appeal | جاذِبيَّةٌ جِنْسِيَّة |
| agenda, working plan | جَدْوَلُ أعْمال |

| | |
|---|---|
| school schedule | جَدْوَلُ دِراسَة |
| town gossip (person) | جَعْبَةُ أَخْبار |
| reunion | جَمْعُ الشَمْل |
| charitable organization | جَمْعِيَّةٌ خَيْرِيَّة |
| eternal Paradise | جَنَّةُ الْخُلْد/دارُ الْخُلْد |
| a horse of perfect beauty | جَوادٌ مُطَهَّم |
| coconut | جَوْزُ الهِنْد |
| Wailing Wall (in Jerusalem) | حائِطُ الْمَبْكى |
| curiosity, inquisitiveness | حُبُّ الاسْتِطْلاع |
| worst people, scum, trash | حُثالَةُ الناس |
| blessed pilgrimage | حَجٌّ مَبْرور |
| cogent argument | حُجَّةٌ دامِغَة |
| impediment, obstacle, stumbling block | حَجَرُ عَثْرَة |
| Prophetic tradition | حَديثٌ نَبَوِيّ |
| psychological warfare | حَرْبُ أَعْصاب |
| cold war | حَرْبٌ بارِدَة |
| liberty of the press | حُرِّيَّةُ الصَحافة |
| freedom of thought | حُرِّيَّةُ الفِكْر |
| freedom of speech | حُرِّيَّةُ الكَلام |
| good behavior, good manners | حُسْنُ السُلوك |
| handbag | حَقيبَةُ يَد |
| dance floor | حَلْبَةُ الرَقْص |
| the last of the Prophets (i.e. Muhammad) | خاتَمُ النَبِيّين |
| postmark | خَتْمُ البَريد |
| eclipse of the moon | خُسوفُ القَمَر |

85

| | |
|---|---|
| stage (of a theatre) | خَشَبَةُ المَسْرَح |
| the equator | خَطُّ الاسْتِواء |
| airline | خَطٌّ جَوِيّ |
| latitude | خَطُّ عَرْض |
| telephone line | خَطٌّ هاتِفِيّ |
| handwriting | خَطُّ يَد |
| easy life | خَفْضُ العَيْش |
| high treason | خِيانَةٌ عُظْمى |
| the hereafter | دارُ البَقاء |
| electric circuit | دارة كَهْرَبائِيّة |
| discord, enmity | ذاتُ البَيْن |
| good taste | ذَوْقٌ سَليم |
| New Year | رَأسُ السَنَة |
| uniform | زِيٌّ رَسْمِيّ |
| watch | ساعَةُ يَد |
| horse race, horse racing | سِباقُ الخَيْل |
| the police | سِلكُ الشُرْطَة |
| filament (in an electric bulb) | سِلكٌ حَراري |
| barbed wire | سِلكٌ شائك |
| menopause | سِنّ اليَأس |
| weak tea | شايٌ خَفيف |
| strangers, foreigners, homeless | شُذّاذُ الآفاق |
| limited company | شَرِكَةٌ مَحْدودَة |
| many thanks | شُكْراً جَزيلاً |
| His Majesty | صاحِبُ الجَلالة |

| | |
|---|---|
| powerful leader, strongman | صاحبُ الحَلِّ والرَّبْط |
| His Excellency | صاحبُ الفَخامَة |
| handicraft | صناعات يَدَوِيَّة |
| income tax | ضَريبَةُ الدَّخْلِ |
| great patience | طولُ الأناة |
| monthly period, menstruation | عادَةٌ شَهْرِيَّة |
| powerful | عَزيزُ الجانب |
| manual work | عَمَلٌ يَدَوِيٌّ |
| bread and salt (socialization) | خُبْزٌ/عيشٌ وملح |
| hazard, risk of war | غِمارُ الحَرْب |
| easy prey | غَنيمَةٌ بارِدَة |
| golden opportunity | فُرْصَةٌ ذَهَبِيَّة |
| within two years | في بَحْرِ سَنَتَيْن |
| success, prize | قَصَبُ السَّبْق |
| bloody shirt, evidence of unlawful action | قَميصُ عُثْمان |
| hand grenade | قُنْبُلَةٌ يَدَوِيَّة |
| completely unfounded | لا أساسَ لَهُ مِنَ الصِّحَّة |
| unobjectionable, not bad | لا بَأسَ بِـ |
| don't worry, you won't be harmed | لا بَأسَ عَلَيْك |
| indisputable | لا جِدالَ فيه |
| disgraceful, despicable, a worthless person | لا خَلاقَ لَهُ |
| indifference | لا مُبالاة |
| unjustifiable | لا مُبَرِّرَ لَهُ |
| unavoidable, inescapable | لا مَحيدَ عَنْهُ |
| inevitable, unavoidable | لا مَعْدَى عَنْهُ |

| | |
|---|---|
| indisputable | لا يَقبَلُ أَخْذاً ولا رَدّاً |
| the Arabic language | لُغَةُ الضاد |
| wedding night | لَيلَةُ الدُخْلَة |
| gentle | لَيِّنُ الجانب |
| a considerable sum of money | مَبْلَغٌ لا بَأْسَ بِه |
| a tiny amount | مثْقالُ ذَرَّة |
| parliament | مَجْلِسٌ نيابي |
| cabinet | مَجْلِسُ الوُزَراء |
| attracting glances, attention | مَحَطُّ الأنْظار |
| telephone call | مُخابَرَةٌ هاتفيّة |
| traffic violation | مُخالَفَةُ مُرور |
| public entrance | مَدْخَلٌ للعُموم |
| chronic disease | مَرَضٌ عُضال |
| incurable disease | مَرَضٌ مُسْتَعْصٍ |
| raw materials | مَوادٌ أوَّليّة |
| ground water | مياهٌ جَوْفيّة |
| soda | مياهٌ غازيّة |
| response to the greeting السَلامُ عَلَيْكُم | وَعَلَيْكُمُ السَلام |
| generosity | يَدُ الإحْسان |
| government's arm, security | يَدُ السُلْطة |
| the handle of the hammer | يَدُ المِطْرَقة |
| beneficent, benevolent | يَدٌ بَيْضاء |
| united | يَدٌ واحدة |

The third category may be those phrases that are adjectival, have an adverbial meaning, or a prepositional structure.

| | |
|---|---|
| of fine character, good reputation | أَبيَضُ الوَجْه |
| for your sake | إكْراماً لَك |
| for his sake, to please him | إكْراماً لَهُ |
| gradually, one by one | أوَّلاً بأوَّل |
| altogether, merely | أوَّلاً وأخيراً |
| in a loud voice, aloud | بصَوْت عالٍ |
| farsighted, foresighted | بَعيدُ النَظَر |
| in vain, of no avail | بلا جَدْوى |
| on probation, in an experimental state | تحتَ التَجرِبَة |
| in s.o.'s honour | تَكْريماً لـ |
| fearless, steadfast | ثابتُ الجَأش |
| courageous | ثابتُ الجَنان |
| shrewd, sagacious | ثاقبُ النَظَر |
| hot-blooded, hot-tempered | حادُّ الطَبْع |
| bare-headed | حاسرُ الرَأس |
| God forbid | حاشا للّه |
| quick-witted | حاضرُ البَديهة |
| unfamiliar, inexperienced | حَديثُ عَهْد بـ |
| wherever, haphazardly, at random | حَيثُما اتَّفَق |
| without his knowledge | خفْيَةً عَنْهُ |
| likeable, nice | خَفيفُ الظلّ/خَفيفُ الروح |
| contrary to | خلافاً لـ |
| famous, well-known | ذائعُ الصيت |
| going and coming, round trip | ذَهاباً وإياباً |
| double-edged | ذو حَدَّيْن |

| | |
|---|---|
| with unswerving courage, unflinchingly | رابِطُ الجَأْش |
| generous, open-minded, candid, magnanimous | رَحْبُ الصَّدْر |
| nice, amiable | رَقيقُ الحاشِيَة |
| guileless, sincere | سَليمُ النِّيَّة |
| courageous, brave | شَديدُ البَأْس |
| empty-handed | صِفْرُ اليَدَيْن |
| at least | على أَقَلِّ تَقْدير |
| heedless, indifferent | غَيْرُ مُبالٍ |
| unlucky | قَليلُ البَخْت |
| shameless, impudent | قَليلُ الحَياء |
| emphatic no, no way | كَلّا ثُمَّ كَلّا |
| heavily armed | مُدَجَّجٌ بالسِّلاح |
| anxious, worried, concerned | مَشْغولُ البال |
| having a free hand | مُطْلَقُ اليَد |
| powerless, impotent, helpless | مَقْصوصُ الجَناح |
| helpless | مَكْتوفُ اليَدَيْن |
| cheerful; happy | مُنْشَرِحُ الصَّدْر |
| I hope you will enjoy it. | هَنيئاً مَريئاً [3] |
| and so on, et cetera | وهَلُمَّ جَرّاً |
| personally, delivered in person, hand-in-hand | يَداً بِيَد |

### 2.4.8 *Prepositional phrases and adverbials*

These may be considered collocations where a preposition collocates with other words or phrases. Like idioms, some of

---

[3] هَنيئاً is used for eating and مَريئاً for drinking.

them have a special meaning (e.g. في خَبَرِ كانَ).

| | |
|---|---|
| in the meantime | أَثْناءَ ذلكَ |
| good bye, see you later | إلى اللقاء |
| and so forth, et cetera | إلى آخِرِه |
| beside, besides | إلى جانبِ |
| God willing | بإذْنِ الله |
| after a great deal of trouble | بَعْدَ جَهْدٍ جَهيد |
| as soon as | بِمُجَرَّدِ |
| in this respect, concerning this | بهذا الخُصوص |
| within his power | بيَدِه |
| from time to time | بَيْنَ آونةٍ وأُخْرى |
| inside, among | بَيْنَ ثَنايا |
| from time to time | بَيْنَ حينٍ وآخَر |
| in front of | بَيْنَ يَدَي |
| amid, among, in the presence of | بَيْنَ أحْضان/في أحْضان |
| hitherto, until now | حَتّى الآن |
| neutral | عَلى الحِياد |
| fully prepared | عَلى أُهْبَة الاستِعْداد |
| at any rate, in any case | على أيِّ حال |
| of a great deal of | على جانِبٍ كَبيرٍ من |
| quickly | عَلى جَناحِ السُرْعَة |
| according to, in accordance with | عَلى حَسَب |
| according to his habit, as usual | عَلى عادَتِه |
| I will accommodate your wish, with pleasure | على عَيْني/رأْسي |
| slowly | على مَهْل |

| | |
|---|---|
| especially, particularly | عَلَى وَجْهِ الخُصوص |
| with his help | على يَدِ فُلان/عَنْ يَدِ فُلان |
| at the same time, simultaneously | في آنٍ واحد |
| during that time | في تلكَ الأَثْناء |
| in the prime of his youth | في عزٍّ/جنِّ شبابه |
| if a case should arise, possibly | في حالٍ مِنَ الأَحْوال |
| in itself, as such | في حَدِّ ذاته/بحَدِّ ذاته |
| in reality, actually | في حَقيقَةِ الأَمْرِ |
| in due time, at the appointed time | في حينه |
| passé, no longer existent | في خَبَرِ كانَ |
| accessible, within reach | في مُتَناوَلِ اليَد |
| for your sake | لأَجْلِ خاطرِك |
| goodbye | مَعَ السَلامَة |
| from A to Z | مِنَ الأَلِف إلى الياء |
| from now on, henceforth | مِنَ الآنَ فَصاعداً |
| from time to time | مِنْ آنٍ لآخَر |
| how to tackle the matter properly | مِنْ أَيْنَ تُؤكَلُ الكَتِفُ |
| on the other hand | مِنْ جانبٍ آخَر |
| on his part | مِنْ جانبه |
| with regard to his interests | مِنْ حَيْثُ اهتماماتُه |
| unknown to him | مِنْ حَيْثُ لا يَدري |
| on the other hand | مِن ناحيةٍ أُخرى |

### 2.4.9 *Phrasal verbs (a verb with a preposition and/or an object)*

Each of the following phrasal verbs is composed of a verb with either a preposition after it, a noun functioning as a direct object, a prepositional phrase, or an *iḍāfa* structure.

| | |
|---|---|
| to destroy everything | أتى عَلى الأخْضَر واليابِس |
| he had the opportunity | أُتيحَتْ لَهُ الفُرصَة |
| to weaken by inflicting wounds | أثْخَنَهُ بالجِراح |
| to influence, have an effect on | أثَّرَ في / أثَّرَ بـ |
| to deliberate, debate | أجالوا الرأيَ فيما بينهم |
| to mull over one's grief | اجْتَرَّ آلامَه |
| to be useful | أجْدى نَفْعاً |
| to struggle with tears, to break into tears | أجْهَشَ بالبُكاء |
| to inform him | أحاطَهُ عِلماً |
| to come through with flying colours | أحرَزَ قَصَبَ السَبْق |
| to punish | أخَذَ فُلاناً بذَنْبِه |
| to regard s.t. as auspicious | اسْتَبْشَرَ خَيْراً |
| to pay attention to | أعارَ انْتِباهاً لـ |
| to be happy to see | اكْتَحَلَتْ عَيْنُهُ بـ |
| to make a decision | بَتَّ الأمْرَ |
| to exert an effort | بَذَلَ جَهْداً |
| to acquit someone | بَرَّأ ساحَتَهُ |
| to extend a helping hand | بَسَطَ يَدَ المُساعَدَة |
| to come of age | بَلَغَ أشُدَّهُ |
| to work havoc on | بَلَغَ مِنْهُ كُلَّ مَبْلَغ |
| it occurred to me | تَبادَرَ إلى ذِهْني |
| to come to power | تَبَوَّأ الحُكْمَ |
| to meddle, interfere | تَدَخَّلَ في (شُؤون) |
| to gain a foothold | ثَبَّتَ قَدَمَيْه |

| | |
|---|---|
| to engage s.o. in conversation | جاذَبَهُ أطْرافَ الحَديث |
| to be preoccupied with | جالَ في خاطِره |
| to take his study seriously | جَدَّ في دِراسَته |
| he went out of his way to seek education | جَدَّ في طَلَب العِلم |
| to become frantic | جُنَّ جُنونُه |
| to be confused, bewildered | حارَ في أمْرِه |
| to gain the admiration of | حازَ إعْجابَ ... |
| God forbid | حاشَ لله |
| to rush into battle, go on a campaign | خاضَ مَعْرَكَةً |
| to act haphazardly, proceed rashly | خَبَطَ خَبْطَ عَشْواءَ |
| it occurred to him | خَطَرَ بِباله |
| to assume the defence of | ذادَ عَنْ حِياض ... |
| to make little of s.t., reject s.t. | ضَرَبَ به عُرْضَ الحائط |
| to make an appointment | ضَرَبَ مَوْعِداً |
| to give an example, be an example, tell a proverb | ضرب مَثلاً |
| to beset s.o. grievously | ضَيَّقَ الخِناقَ (على) |
| ask for a girl's hand (in marriage) | طَلَبَ يَد فُلانَة |
| to pay no attention, disregard, ignore | لبِس أذُنيه |
| to walk slowly, unhurriedly | مَشى الهُوَيْنى |
| to walk briskly | مَشى مَشْياً حَثيثاً |
| to desire, be greedy | نَشر أذُنيه |
| to meet with difficulties | وَقَعَ في حَيص بَيص |
| to flee, run away | وَلَّى دُبَرَهُ، وَلَّوا الأدْبار |
| to put matters in the right position | وَضَعَ الأمورَ في نِصابها |

### 2.4.10 *Verbs which change their meaning*

The meaning of some verbs changes with the use of certain prepositions after them. These constructions are similar to English phrasal verbs.

أتى

| | |
|---|---|
| to come, arrive, conclude | أتى إلى |
| to bring, produce, accomplish s.t. | أتى بِـ |
| to finish off, destroy, annihilate, wipe out | أتى على |
| to exhaust, use up, consume | أتى على |

أحالَ

| | |
|---|---|
| to transform, convert, translate | أحالَ إلى |
| to remit, assign | أحالَ عَلى |

أخَذَ

| | |
|---|---|
| to treat with kindness | أخَذَ بالحُسْنى |
| to show s.o. compassion | أخَذَ بخاطِرِه |
| to grab s.o. by the throat | أخَذَ بخِناقِه |
| to grab, take hold of, take up, adhere to, adopt | أخَذَ بِـ |
| to punish s.o. for his offence | أخَذَهُ بذَنْبِه |
| to captivate the hearts, fascinate | أخَذَ بمَجامِعِ القُلوب |
| to help someone | أخَذَ بيَدِه |
| to be on one's guard, to take precautions | أخَذَ حيطَتَهُ |
| to take s.t. seriously | أخَذَ شَيْئاً على مَحْمَلِ الجَدِّ |
| to reproach, blame, hold against | أخَذَ على |
| to take by surprise | أخَذَ على حينِ غِرّة |
| to undertake | أخَذَ على عاتِقِه |

| | |
|---|---:|
| to study under s.o. | أَخَذَ عَن |
| to prepare, set out, be about, begin | أَخَذَ في |

أدّى

| | |
|---|---:|
| to lead to, bring about, cause | أدّى إلى |
| to give s.t. to | أدّى لـ |

أَذِنَ

| | |
|---|---:|
| to listen | أَذِنَ إلى |
| to permit, allow | أَذِنَ في |
| to allow (s.o.) | أذن له |
| to hear, learn, be informed | أَذِنَ بـ |

استَأْذَنَ

| | |
|---|---:|
| to ask permission | استَأْذَنَ في |
| to ask permission to enter | استَأْذَنَ على |
| to say goodbye | استَأْذَنَ مِن |

أغارَ

| | |
|---|---:|
| to help, rescue, seek help | أغارَ إلى |
| to kill, attack | أغارَ عَلى |
| to go away | أغار في (الأرض) |

اِنْخَرَط

| | |
|---|---:|
| to break into tears | اِنْخَرَطَ في البُكاء |
| to enter the field of education | اِنْخَرَطَ في سِلْكَ التَعْليم |

انقَطَع

| | |
|---|---:|
| to dedicate, apply oneself to s.t. | انقَطَع إلى |
| to dissociate oneself from, to break up or part with | انقَطَع عَن |

96

| | |
|---|---|
| to desist, abstain from, cease | اِنْقَطَعَ عَن |

راغَ

| | |
|---|---|
| to depart, leave | راغَ إلى |
| to come, approach | راغَ عَلى |
| to evade, turn away furtively from | راغَ عن |

طَلَعَ

| | |
|---|---|
| to leave, go away | طَلَعَ عَلى |
| to come, draw near, approach | طَلَعَ إلى |

بَحَثَ

| | |
|---|---|
| to search for, seek | بَحَثَ عَن |
| to research, investigate, explore | بَحَثَ في |
| to confer, have a talk | بَحَثَ مَعَ |

جَرى

| | |
|---|---|
| to wend one's way | جَرى إلى |
| to be in force | جَرى بِهِ العَمَل |
| to proceed in accordance with | جَرى عَلى |
| to be on everyone's lips | جَرى عَلى كُلِّ لِسان |
| to happen to, befall | جَرى لِ |
| to follow | جَرى مَعَ |
| it has become second nature to him | جَرى مِنْهُ مَجْرى الدَم |

حالَ

| | |
|---|---|
| to become, to undergo a change | حالَ إلى |
| to make s.t. inaccessible to s.o. | حالَ بَيْنَ فُلانٍ وبَيْنَ |
| to prevent | حالَ دونَ |

| | |
|---|---|
| to deviate, from (e.g. a commitment) | حالَ عَن |

خَرَجَ

| | |
|---|---|
| the matter is out of my hand | خَرَجَ الأمْرُ مِن يَدي |
| to attack, rise, fight, rebel | خَرَجَ على |
| to deviate, depart from an arrangement | خَرَجَ عَنْ |
| to get out, step out, disembark | خَرَجَ مِنْ |

خَلا

| | |
|---|---|
| to retire for deliberation with s.o. | خَلا إلى/مع |
| to be alone with s.o. | خَلا بـ |
| to restrict oneself to something; depend on s.o. | خَلا على |
| to be devoid of | خَلا مِنْ |

دَخَلَ

| | |
|---|---|
| to come to the point | دَخَلَ في المَوْضوع |
| to penetrate | دَخَلَ (المسمارُ) في (الخَشَب) |
| to consummate the marriage, cohabit | دَخَلَ بـ (زَوْجَته) |
| to introduce, be added (in grammar) | دَخَلَ على (شَيْء) |
| to drop in, call on, come to see s.o. | دَخَلَ على (فُلان) |
| to seek s.o.'s protection | دَخَلَ على (فُلان) |
| to belong to, fall under | دَخَلَ في باب كَذا |
| to have the perception that | دَخَلَ في رَوْعِه |

دَرَجَ

| | |
|---|---|
| to proceed slowly | دَرَجَ إلى |
| to be severely exposed | درج بـ (درجت الريح به) |
| to follow a course, proceed along the lines of | دَرَجَ على |

| | |
|---|---:|
| to go away, leave, depart | دَرَجَ مِنْ |
| | دَعا |
| to appeal, invite, prompt | دَعا إلى |
| to name, call | دَعا بـ |
| to pray for, to wish well, invoke God in favour of | دَعا لـ |
| to invoke God against, curse, call down evil | دَعا على |
| | دَلَّ |
| to show, point out, demonstrate | دَلَّ على |
| to lead, guide, direct | دَلَّ إلى |
| | ذَهَبَ |
| to go, travel, depart | ذَهَبَ إلى |
| to carry s.t. away, abduct, steal, destroy | ذَهَبَ بـ |
| to escape one's mind, lose sight of, forget | ذَهَبَ عَن |
| | رَجَعَ |
| to come back, return, recur, resort | رَجَعَ إلى |
| to be attributable to s.t., ascribe to, stem from | رَجَعَ إلى |
| to be under s.o.'s jurisdiction | رَجَعَ لـ |
| to desist, refrain, retract, revoke, repent | رَجَعَ عَن |
| to entail, involve, bring about | رَجَعَ بـ |
| to turn against s.o., claim restitution from s.o. | رَجَعَ على |
| to go back on one's word, to cancel | رَجَعَ في |
| | رَغِبَ |
| to desire, want, covet | رَغِبَ في |
| to ask, request | رَغِبَ إلى |

| | |
|---|---|
| to be disinclined, dislike, detest, loathe | رَغِبَ عَن |
| to wish | رَغِبَ بِـ |
| to favour s.o. over another | رغب بفلانٍ عن غيره |
| to be far above, too proud for, disdain | رغب بنفسه عن شيء |

رَفَعَ

| | |
|---|---|
| to petition | رَفَعَ الشيءَ إلى |
| to proceed forward | رفع في (الأرض) |
| to walk briskly | رفع في (سيره) |
| to spot s.t. from a distance, point out s.t. | رفع له الشيء |

رَمى

| | |
|---|---|
| to throw, toss, cast, pelt, hurl | رَمى بِـ (شَيْءٍ) |
| to shoot, fire, bombard | رَمى بِـ (طَلَقٍ ناريّ) |
| to accuse, charge with | رَمى بِـ (صِفَةٍ) |
| to aim at, drive at, intend | رَمى إلى |
| to sow dissension, stir up discord | رَمى بَيْنَ |

سَجَّلَ

| | |
|---|---|
| to record on tape | سَجَّلَ على شَريط |
| to credit with | سَجَّلَ لحساب فُلان |
| to debit with, charge | سَجَّلَ على حِساب فُلان |

سَقَطَ

| | |
|---|---|
| to fall down, tumble, trip | سَقَطَ على الأرض |
| to come across, hit upon | سَقَطَ على خَبَر |
| to fail, flunk | سَقَطَ في الامتحان |
| to fall in battle, be killed, die | سَقَطَ في المعركة |

سَلَّمَ

| | |
|---|---|
| to hand over, turn over, turn in, deliver | سَلَّمَ إلى |
| to submit, give in, surrender | سَلَّمَ إلى |
| to salute, greet | سَلَّمَ على |
| to accept, approve of, admit, acknowledge | سَلَّمَ بـ |

ضَرَبَ

| | |
|---|---|
| to shade into red | ضَرَبَ إلى الحُمْرة |
| to point at s.t., be inclined toward s.t. | ضَرَبَ إلى الشَيْءِ |
| to throw s.o. or s.t. to the ground | ضَرَبَ به الأرضَ |
| to cower, cringe, lose heart, be a coward | ضَرَبَ بذَقْنه الأرض |
| to shoot at, fire | ضَرَبَ على |
| to strike out, efface, erase a word | ضَرَبَ على كلمة |
| to type on a typewriter | ضَرَبَ على الآلة الكاتبة |
| to prevent s.o. from doing s.t. | ضَرَبَ على يده |
| to impose a tax on s.o. | ضَرَبَ عليهم ضَريبة |
| to turn away from s.t. | ضَرَبَ عَن (شَيْء) |
| to turn away s.o. | ضَرَبَ عَنْهُ صَفْحاً |
| to be in the clouds, be unrealistic | ضَرَبَ في الخَيال |
| to swim | ضَرَبَ في الماء |
| to travel seeking work | ضَرَبَ في الأرض |
| to take futile steps | ضَرَبَ في حديدٍ بارد |

ظَهَرَ

| | |
|---|---|
| to disparage, make little of; be proud of | ظهر بـ |
| to become visible, be apparent, clear, appear | ظَهَرَ لـ |
| to get the better of, overcome, conquer | ظَهَرَ على |

| | |
|---|---|
| to know, be aware, acquainted | ظَهَرَ على |
| to disappear, go away, come to an end | ظهر عن |

قامَ

| | |
|---|---|
| to perform, make carry out | قامَ بـِ |
| to assume, undertake, shoulder | قامَ بـِ |
| to support, provide, sustain | قامَ بـِ |
| to rise, revolt, rebel | قامَ على |
| to rest on, be based on | قامَ على |
| to take care of, look after, attend to, tend | قامَ على |
| to rise in honour of s.o. | قامَ لـ |

قَضى

| | |
|---|---|
| to decide, decree, rule | قَضى بـِ |
| (of God) to foreordain, predestine | قَضى بـِ |
| to act as a judge, decide judicially | قَضى بَيْنَ |
| to pronounce a judgement in favour of s.o. | قَضى لـ |
| to root out, annihilate, exterminate, to kill, do in s.o. | قَضى على |

### 2.4.11 *Verbs which change meaning based on the direct object*

Verbs may change their meaning on the basis of their direct objects. The direct object may be a noun, a prepositional phrase, or an *iḍāfa* structure. The majority of these phrases are R3. Lower registers are marked.

أدّى

| | |
|---|---|
| to take an examination | أدّى امتحاناً |
| to perform a prayer | أدّى الصَلاةَ |

| | |
|---|---|
| to do one's duty | أدَّى واجِبَه |
| to fulfil a task or mission | أدَّى رسالةً |
| to accomplish a mission | أدَّى مُهِمَّةً |
| to salute, greet | أدَّى تَحِيَّةً أو سَلاماً |
| to render a service, do a favour | أدَّى خِدْمَةً |
| to pay, settle a debt | أدَّى دَيْناً |
| to testify, give testimony | أدَّى شَهادةً |
| to express a meaning, denote | أدَّى مَعْنىً |

أسْقَطَ

| | |
|---|---|
| to drop, let fall | أسْقَطَ شيئاً |
| to shoot down (a plane) | أسْقَطَ طائرةً |
| to fail, flunk | أسْقَطَ في الامتِحان |
| to deduct, subtract | أسْقَطَ عَدَداً |
| to omit, leave out, skip, eliminate, cancel | أسْقَطَ كلمةً |
| to deprive of citizenship | أسْقَطَ جِنسِيَّةَ فُلان |
| to waive, forgo, relinquish, disclaim | أسْقَطَ حَقَّهُ |
| to drop, withdraw a case | أسْقَطَ دَعْوى |
| to abort, cause an abortion | أسْقَطَ جَنيناً |
| to project | أسْقَطَ (في الهندسةِ وعلمِ النَفْس) |

أطْلَقَ

| | |
|---|---|
| to divorce | أطْلَقَ (المرأة) |
| to release, set free | أطْلَقَ (الأسير) |
| to let cattle graze, pasture | أطْلَقَ (المَواشي) |
| to be generous, liberal, openhanded | أطْلَقَ يَدَه (بخَيْر) |
| to give a free hand, give unlimited authority | أطْلَقَ يَدَه |

| | |
|---|---|
| to poison one's enemy | أَطْلَقَ عَدُوَّه |
| to pollinate, impregnate | أَطْلَقَ نَخْلَة |
| to generalize | أَطْلَقَ (في الكلام) |
| to hurry | أَطْلَقَ رِجْلَه |
| to loosen or relax the bowels | أَطْلَقَ الدَّواءُ بَطْنَه |
| to fire, shoot | أَطْلَقَ الرَصاص/أَطْلَقَ النار |
| to launch a rocket | أَطْلَقَ صاروخاً |
| to run away head over heels | أَطْلَقَ ساقَيْه للريح |
| to emit, utter, send | أَطْلَقَ (صَيْحة/ضِحْكة) |
| to name, call, dub | أَطْلَقَ اسمَ كَذا (على فُلان) |
| to grow a beard | أَطْلَقَ لِحْيَتَه |
| to shell, bombard | أَطْلَقَ (مَدْفَعاً/قُنْبُلة) |
| to give free or full rein to, unleash | أَطْلَقَ العنانَ لـ |

بَذَلَ

| | |
|---|---|
| to go to any length, to spare no effort | بَذَلَ الغالي والرَخيص |
| to take pains, to exert effort | بَذَلَ جَهْدَه |
| to do one's best | بَذَلَ وُسْعَهُ |

خَلَعَ

| | |
|---|---|
| to grant, bestow | خَلَعَ على (فُلانٍ شَيْئاً) |
| to extract a tooth | خَلَعَ ضِرْساً |
| to pull a nail | خَلَعَ مِسْماراً (R2) |
| to remove / discharge from office | خَلَعَ (فلاناً مِنْ مَنْصِبه) |
| to repudiate one's son | خَلَعَ ابنَهُ |
| to refuse to obey | خَلَعَ الطاعَة |
| to divorce one's wife in return for payment | خَلَعَ زَوْجَتَهُ |

| | |
|---|---|
| to cast off one's restraints | خَلَعَ عِذارَهُ |
| to take off one's clothes, undress | خَلَعَ مَلابِسَهُ |

رَفَعَ

| | |
|---|---|
| to lift, raise, pick up | رَفَعَ شَيْئاً |
| to hoist, fly | رَفَعَ عَلَماً/رَفَعَ رايَةً |
| to tip one's hat | رَفَعَ قُبَّعَتَهُ |
| to eliminate, abolish an injustice | رَفَعَ ظُلْماً |
| to raise one's voice | رَفَعَ صَوْتَهُ |
| to put an end to sanctions | رَفَعَ الحَظْرَ |
| to submit a petition | رَفَعَ عَريضَةً |
| to file a report | رَفَعَ تَقريراً |
| to put a word in the nominative or indicative | رَفَعَ كَلِمَةً |
| to initiate, bring legal action, to sue | رَفَعَ قَضِيَّةً/رَفَعَ دَعْوى |
| to desist, refrain from | رَفَعَ يَدَهُ عَن شَيْء |

سَجَّلَ

| | |
|---|---|
| to register, record, make an entry | سَجَّلَ (شَيْئاً) |
| to enrol, register, list as member | سَجَّلَ عُضواً |
| to patent | سَجَّلَ اخْتِراعاً |
| to set a record | سَجَّلَ رَقْماً قِياسِيّاً |

سَقَطَ

| | |
|---|---|
| to fall out | سَقَطَ (شَعْرُهُ)، سقطت (أَسنانُه) |
| to prescribe | سَقَطَ (حَقُّه) |
| to cease to be valid or effective | سَقَطَ حُكْمُه |
| he was deprived of his citizenship | سَقَطَتْ جِنْسِيَّتُه |

سَلَّمَ

| | |
|---|---|
| to extradite a criminal | سَلَّمَ مُجْرِماً |
| to surrender, give oneself up | سَلَّمَ نَفْسَهُ |
| to die | سَلَّمَ روحَهُ |

شَهَرَ

| | |
|---|---|
| to make famous or notorious | شَهَرَ (شَيْئاً أو شَخصاً) |
| to unsheathe, point | شَهَرَ سِلاحاً |
| to declare war | شَهَرَ الحَرْبَ |
| to declare one's conversion to Islam | شَهَرَ إِسْلامَه |

ضَرَبَ

| | |
|---|---|
| to hull rice | ضَرَبَ الأُرُزَّ |
| to knock on the door | ضَرَبَ البابَ |
| to ring the bell | ضَرَبَ الجَرَسَ (R1) |
| to throw a stone | ضَرَبَ حَجَراً (R1) |
| to give an injection | ضَرَبَ حُقنةً/ضَرَبَ إِبْرَةً (R1) |
| to pitch a tent | ضَرَبَ خَيْمَةً (R1) |
| to be separated by the passage of time | ضَرَبَ الدَهْرُ بيننا |
| to break a record | ضَرَبَ رَقْماً قِياسِيّاً |
| to strike, beat s.o. | ضَرَبَ شَخْصاً (R1, 2) |
| to give a military salute | ضَرَبَ سَلاماً (R1) |
| to multiply a number by another | ضَرَبَ عَدَداً في عَدَدٍ (R2) |
| to behead, decapitate s.o. | ضَرَبَ عُنُقَهُ |
| to be stung, bitten | ضَرَبَته العَقْرَب (R2) |
| to imitate | ضَرَبَ قالَبَهُ |
| to slap s.o.'s face | ضَرَبَ (له) كَفّاً (R1) |

| | |
|---|---|
| to strike both hands to express despair | ضَرَبَ كَفّاً بِكَفّ |
| to give an example, quote as an example | ضَرَبَ مَثَلاً (R2) |
| to mint money | ضَرَبَ نُقوداً |
| to make an appointment | ضَرَبَ مَوْعداً |
| to blockade, besiege | ضَرَبَ حصاراً |
| to throb | ضَرَبَ القَلْبُ |
| to take root | ضَرَبَ أطنابَهُ |
| to whip, beat, whisk eggs | ضَرَبَ البَيْضَ |
| to be a long night | ضَرَبَ الليلُ عليهم |
| to have intense toothache | ضَرَبَ الضرْسُ (R1) |
| to shade into red | ضَرَبَ إلى الحُمْرة |
| to point at s.t., be inclined toward s.t. | ضَرَبَ إلى الشَيْءِ |
| to throw s.o. or s.t. to the ground | ضَرَبَ به الأرضَ |
| to cower, cringe, lose heart, be a coward | ضَرَبَ بذَقْنه الأرض |
| to shoot at, fire | ضَرَبَ على |
| to strike out, efface, erase a word | ضَرَبَ على كلمة |
| to type on a typewriter | ضَرَبَ على الآلة الكاتِبة |
| to prevent s.o. from doing s.t. | ضَرَبَ على يده |
| to impose a tax on s.o. | ضَرَبَ عليهم ضَريبة |
| to turn away from s.t. | ضَرَبَ عَن (شَيْء) |
| to turn away s.o. | ضَرَبَ عَنْهُ صَفْحاً |
| to be in the clouds, be unrealistic | ضَرَبَ في الخَيال |
| to swim | ضَرَبَ في الماء |
| to travel seeking work | ضَرَبَ في الأرض |
| to mint coins | ضَرَبَ نقداً |

| | |
|---|---|
| to take futile steps | ضَرَبَ في حديدٍ بارِدٍ |
| to settle down | ضَرَبَ الوَتَدَ |
| to attain glory | ضَرَبَ المَجْدَ |

قامَ

| | |
|---|---|
| the truth became manifest | قامَ الحَقُّ |
| the time of prayer has come | قامَت الصَلاةُ |
| to take the place of s.o., substitute | قامَ مَقامَ |

قَضى

| | |
|---|---|
| to die, pass away | قَضى أجَلَهُ/نَحْبَهُ |
| to attain one's aim, fulfil one's wish or desire | قَضى وَطَرَهُ |
| to pay off a debt | قَضى دَيْناً |
| to pass time | قَضى وَقْتاً |
| to accomplish s.t. | قَضى أمْراً |
| to relieve oneself, defecate | قَضى حاجَتَهُ |

## 2.4.12 *Idioms*

An idiom is an expression of a given spoken or written language that has acquired a meaning peculiar to itself. It cannot be understood from the individual meanings of its elements. In addition, the distinction between phrasal verbs and idioms lies in that all phrasal verbs start with a verb and that idioms may have any structure, including complete sentences.

| | |
|---|---|
| everything became confused | اخْتَلَطَ الحابِلُ بالنابِل |
| to follow in close succession | أخَذَ بَعْضُهُم بِرِقابِ بَعْضٍ |
| to be at a loss, be bewildered | أُسْقِطَ في يَده |
| his hair turned white | اشتَعَل رأْسُه شَيباً |

108

| | |
|---|---|
| to crane, stretch out one's neck | اشرأَبَّت الأعناق |
| to be at a loss | أعْيَتْهُ الحيلة |
| to be very old | أكل الدَهْرُ عليه وشرب |
| it is up to him, he has the power | الأمْرُ بيَده |
| you are wrong | الحَقُّ عَلَيْك |
| you are right | الحَقُّ مَعَك |
| to give free rein, give a free hand | ألقى الحَبْلَ على الغارب |
| to stop, settle down | ألقى الرحال |
| to be overcome with longing | تَحَرَّقَ شَوْقاً |
| to pass unnoticed without leaving a trace | ذَهَبَ أدراجَ الرياح |
| to be futile, in vain | ذَهَبَ سُدىً |
| to act at one's discretion, rashly, follow a whim | ركبَ رأسَهُ |
| thank you | سَلِمَتْ يَداك |
| to set out | شَدَّ الرحال |
| to be unable to accomplish s.t., fed up with | ضاقَ ذَرْعاً بـ |
| to have nothing to do with the matter | غَسَلَ يَدَهُ من |
| powerless | لَيْسَ بيَده حيلة |
| he can do nothing, can't get anywhere | ما بيَده حيلة |
| unavoidable | ما عَنْهُ مَحيص |
| he died instantly | ماتَ لساعَته |
| they are the same, alike | هُما سِيّان |
| they stand worlds apart | هُوَ في وادٍ وهِيَ في وادٍ |
| to straighten things out | وَضَع الأمورَ في نِصابها |

The majority of idioms are, however, at the phrase level.

| | |
|---|---|
| great calamity, disaster, catastrophe | الطامّةُ الكُبْرى |

| | |
|---|---|
| to a great extent | إلى حَدّ بَعيد |
| first of all, in the first place | بادِئ ذي بَدْء |
| gradually | بالتَدريج |
| verbatim, to the letter | بالحَرْف الواحد |
| a very short time, a moment | بُرْهَة وَجيزَة |
| undoubtedly, without doubt | بلا شَكّ |
| one in a powerful position | بيَده الحَلُّ والرَبْط |
| sometimes here, sometimes there | تارَةً هُنا وتارَةً هُناك |
| as much as he can, to the limit of his abilities | جُهْدَ طاقَته |
| it would be nice if | حَبَّذا |
| of no effect, inconsequential | حبرٌ عَلى وَرَق |
| literally, word for word | حَرْفاً بحَرْف |
| as chance will have it | حَسْبَما اتَّفَق |
| at his discretion, as he pleases | حَسْبَما يَحْلو لَهُ |
| empty-handed, with an empty pouch | خاوي الوفاض |
| witty, humorous, funny, amiable | خفيف الظل/الدَم |
| it is apt for him to, incumbent upon him to | خَليقٌ به أَنْ |
| without distinction; equally; alike | رأسٌ برأَس |
| upside down, head over heels | رأساً عَلى عقب |
| short notes | رُؤوس أقلام |
| in spite of, despite | رَغْماً عَن |
| willy-nilly, whether he likes it or not | شاءَ أَمْ أبى |
| Thank you very much! | شُكراً جزيلاً |
| a thorn in his side | شَوكَةٌ في خاصرَته |
| poverty, destitution | ضيقُ اليَد |

110

| | |
|---|---|
| sooner or later | عاجِلاً أو آجِلاً |
| at least | على أَقَلّ تَقْدير |
| imminent, near | على الأَبْواب |
| very gladly, with pleasure | على الرَأْس والعَيْن |
| in spite of, despite | على الرَغْم من |
| a question being raised, discussed | على بِساط البَحْث |
| equally, likewise, in the same manner | على حَدّ سَواء |
| publicly, for everybody to see | على رُؤوس الأَشْهاد |
| slowly! gentle! take it easy! | على رِسْلِك |
| exclusively | عَلَى سَبيل الحَصْر |
| in opposition, in contradiction | على طَرَفَي نَقيض |
| in full swing, fully effective | على قَدَمٍ وساق |
| done all over again, begun anew | عَوْداً على بَدْء |
| at first; in the beginning | في بِدايَة/بادِئ الأَمْر |
| as good as nothing | في حُكْم العَدَم |
| all but decided | في حُكْم المُقَرَّر |
| to be thoroughly established in, involved in | قَدَمٌ راسخةٌ في |
| it is inevitable, necessary | لا بُدَّ من |
| he is free from blame | لا جُناحَ عَلَيْه |
| nothing stands in your way | لا حَرَجَ عَلَيْك |
| there is no power save in God | لا حَوْلَ ولا قُوَّةَ إلاّ بالله |
| he is completely helpless | لا حَوْلَ لَهُ ولا حيلَة |
| fortunately | لحُسْن الحَظّ |
| to the extent that | لدَرَجَة أَنْ |
| unfortunately | لِسوء الحَظّ |

| | |
|---|---|
| well-planned, well-contrived | مُحْكَمُ التَدْبير |
| insincere flattery | مَسْحُ جوخ |
| the more so, s.t. having priority | مِنْ باب أوْلى |
| blindly, without forethought, at random | مِنْ غَيْر حساب |
| at any rate, in any case | مِن كُلٍّ بُدَّ |
| whatever may happen | مَهْما يَكُنْ مِنْ أمْر |
| inequitable treatment of people | ناسٌ وناس |

## 2.4.13 *Homonyms*

A homonym is defined as a word whose standard written form is identical to another word, but they differ in one or more of the diacritics which are not normally indicated. There are many such words in Arabic. Examples are:

| | | | |
|---|---|---|---|
| August | آب | to return, go back | آبَ |
| permission, leave | إذْن | to allow, permit | أذِنَ |
| therefore, hence | إذَن | ear, handle | أذُن |
| to inform, notify | آذَنَ | to call to prayer | أذَّنَ |
| beds | أسِرّة | family | أُسْرة |
| the letter *alif* | ألِف | thousand | ألْف |
| to form, compose | ألَّفَ | close, intimate friend | إلْف |
| or | أمْ | mother, most important | أمّ |
| to become a widower | آمَ | to travel to, lead | أمَّ |
| human being | بَشَر | to grate | بَشَرَ |
| sufficiency, calculation | حَسْب | ancestry, lineage | حَسَب |
| to suppose, assume | حَسِبَ | to calculate, count | حَسَبَ |
| patience, toleration | حِلْم | dream, puberty | حُلْم/حُلُم |

| | | | |
|---|---|---|---|
| to dream | حَلَم | to be patient | حَلُم |
| behind, rear | خَلْف | bad offspring | خَلْف |
| dissimilarity, difference | خُلْف | good offspring | خَلَف |
| ethical, moral | خُلُقيّ | congenital, inborn | خَلْقيّ |
| brokerage, commission | دلالة | sign, meaning | دَلالة |
| slavery; tambourine | رق | parchment; turtle | رَق |
| travel, journey | سَفَر | book | سِفْر |
| sister-in-law | سِلْفة | loan, advance payment | سُلْفة |
| example, lesson | عِبْرة | tear | عَبْرة |
| upper, higher, supreme | عُلْويّ | Alawite, sect of Ali | عَلَويّ |
| building, edifice | عِمارة | fleet, head gear, tribe | عَمارة |
| mecca, centre of attraction | قِبْلة | kiss | قُبْلة |
| magnitude, size, bigness | كِبَر | eminence, dignity | كُبْر |
| amphitheatre, stadium | مُدَرَّج | runway, tarmac | مَدْرَج |
| filter; nominator | مُرَشِّح | candidate, nominee | مُرَشَّح |
| quorum | نِصاب | swindler | نَصّاب |
| vermin, important (f.) | هامّة | head, summit | هامة |
| gust, blast, blow | هَبّة | gift, donation | هِبة |
| evening prayer, odd # | وِتْر | string, cord | وَتَر |

### 2.4.14 *Polysemy*

Polysemy is the situation when the same word has two or more different meanings. A selection of such words follows.

(1) allowance, sanction    إجازة

(2) permission, leave

(3) permit, licence, authorization

(4) academic degree

أَجَدُّ   (1) newer, more recent

(2) more intent, more serious

أَدَب   (1) good manners, politeness, civility, courtesy

(2) literature, belles-lettres

أَسْفار   (1) books

(2) trips, travels

تَرْشيح   (1) filtering, purification

(2) nomination, candidacy

(3) getting a cold

جَدْوَل   (1) schedule, chart, table, list, roster, register

(2) stream, creek, brook, rivulet

(3) agenda

جَواد   (1) steed, horse

(2) generous, liberal, openhanded

حُبّ   (1) love, affection

(2) vat, tun, cask

حُجَّة   (1) proof, evidence

(2) argument, pretext, excuse

(3) authority, source, expert

(4) deed, document, record

حَرَّرَ   (1) to write

(2) to liberate, set free

حَديث   (1) new, novel, recent, modern, fresh, up-to-date

(2) speech, talk, conversation

(3) report, account, tale, narrative

(4) interview

(5) Prophetic tradition

(1) shoe, footwear                                     حِذاء

(2) face to face with, opposite; next to, beside

(1) one milking                                        حَلْبَة

(2) race track, arena, dance floor

(1) to propose to a girl                               خَطَبَ

(2) to deliver a public address, make a speech

(1) speaker, orator, preacher                        خَطيب

(2) fiancé

(1) to go to, head for                                  ذَهَبَ

(2) to go away, leave, depart

(3) to take away, remove, eliminate

(4) to be of the opinion, believe

(1) head                                               رَأْس

(2) tip, apex, point

(3) top, summit, peak

(4) cape, headland

(5) clove (of garlic)

(6) beginning, start, onset

(7) main part, principal part

(8) chief, leader, commander

(1) to comply with, observe, conform to, adhere to       راعى

(2) to take into consideration

(3) to humour, indulge, respect, be willing to please

(4) to listen to, hearken to, pay attention to

(5) to observe, regard, watch, gaze, keep looking at

(1) drawing, sketching, delineation, painting     رَسْم

(2) description, depiction, portrayal, representation

(3) planning, designing, projecting

(4) drawing, figure, picture, illustration, painting

(5) trace, track, vestige, sign, imprint

(6) fee, rate, charge, dues, duty, impost, toll, excise

(1) to take care of, look after     رَعى

(2) to patronize, sponsor, cultivate, develop, promote

(3) to govern, rule, regulate, control

(4) to graze, pasture, shepherd, herd

(1) to be high, become high-ranking     رَفُعَ

(2) to be or become thin, fine, delicate

(1) parchment, scroll     رَقّ

(2) turtle

(1) slavery, bondage     رِقّ

(2) tambourine

(1) professional dancer     رَقّاص

(2) pendulum

(1) patch, piece of cloth     رُقْعَة

(2) piece of land, area, lot, plot

(3) chessboard

(4) slip of paper, note, brief message

(5) a cursive style of calligraphy

(1) pawn, mortgage      رَهِينَة

(2) hostage

(1) to unveil, uncover, disclose      سَفَّرَ

(2) to send on a journey, put on board, deport

(1) to fall down, tumble, decline      سَقَطَ

(2) to slip, lapse, err, blunder, make a mistake

(3) to sink, deposit, subside

(4) to fail, flunk

(1) loan, advance payment      سُلْفة

(2) inner sole, inner lining of shoes

(1) belt, drive belt      سَيْر

(2) traffic

(3) behaviour

(1) to become white-haired, grow old      شابَ

(2) to mix, blend, corrupt, spoil

(1) drinker      شارِب

(2) moustache

(1) alum      شَبَّة

(2) young woman

(1) to become a young man      شَبَّ

(2) to jump, prance

(3) to burn, blaze

(1) wooden bar, bolt      شِجار

(2) quarrel, fight, dispute, argument

| | |
|---|---|
| (1) slipper | شَحّاطَة |
| (2) match | |
| (1) deck of playing cards | شَدَّة |
| (2) a pull, drag, tug | |
| (3) diacritical mark indicating doubling of a consonant | |
| (1) to slit open, make an incision | شَرَطَ |
| (2) to stipulate, impose as a condition | |
| (1) to begin, start | شَرَعَ |
| (2) to point a weapon | |
| (3) to introduce, enact (a law) | |
| (1) to rise, shine, radiate | شَرَقَ |
| (2) to choke | |
| (1) rag, shred, tatter | شَرْموطة (R1) |
| (2) prostitute, whore | |
| (1) migraine | شَقيقَة |
| (2) full sister (from both parents) | |
| (1) to fix, prick, transfix, stab | شكّ |
| (2) to doubt, suspect | |
| (1) testimony, statement, affidavit | شَهادَة |
| (2) certificate, degree, diploma | |
| (3) martyrdom | |
| (4) profession, expression of faith (in Islam) | |
| (1) friend, companion | صاحِب |
| (2) owner, master, lord | |
| (1) aloe | صَبْر |

(2) patience, forbearance

(1) hard, firm, stiff, rigid     صُلْب

(2) steel

(3) spinal column, backbone

(4) text body (of a book, article)

(1) beating, striking, hitting, knocking     ضَرْب

(2) minting (money)

(3) typing

(4) kind, sort, species, variety

(1) whitewashing     طَرْش

(2) flock of sheep, herd of cattle

(1) envelope, vessel     ظَرْف

(2) circumstance, condition

(3) humour, wit, charm, elegance

(4) adverb

(1) dependent, parasite     عالة

(2) burden, charge

(3) poverty, destitution, need

(4) family, household     (ج عَيِّل)

(1) slave, serf, bondsman     عَبْد (ج عَبيد)

(2) human being, man     عَبْد (ج عِباد)

(1) to find, hit upon, come across     عَثَرَ

(2) to stumble, trip, tumble

(1) head gear, turban     عَمْرَة

(2) repair, repair work, overhaul

119

(3) minor pilgrimage to Mecca

(1) neck عُنُق

(2) precedence (لَه عُنُقٌ في الخَيْر)

(3) adversaries, group of people    (rare in MSA) (هم عُنُقٌ عليه)

(4) piece of property, money

(5) task, work

(6) the beginning of s.t.

(1) life, living, existence عَيْش

(2) bread

(1) eye عَيْن

(2) spring, source, fountainhead

(3) spy

(4) scout, reconnoiterer, explorer

(5) overseer, inspector, supervisor, superintendent

(6) lookout, guard, watchman

(7) ready money, cash

(8) property, assets

(9) usury, interest

(10) notable, dignitary, prominent person, celebrity

(11) chief, lord, master

(12) essence

(13) the same

(1) dismissal فَصْل

(2) season

(3) school term

(4) classroom

قابِلِيَّة

(1) appetite

(2) faculty, power, ability, capability

قَرْض

(1) loan

(2) nibbling, biting, gnawing

(3) writing (poetry)

قَرْعة

(1) pumpkin, gourd

(2) knock, rap, blow

قَرْن

(1) century

(2) horn (of an animal)

قِطْعَة

(1) portion, piece

(2) military unit

قَلْب

(1) heart

(2) middle

(3) center, core

(4) gist, essence

(5) the best part

(6) mind, soul, spirit

كادَ

(1) to deceive, dupe, outwit, conspire against

(2) to be about to, be on the verge of

كَشْف

(1) uncovering, revelation, vision, apocalypse

(2) list, roll, roster, register, statement of account

(3) inquiry, search, quest

كَشْف (البَخْت)

(4) fortune-telling

كَشْف (حِساب)

(5) bill, statement of account

(1) heel, heel bone        كَعْب

(2) anklebone

(3) knot, knob, node

(4) bottom, tail, end, lower part

(5) glory, dignity, honour, distinction, high rank

(1) to hide, cover, conceal        كَفَرَ

(2) to disbelieve in God

(3) to curse, swear

(1) college, faculty, school, academy        كُلِّيّة

(2) totality, entirety, universality

(1) brick        لَبِنة

(2) giving milk, milker

(1) glance, glimpse        لَحْظة

(2) moment

(1) mending, soldering, welding        لَحْم

(2) flesh, meat

(1) weft, woof of a fabric        لُحْمة

(2) stroma (anatomy)

(3) parenchyma (botany)

(4) relationship, kinship

(5) bond, tie, connection, link

(1) grammatical error        لَحْن

(2) shrewdness, wit, sagacity, intelligence

(3) tune, melody

(1) to adhere, belong, persist, stick        لَزِمَ

(2) to be necessary, requisite, imperative, indispensable

(1) striped مُخَطَّط

(2) plan, map, design

(1) named (person) مَدْعو

(2) guest

(1) project, enterprise, plan, scheme, venture مَشْروع

(2) legal, lawful

(3) legislated, enacted, passed (by the parliament)

(1) intestine, gut مَصير

(2) fate, destiny, lot

(3) outcome, consequence

(4) self-determination (تقرير المصير)

(1) interview مُقابَلَة

(2) audience (with an important person)

(3) comparison

(1) separation, break, boycott مُقاطَعَة

(2) interruption

(3) area, province, district, region

(1) time, occasion مَعْرِض

(2) exhibition, showroom, fair, exposition

(1) meathouse, butchery مَلْحَمَة

(2) slaughterhouse

(3) bloody fight, fierce battle, massacre, carnage

(4) epic poem, heroic poem, epopee

(1) clinging, inseparable, adhering مُلازِم

(2) lieutenant

(1) vice (vise, Amer.), press مَلزَمة

(2) section (of a book)

(1) task, function, duty مُهِمَّة

(2) important (f.)

(3) equipment (ج) مُهِمَّة

(1) prose نَثْر

(2) scattering, dispersal, dissemination

(1) direction, method, course, manner نَحْوٌ

(2) grammar, syntax

(1) ascription, attribution نِسْبَة

(2) connection, relationship

(3) proportion, ratio, rate

(4) percentage

(1) to spread, emit, send out, release نَشَرَ

(2) to spread, propagate, disseminate, circulate, promulgate

(3) to publish, issue, put out, produce, release

(4) to deploy (forces)

(5) to resurrect, raise from the dead

(6) to saw

(1) to erect, raise, set up, install نَصَبَ

(2) to pitch (a tent)

(3) to plant (a tree)

(4) to hoist, raise (a flag)

(5) to mount or emplace (a gun)

(6) to swindle, dupe, defraud

(7) to embezzle, misappropriate

(8) to exhaust, fatigue, wear out

(1) expulsion, exile, banishment نَفْي

(2) negation, negative

(3) denial, disavowal, disclaimer, refutation

(4) to walk, proceed slowly

(1) to shake off, dust off نَفَضَ

(2) to fade, lose colour

(3) to make shiver

(4) to recover, recuperate

(1) remoteness نَوىً

(2) destination

(3) kernels, pits, stones, seeds

(1) to intoxicate, inebriate هَوَّدَ

(2) to lullaby

(3) to make Jewish, Judaize

(1) front, façade وَجْه

(2) surface, outside, exterior

(3) right side, outside (of cloth)

(4) dial (of a watch, clock)

(5) obverse (of a coin)

(6) phase (of a moon)

(7) appearance, look, aspect, guise, semblance

(8) manifestation, expression, indication

(9) aspect, facet, point, respect, regard, standpoint, viewpoint

(10) side, direction

(11) meaning, sense, signification

(12) intention, design, purpose, aim, end, goal

(13) way, manner, mode

(14) coat, coating, outer layer

(15) notable (person), celebrity

(1) to connect, link, join, couple      وَصَلَ

(2) to reach, amount to, add up to

(3) to extend to, stretch to, spread to

(4) to come, arrive, show up

(5) to give, award, grant, bestow upon, confer upon

(1) connecting, joining, uniting      وَصْلٌ

(2) receipt, voucher

(3) reunion of lovers, communion, (sexual) intercourse

(1) to be next, close, near, adjacent      وَلِيَ

(2) to follow

(3) to be friends

(4) to be in charge, manage, run, administer, govern, rule

(1) easy, facile      يَسِير

(2) to walk, go on foot, tread, march

### 2.4.15 *Words with two opposite meanings*

Arabic contains words that have opposite meanings (أضْـداد).
Their existence in the language is attributed to several factors,
including the different dialects in pre-Islamic Arabic, semantic

change, phonological change, mispronunciation, social and
psychological motivation, context, and the following preposition. Words that are rare in MSA are eliminated.

(1) to keep a secret, hide, conceal أَسَرَّ

(2) to declare, announce, make public

(1) to deposit (money) أَوْدَعَ

(2) to accept a deposit

(1) separation, division, disunity بَيْن

(2) uniting, getting together

(1) one who repents تَوَّاب

(2) one who pardons (God)

(1) important, significant, momentous, great جَلَل

(2) low, base, vile, ignoble, menial, inferior

(1) one asking for help صَارِخ

(2) one providing help

(1) to increase ضَعُفَ

(2) to decrease, weaken, slacken, decline

(1) doubt, suspicion, uncertainty ظَنّ

(2) certainty, assurance

(1) to darken, grow dark عَسْعَسَ (اللَّيْل)

(2) to grow light

(1) eminence, prestige, glory, high rank كِبْر

(2) great sin, grave offence, atrocious crime

(1) committing a grammatical error لَحْن

(2) shrewdness, wit, sagacity, intelligence

(1) standing مَائِل

(2) lying close to the ground

(1) the one who selects      مُختار

(2) the one who is selected

(1) victor, conqueror, winner, triumphant      مُغَلَّب

(2) defeated, beaten, conquered, vanquished

(1) master, lord      مَولى

(2) slave, freed slave

### 2.4.16 *Synonyms and related words*

A synonym is a word having the same or nearly the same meaning as another word or words in a language. Nonetheless, two words, rarely if ever, have exactly the same meaning, whereby they can be used interchangeably. In this section, synonyms are listed in each entry along with other words which are not as closely related. The choice is not as wide as that under categorization above, nor is it restricted only to identical synonyms. Lexical items that can be associated meaningfully together in one way or another are grouped in one entry. The Arabic head-word (highlighted), represents the general meaning of the associations included in the entry. Its English meaning or meanings are provided on the same line on the left-hand side. Its synonym or synonyms and related words are listed in the same manner. If there is a need for a sentence or phrase containing an item in order to explain its use, it is provided next to it. There are many synonyms in Arabic, but only those that are common in modern usage and deemed most useful to students of Arabic are provided.

to blend, mix      خَلَطَ –

to mingle, combine      مَزَجَ

congenital, inborn      خَلقي –

| | |
|---|---|
| natural, innate | فِطْرِيّ |
| natural, native | طَبِيعِيّ |
| doctor, physician | طَبِيب - |
| wise man, sage, philosopher, physician | حَكِيم |
| surgeon | جَرّاح |
| specialist | اخصّائِيّ |
| board, blackboard, slate, panel, tablet | لَوْح - |
| painting, picture, signboard, billboard, plaque | لَوْحة |
| signboard, sign, billboard | لافِتة |
| announcement, advertisement, commercial | إعْلان |
| garbage, rubbish, waste, refuse | زُبالة - |
| garbage, rubbish, waste, refuse | قُمامة |
| junk, waste, refuse, offal, scrap | نُفايات |
| rubbish, trash, junk, scrap, waste | فَضَلات |
| to fold, double, roll up | طَوى الصَّفْحَةَ — طَوى - |
| to pleat, tuck, flex | ثَنى طَرَفَ الثَوبِ — ثَنى |
| to bend, curve | عَطَفَ الوِسادة — عَطَفَ |
| father | أب - |
| father, parent | والِد |
| cold, coldness, chilliness | بَرْد - |
| cold, coldness, chilliness | قُرّ |
| frost, freeze | صَقيع |
| scissors, shears | مِقَصّ - |

| | |
|---|---|
| scissors | مِقْراض |
| table, dining table | – مائِدَة |
| buffet, sideboard, table, dining table | خُوان |
| table | طاوِلَة |
| table | مِنضَدة |
| tiredness, weariness, fatigue, toil, labour | – تَعَب |
| fatigue, exhaustion | نَصَب |
| pains, hardship | عَناء |
| drudgery, toil, exertion | كَدّ |
| to return, come back, go back | رَجَعَ إلى وَطَنِه | – رَجَعَ |
| to return, repent | آبَ إلى الله | آبَ |
| to be due to, attributed to | عاد الفشَلُ إلى التأخير | عادَ |
| ugly, unsightly, hideous, repulsive | – قَبيح |
| ugly, unsightly, repellent, disagreeable | بَشِع |
| ugly, repugnant, abominable, atrocious, horrible | شَنيع |
| praise, commendation, tribute, compliment | – مَدْح |
| praise, panegyric, tribute, compliment | ثَناء |
| praise, laudation, extolment, eulogy | تَقْريظ |
| praise, panegyric, tribute, compliment, flattery | إطْراء |
| to contrive, devise, design, invent, create | – ابْتَدَعَ |
| to invent, contrive, innovate, originate | ابْتَكَرَ |
| to contrive, devise, design, invent, create | اسْتَنْبَطَ |
| to fear, dread, apprehend, be afraid, alarmed | – خافَ |

| | |
|---|---|
| to become afraid, scared | فَزِعَ |
| to panic, fear, dread, be terrified, frightened | ذُعِرَ |
| to fear, be afraid of, to feel awe or reverence for | خَشِيَ |
| to nullify, cancel, abolish, repeal, void | أَبْطَلَ – |
| to cancel, annul, abolish, void, call off, negate | أَلْغَى |
| to revoke, repeal, rescind, defeat, make null | فَسَخَ |
| to revoke, countermand, reverse, overrule | نَقَضَ |
| to break, breach, violate, infringe, transgress | خَرَقَ |
| betrayal, treachery, faithlessness, deception | غَدْر – |
| treason, betrayal, disloyalty, unfaithfulness | خِيانة |
| cheating, double-cross, treachery, disloyalty | خَتْر |
| diligence, industry, hard work, exertion | اجْتِهاد |
| toil, labour, hard work, travail | كَدّ |
| to work hard, exert oneself, toil, labour | ثابَرَ |
| to be or become tired, fatigued, exhausted | تَعِبَ |
| dissolution, melting | ذَوَبان الثلج | ذَوَبان – |
| dissolution, decomposition | انحلال السُكَّر | انحلال |
| fusion, melting | انصهار المَعدِن | انصهار |
| liquefaction | تَمْييع الغاز | تَمْييع |
| liquidity, fluidity | | سُيولة |
| obedience, compliance, yielding, submission | | انْقِياد – |
| yielding, submissiveness, acquiescence | | انْصِياع |
| submission, surrender, giving in, obedience | | خُضوع |

131

| | |
|---|---|
| submission, surrender, giving in, obedience | إِذْعان |
| far, distant, remote, secluded | قاصٍ – |
| remote, distant, far-off, outlying | ناءٍ |
| force, coercion, compulsion | عَنْوَة – |
| force, coercion, compulsion | قَسْر |
| coercion, compulsion | إكراه |
| force, constraint, compulsion | إرْغام |
| violence, vehemence, severity | عُنْف |
| gold | ذَهَب – |
| gold (rare) | عَسْجَد |
| kind, sort, type, species, form | نَوْع – |
| kind, type, sort, variety | ضَرْب (ضُروب الفَنّ) |
| class, grade, category, type, kind, variety | صِنْف |
| form, shape, figure | شَكْل – |
| form, shape, aspect, mien, appearance | هَيْئة |
| appearance, mien, visage, facial features | سَحْنة |
| form, shape, appearance | صورة |
| like, similar, identical | مَثيل |
| match, like, parallel, double, duplicate | شَبيه |
| counterpart, parallel, equivalent | نَظير |
| peer, equal, equivalent | نِدّ |
| similar, equal, like (rare, though the verb is not) | ضِرْع |
| twin, double, brother, duplicate, equal, peer | صِنْو |

| | |
|---|---|
| full brother | شَقيق |
| to have sexual intercourse with, to make love | ضاجَعَ – |
| to have sexual intercourse with, copulate with | جامَعَ |
| damage, harm, injury, detriment | ضَرَر – |
| nuisance, trouble, damage, hurt, injury | أذىً |
| breast, bosom | ثَدْيٌ – |
| breast, bosom, bust | نَهْد |
| udder, dug | ضَرْع |
| necessity, need, exigency, demand, requirement | ضَرورة – |
| need, want, necessity, exigency, requisite | حاجة |
| necessary, requisite | ضَروري – |
| necessary, requisite, indispensable, required | لازِم |
| sleep, slumber | نَوْم – |
| sleep, slumber, dormancy, repose, resting | رُقاد |
| sleep, lethargy, coma, hibernation | سُبات |
| grave, tomb, burial, burying, interment | قَبْر – |
| grave, tomb, sepulchre | لَحْد |
| grave, tomb, sepulchre (rare) | جَدَث |
| grave, tomb, sepulchre (rare) | رَمْس |
| grave, tomb, sepulchre | ضَريح |
| shrine, sanctuary | مَقام |
| wine | خَمْر – |
| wine | نَبيذ |

| | |
|---|---|
| wine | راح |
| book, compilation, publication | – كِتاب |
| book | سِفْر |
| book, work, publication | مُؤَلَّف |
| paper | – وَرَق |
| paper, sheet | قُرْطاس |
| to fall down, stumble | – وَقَعَ |
| to fall down, drop, stumble, decline | سَقَطَ |
| to fall down, drop, stumble, decline | تَرَدّى |
| easy, facile, simple, uncomplicated | – سَهْل |
| easy, facile, flowing, fluent | سَلِس |
| easy, simple, uncomplicated | يَسير |
| simple, plain | بَسيط |
| easy, facile | هَيِّن |
| blind | – أَعْمى |
| blind | ضَرير |
| blind | كَفيف |
| people, human beings, mankind | – ناس |
| people, creatures, mankind | الوَرى |
| human being, man, people | بَشَر |
| people, Adam's offspring | بَنو آدَم |
| mankind | الأَنام |
| tooth | – سِنّ |

tooth, molar ضِرْس

## 2.4.17 *Antonyms*

An antonym is a word having a meaning opposite to that of another word. In this section, each pair of words on the same line represents two opposite meanings.

| | | | |
|---|---|---|---|
| separation, parting | افْتِراق | meeting, gathering | اِجْتِماع |
| offence, harm | إساءَة | kindness, good deeds | إحْسان |
| evil, bad people | أشْرار | good people | أخْيار |
| to avoid, shun | اِجْتَنَبَ | to observe, adhere to | اِلْتَزَمَ |
| abstention, refraining | اِمْتِناع | obedience, compliance | اِنْقِياد |
| heat | حَرّ | coldness | بَرْد |
| near, close | قَريب | far | بَعيد |
| restfulness | راحَة | weariness | تَعَب |
| joking, jesting | هَزْل | seriousness | جِدّ |
| bad | فاسد | good | جَيِّد |
| ugly | قَبيح | good-looking | حَسَن |
| pride, glory | فَخْر | lowness, abjectness | حَقارة |
| remote, far | قاصٍ | close, near | دانٍ |
| respect, regard | اِحْتِرام | sarcasm, mockery | سُخْرِية |
| slowness | بُطْء | speed | سُرْعَة |
| certainty | يَقين | doubt | شَكّ |
| ungratefulness | جُحْد | thankfulness | شُكر |
| ingratitude | كُفْران | thankfulness | شُكْر |
| blame, censure | مُؤاخَذة | forgiveness | صَفْح |
| disobedience | عِصْيان | obedience | طاعَة |

| | | | |
|---|---|---|---|
| satisfaction | قَناعَة | greed | طَمَع |
| shortness | قِصَر | height, tallness | طول |
| ignorance | جَهْل | knowledge | عِلْم |
| abundant, plenty | كَثير | little, few | قَليل |
| disgrace | ذُلّ | pride | كِبْرِياء |
| disclosure, divulgence | إفْشاء | secrecy, suppression | كَتْم |
| truthfulness, veracity | صِدْق | lying, falseness | كَذِب |
| love | مَحَبَّة | hatred, aversion | كُرْه |
| activity, vigour | نَشاط | laziness, lethargy | كَسَل |
| faith, belief | إيمان | disbelief | كُفْر |
| rude, ungracious | غَليظ | gentle, amiable | لَطيف |
| excuse, forgiveness | مَعْذِرَة | blame, reproach | لَوْم |
| moral, immaterialist | مَعْنَوِيّ | materialist | مادِّيّ |
| remote, distant | ناءٍ | close, near | مُجاوِر |
| isolation, seclusion | عُزْلَة | sociability, company | مُخالَطة |
| censure, slander | ذَمّ | praise | مَدْح |
| satirical poem, lampoon | هِجاء | praise, panegyric | مَديح |
| innocent | بَريء | guilty | مُذْنِب |
| despotism, autocracy | اسْتِبْداد | consultation, counsel | مُشاوَرَة |
| devil | شَيْطان | angel | مَلاك |
| empty | فارِغ | full | مَمْلوء |
| indignation, malice | نَقْمَة | blessing, grace | نِعْمَة |
| damage, harm | ضَرَر | benefit, usefulness | نَفْع |
| denial, deprivation | حِرْمان | gift, donation | هِبَة |
| betrayal, treachery | غَدْر | faithfulness, fidelity | وَفاء |

| soft, tender, supple | طَرِيّ | dry, stiff | يابِس |
|---|---|---|---|

### 2.4.18 *Similes* التَشْبيه

A simile is a figure of speech in which two essentially different things are compared, often in a phrase introduced by مِثل or the preposition كَ. Other words may also be used to introduce similes, such as أشْبَه. ,كَأنَّ ,حاكى ,حَكى Similes enrich a text and add imagery. Some examples follow.

| Brave as a lion. | شُجاعٌ كالأسَد. |
|---|---|
| His memory is as deep as the sea. | ذاكِرَتُه مثلُ البحرِ عُمْقاً. |
| As though the sea is human memory. | كأنَّ البحرَ ذاكِرةٌ إنسانية. |
| Loyal as a dog. | وَفِيٌّ كالكلب. |
| The drink sparkles like stars. | يتَلألأ الشَرابُ كالنُجوم. |
| A good word is like a good tree. | الكلمةُ الطيِّبةُ كالشجرةِ الطيِّبة. |
| From the frying pan into the fire. | كالمُسْتَجير مِنَ الرَمْضاءِ بالنار. |
| Like a shepherd without a stick (said about | كالراعي بلا عصا. |

one who is not prepared for what is expected of him).

| As if her smile reveals pearls. | كأنَّما تَبَسَّمُ عن لُؤْلُؤٍ. |
|---|---|
| The truth is as evident as the sun. | الحَقيقةُ واضحةٌ كالشَمْس. |
| More cunning than a fox. | أرْوَغُ مِن ثَعْلَب. |
| More deceptive than a mirage. | أغَرُّ مِن سَراب. |

Arabic poetry has a plethora of imagery. Some examples:

أرى كُلَّ ذي جودٍ إليكَ مَصيرُه     كأنَّكَ بَحْرٌ والمُلوكُ جَداوِلُ

*I think all generous men flock to you; you seem to be a sea and all other kinds like streams.*

كأنَّ مِشْيَتَها مِن بَيْتِ جارَتِها     مَرُّ السَحابَة لا رَيْثٌ ولا عَجَلُ

*She walks like the passing of a cloud; neither slow nor fast.*

إنَّ القُلوبَ إذا تَنافَرَ وُدُّها          مِثلُ الزُجاجَة كَسْرُها لا يُجْبَرُ

*Alienated hearts are like a pane of glass; if broken, it cannot be repaired.*

إذا قامَتْ لِحاجَتِها تَثَنَّتْ          كَأنَّ عِظامَها مِن خَيْزُران

*When she gets up to get something, she walks with a swinging gait as though her bones were made from bamboo.*

From Muslim Spain, the poet describes his beloved.

يا مَنْ حَوى وَرْدَ الرِياض بِخَدِّهِ          وَحَكى قَضيبَ البَيْلَسان بِقَدِّه

جاءَت مُعَذِّبَتي في غَيْهَب الغَسَقِ          كَأنَّها الكَوكَبُ الدُرِّيُّ في الأُفُقِ

*Her cheeks are the colour of garden roses and her figure is like a limb of the balm tree.*

*My tormentor (beloved one) showed up at dusk as though she were the glistening evening star.*

As in all poetry, similes abound in modern Arabic poetry. Here are some verses by Sa°īd °Aql, praising Syria. They were made popular by the renowned Lebanese singer Fairouz.

بي كَما العودُ إلى الطَرَب؟          طابَت الذكْرى فَمَنْ راجِعٌ

مِثْلَما سَيْفي وَسَيْفُ أبي.          أنا أحبابيَ شِعْري لـهُمُ

مِثْلَما نَبْعُكَ مِنْ سُحُبي.          أنا صَوْتي مِنكَ يا بَرَدى،

شامِخاً كَالعِزِّ في القُبَب.          ثَلجُ حَرْمونَ غَذانا مَعاً،

*Those were fine memories. Who is going to bring them back to me, just as the lute brings joy and ecstasy?*

*My poetry is for those I love, just as my sword and my father's sword support them.*

*My voice comes from you, River Barada, just as your spring is nourished by my clouds.*

*The snows of Mount Hermon nourish us both, towering like glory in the sky.*

### 2.4.19 *Plural nouns which have no singular*

The singular forms of these nouns are either not used at all (e.g. حَـذافِـيـر), used in contexts other than those of the plurals (e.g. رؤوس أقـلام), or they are not the real singular forms of the plurals (e.g. أُحْدوثة ج أحاديث, not حديث).

| | |
|---|---:|
| battalions, brigades | أبابيل |
| lies, untruths | أباطيل |
| furniture | أثاث |
| tricks, wiles, stratagems | أحابيل |
| talks, conversations, chats | أحاديث |
| facial features (when one is happy) | أسارير |
| severed limbs (lit.), corpse, body | أشْلاء |
| debris, rubble, wreckage | أنقاض |
| foretokens, omens, first indications | تَباشير |
| direction, instructions | تَعْليمات |
| equipment | تَجْهيزات |
| sides; entirety; lock, stock, and barrel | حَذافير (بحَذافيرِه) |
| needs, necessities, belongings | حَوائِج |
| short notes | رُؤوس أقْلام |
| red anemones | شَقائقُ النُعْمان |
| advantage, merit, good characteristics | مَحاسِن |
| risks, perils, dangers, hazards | مَخاطِر |
| pores | مَسامّ |

| features, countenance | مَلامِح |
| wedding gift | نُقوط |

### 2.4.20 *Nouns which are singular, plural, masculine, and feminine*

This class of nouns includes nouns that are singular and plural at the same time, and also masculine and feminine. So, unlike regular nouns, they do not have to agree with the antecedent in number and gender. One of them (وَلَد) can be pluralized (وِلْدان). Examples:

هو جُنُب، هي جُنُب، هما جُنُب، هم جُنُب، هنّ جُنُب.

| in a state of a major ritual impurity | جُنُب |
| guest, visitor | ضَيْف |
| enemy, adversary | عَدُوّ |
| boat, vessel, ship | فُلْك |
| offspring, children | وُلْد |

### 2.4.21 *Words of emphasis*

There are specific words used to emphasize utterances. Note that if the intention is emphasis, then the emphasized noun must *precede* the word of emphasis, e.g.

| I saw the man <u>himself</u>. | رَأَيْتُ الرجلَ نَفسَه. |

However, even if the word نفس is used, which is a word of emphasis, but is placed before the noun it modifies (e.g. رأيتُ نَفسَ الرجُلِ), not after it, it would function as the direct object of the verb and would not signify emphasis. Other words include:

| This is the <u>same</u> book. | هذا هو الكتابُ عَيْنُه. |
| That is my colleague <u>herself</u>. | تلكَ هي زَميلتي ذاتُها. |

140

| | |
|---|---|
| I read <u>both</u> books. | قرأتُ الكتابَيْنِ كِليهِما. |
| <u>Both</u> cars are Japanese. | السّيّارتانِ كِلتاهُما يابانيّتانِ. |
| <u>All</u> the students are in class. | الطُّلابُ كُلُّهُم في الصَّفِّ. |
| <u>All</u> the girls are on the playfield. | البَناتُ كُلُّهُنَّ في المَلعَبِ. |
| Not <u>all</u> Arabs are Muslims. | لَيسَ العَرَبُ جَميعُهُم مُسلمينَ. |
| | الطُّلابُ عامَّتُهُم يدرسونَ في المكتَبةِ. |

<u>All</u> students study in the library.

Three additional words express comprehensive emphasis. They may be used with or without the other words of emphasis.

| | |
|---|---|
| I read the book <u>in its entirety</u>. | قرأتُ الكتابَ بِأجمَعِهِ. |
| <u>All</u> the students came. | حَضَرَ الطُّلابُ كُلُّهُم أجمَعونَ. |
| I like <u>all</u> German cars. | تعجِبُني السياراتُ الألمانيةُ جَمْعاءَ. |

### 2.4.22 *Verbs of transformation*

Some of the so-called defective verbs express transformation. That is, they express a change from one state to another. They are members of the كان set. Briefly, members of this set introduce nominal sentences, causing the predicate to have the accusative case (نصب) instead of the nominative (رفع).

| | |
|---|---|
| The weather has become cold. | أصبَحَ الجَوُّ بارداً. |
| Prices have risen. | أضْحَت الأسعارُ عاليةً. |
| The labourer has become exhausted. | أمسى العامِلُ تَعباناً. |
| The people have become concerned. | باتَ الشَّعْبُ قَلِقاً. |
| The market has become free. | صارَت السوقُ حُرَّةً. |
| Cooperation became impossible. | استَحالَ التعاوُنُ مُستحيلاً. |
| Other words include: | غَدا، عاد، آض، ارتَدَّ، انقَلب، تبدَّل، تحوَّل، حار. |

### 2.4.23 *Proverbs*

Selected Arabic proverbs are explained and listed along with their closest English counterparts. If no such counterparts exist, a close translation is provided.

A friend in need is a friend indeed. الصَّديقُ عندَ الضِّيق.

A man can do no more than he can. الإناءُ يَنضَحُ بما فيه.

War is deception. الحَرْبُ خُدْعة.

It's greener on the other side of the fence. زامِرُ الحَيِّ لا يُطرِب.

A stitch in time saves nine. دِرْهَمُ وقايَة خَيرٌ من قنْطار علاج.

A word to a wise man is enough. إنَّ اللَّبيبَ مِنَ الإشارة يَفهَمُ.

Birds of a feather flock together. الطُّيورُ على أشْكالِها تَقَع.

Charity begins at home. الأقرَبونَ أوْلى بالمَعروف.

Cleanliness is next to godliness. النَظافةُ مِنَ الإيمان.

Deeds, not words. أسْمَعُ صَوْتاً وأرى فَوْتاً.

Nothing blunts steel but steel. لا يَفِلُّ الحَديدَ إلاَّ الحَديد.

I have nothing to do with this. لا ناقةَ لي في هذا ولا جَمَل.

Need is the mother of invention. الحاجةُ تُفَتِّقُ الحيلة.

Forgetfulness is the blight of knowledge. آفةُ العلم النسيان.

Much ado about nothing. أسمعُ جَعْجَعةً ولا أرى طحْناً.

Having nothing to do with it. لا في العِير ولا في النَفير.

Forbidden fruit is sweet. كُلُّ مَمنوعٍ مَرغوب.

Money begets money. الدَراهِمُ بالدَراهِم تُكسَب.

A good neighbour is better than a good house. الجارُ قَبْلَ الدار.

Some friends are closer than brothers. رُبَّ أخٍ لَم تَلِدْهُ أمُّك.

He returned evil for good. جَزاهُ جَزاءَ سِنِّمار.

142

He returned empty-handed.      رَجَع بِخُفَّي حُنَيْن.

To be happy to save one's skin.      رضِيَ مِنَ الغنيمة بالإياب.

Scarcer than a white camel.      أعَزُّ من بيض النوق.

عَدُوٌّ عاقِلٌ خَيْرٌ من صَديقٍ جاهِل.

Better an open enemy than a false friend.

ضَرَب أخْماساً لأسْداس.

To rack one's brain in search of a way out (to scheme).

كالمُسْتَجيرِ مِنَ الرَمْضاءِ بالنار.

To escape the heat by jumping into the fire.

مَنْ أنْكَرَ أصلهُ فلا أصْلَ له.

He who denies his heritage is not worthy of one.

سلامةُ الإنسانِ في حفظِ اللسان.

Speech is silver, but silence is gold.

إذا كُنتَ في قَوْمٍ فاحلِبْ في إنائِهِم.

When in Rome do as the Romans do.

لَيْسَ لِرَجُلٍ لُدِغَ من جُحْرٍ مَرَّتَيْن عُذْرٌ.

A fox is not taken twice in the same snare.

### 2.4.24 *English prefixes and suffixes and their Arabic meanings*

The focus in this section is on derivational suffixes rather than on inflectional ones (e.g. *-ing*, *-ed*, *-s*), because derivational suffixes can change the meaning of a word. Some English prefixes which denote a negative meaning (e.g. *non-*, *un-*, *in-*, *-less*, *anti-*, *ir-*, *im-*, *de-*, *a-*, *il-*) have the negative particle ﻻ as their equivalent.

the non-ego      اللاأنا

unconscious mind, unconsciousness      اللاشُعور

| | |
|---|---|
| the infinite | اللاتِهائِيّة |
| the unconscious, unconsciousness | اللاوَعْيَ |
| skepticism, agnosticism | لاأَدرِية |
| unintentional, involuntary, reflex | لاإرادي |
| selflessness, unselfishness | لاأنانِيّة |
| stateless | لاجِنْسِيّة |
| indeterminism | لاحَتْمِيّة |
| nonpartisan | لاحِزْبيّ |
| antireligious, irreligious, without a religion | لاديني |
| irreligion, godlessness | لادينِيّة |
| anti-Semitic, anti-Semite | لاسامِيّ |
| anti-Semitism | لاسامِيّة |
| wireless, radio | لاسلكيّ |
| unconscious, unaware | لاشُعوريّ |
| nothing, nil | لاشيْء |
| nonexistence, nothingness, nihility | لاشَيْئِيّة |
| irrational, nonrational | لاعَقْلانيّ |
| nonviolence | لاعُنْف |
| immaterialism, immateriality | لامادِيّة |
| indifference | لامُبالاة |
| amorphous, uncrystallized | لامُتَبَلْوِر |
| infinite, limitless, boundless, eternal | لامُتَناهٍ |
| unlimited, limitless, infinite, immeasurable | لامَحْدود |
| decentralization | لامَرْكَزِيّة |
| irresponsibility | لامَسْؤوليّة |

| | |
|---|---|
| absurd | لامَعْقول |
| (theatre) of the absurd | (مَسْرَح) اللامَعْقول (العَبَث) |
| illogicality, irrationality | لامَنْطقيّة |
| nonunion | لانقابيّ |
| astigmatism | لانُقْطيّة |
| infinite | لانهائيّ |
| unconscious | لاواعٍ |
| nonexistence, nonbeing, nonentity, nothingness | لاوُجود |

However, if an antonym exists, as in the case of 'possible' مُمْكن and 'impossible' مُسْتَحيل, it is used without the need for the negative particle لا.

| | |
|---|---|
| impolite | فَظّ، جِلف |
| disappear | اختفى |
| discharge | فرّغ |
| discourteous | فَظّ، غَليظ |
| disfigure | شَوّه |
| dishonourable | مُخْزٍ، شائن |
| imperfect | ناقص |
| inattention | غفلة |
| inconsonant | مُتنافر |
| misdeed | ذَنْب |
| mislead | ضَلَّل، خَدَع |
| misrepresent, distort, corrupt | حَرّف |
| nonconductor | عازِل |
| nonsense | هُراء |

| rebirth | تَجَدّد، تقمُّص، انبعاث |
| retouch | يهذِّب، ينقِّح، ينمِّق |
| unaware | غافِل |
| unclothe | عَرَّى |

The derivational prefix *mis-* is sometimes translated as أَسَاءَ. Similarly, the prefix *dis-* is translated into a number of Arabic words, such as عَدَم، جَرَّدَ، حَرَمَ، غَيْر، لا. The nouns عَدَم and غَيْر form an *iḍāfa* structure with the following noun.

| miscount | أخطأ في العَدِّ أو الحِساب |
| mistreat | أساءَ المُعامَلة |
| disfranchise | حُرِم حَقّ التَصويت |
| dispensable | غَيْر ضَروري |
| disengaged | غَيْر مَشغول |

The prefix *re-* is frequently translated as a verb (أعاد) followed by a verbal noun (مصدر).

| reprinting | إعادة الطَبْع |
| rearm | يتسلَّح من جديد/يعيد التسلُّح |

Note also that certain nouns in English are translated as a technical participle (مَصْدَر صِناعي) such as إنسانيّة, a noun which resembles in form a feminine relative adjective (نِسْبة). The difference between the two is in the intention of use. If such a noun is used to describe, then it is a *nisba*, but if it is used to refer to an attribute or concept, it is a technical participle.

| neo-impressionism | الانطِباعية المُحدَثة/الانطِباعية الجديدة |
| cubism | التكعيبيّة |
| opportunism | إنتهازيّة |

For other English prefixes, a word representing the meaning of the prefix is combined with another word for the item.

| | |
|---|---|
| self-defence | الدفاع عن النفس |
| self-recording | تَسْجيل ذاتيّ |
| monocracy | حُكم الفَرْد |
| subaverage | دون المتوسِّط |
| preconception | فكرة مُكوَّنة سَلَفاً |
| pro-choice | مُؤَيِّد لحرية اختيار المرأة بشأن الإجهاض |
| pre-mix | مَزج قبل الاستعمال |
| prelude | مُقَدِّمة، استهْلال |

English derivational suffixes, on the other hand, generally do not require a word to reflect their meanings. Only three suffixes (*-ly, -less, -able*) require the use of a word or a preposition. Adverbs with *-ly* need either the preposition بـ prefixed to a noun or a noun phrase.

| | |
|---|---|
| quickly | بِسُرعة |
| effectively | بصورة فعّالة |

The *-ly* prefix may also translate into a circumstantial adverb (حال), cognate accusative (مفعول مطلق), or prepositional phrase.

| | |
|---|---|
| quickly | سريعاً |
| intently, deeply | (فكَّر) مليّاً |
| intently, deeply | (فكَّر) تفكيراً (عميقاً) |
| currently | في الأحوال الراهنة |

However, adjectives with *-ly* translate as nouns.

| | |
|---|---|
| friendly | وَدود /ودّيّ، مُحبّ /حبيّ |

For the suffix *-less*, the words غـيـر، لا، فـاقـد and عديم are usually used if there is no single-word equivalent.

| | |
|---|---|
| odourless | عديم الرائحة، غير ذي رائحة، لا رائحة له |
| stateless | فاقد الجنسية، لا جنسية له |
| sleepless | أرِق، يقظ |

The suffix *-able/-ible* is normally translated جدير or قابل، صالح in some words and not translated in others.

| | |
|---|---|
| potable | صالح للشرب |
| provable | قابل للإثبات |
| dependable | مَوثوق، يُعتمد عليه |
| acceptable | مَقبول |

The suffix *-logy* is usually translated عِلم.

| | |
|---|---|
| sociology | علم الاجتماع |
| philology | فقه اللغة |

The suffix *-itis* is translated invariably as التهاب.

| | |
|---|---|
| pharyngitis | التهاب البُلعوم |

No other suffixes are translated by specific elements in Arabic. The meaning is reflected in the word form (e.g., verbal noun, attributive adjective, participle, etc.). Adjectival suffixes such as *-ous*, *-ary*, *-ic*, *-ive*, and *-al* generally make the Arabic equivalent an attributive adjective (نسبة), active participle (اسم فاعل), passive participle (اسم مفعول), or an adjective (صفة مشبهة).

| | |
|---|---|
| tumultuous | هائِج، مُضطرِب |
| customary | عُرفيّ، عاديّ |
| angelic | ملائكيّ |
| vindictive | حَقود، انتقاميّ |
| comical | هَزليّ، مُضحِك |

148

### 2.4.25 *Loan words*

Although Arabic has resisted the importation of lexical items and depended on its derivational system and other means to express new concepts, the influx of technological and other terms found their way into the language (see next section). Loan words are foreign words used with no or minimal change. They follow Arabic rules of pluralization and derivation.

| strategy | استراتيجيَّة | telephone | تَلِفون |
| --- | --- | --- | --- |
| democratic | ديُقْراطي | aristocratic | أَرِسْتُقْراطي |
| academic | أكاديمي | bank | بَنْك |
| line, queue | طابور | ideology | إديولوجية |
| bus | أتوبوس/أوتوبيس | chalk | طَبْشورة |
| baccalaureate | بكالوريا | bus | باص (أتوبيس) |
| television | تلفزيون | computer | كمبيوتَر |
| imperialism | إمبرياليَّة | video | فيديو |
| butane gas | غاز | policy (insurance) | بوليصة |
| radio | راديو | radar | رادار |
| cigarette | سيكارة | oven | فُرْن |
| cinema, movies | سينَما | cigar | سيكار |
| pasta | مَعْكَرونة | sandwich | سَندويش |
| panties | كلوت | madam | مَدام |
| centimetre | سَنتيمتر | kilo | كيلو |
| kilometre | كيلومتر | millimetre | ميليمتر |
| billion | مليار | million | مليون |
| lithium | لِثيوم | calcium | كَلْسيوم |
| volt | فولط | oxide | أُكْسيد |

| | | | |
|---|---|---|---|
| oxygen | أُكْسِجين | chloride | كْلُوريد |
| dictator | دِكْتاتور | Bachelor of Arts | بَكالوريوس |
| balcony | بَلْكَون | trousers, pants | بَنْطَلون |
| central heating | شوفاج | reception room, salon | صالون |
| doctor | دُكْتور | film, movie | فيلم |

### 2.4.26 *Derived and translated technical terms*

This is probably the most productive process in the effort to transfer the terminology of Western sciences. Dictionaries were compiled and innumerable studies were conducted in this area. Some of the selected terms have enjoyed currency even among lay people, others are rarely used.

Telephone related

| | | | |
|---|---|---|---|
| portable phone | هاتف نَقّال/مَحْمول | telephone | هاتف |
| wireless phone | هاتف لاسِلْكي | cellular phone | هاتف خَلَوي |
| (telephone) call | مُكالَمة (هاتفيّة) | switchboard | مَقْسَم |
| local calling | النداء الداخِلي | telephone directory | دَليل هاتف |
| privacy | عَدَم الإزعاج | calling tone | نَغْمة النداء |
| voice mail | مُكالَمة مُسَجَّلة | call waiting | انتِظار النداء |
| receiver | سَمّاعة الهاتف | caller ID | الكاشِف |

Computer related

| | | | |
|---|---|---|---|
| port | مَسار مَعْلومات | computer | حاسوب/حاسِب |
| disk drive | قارِئ الأقْراص | disk | قُرْص |
| interface | وَصْلة | booting up | تَشْغيل/إقلاع |
| byte | مَجْموعة مُفرَدات بَيان | bit | مُفْرَدة بَيان |
| file | مَلَفّ | card | بِطاقة أو لَوْحة |

150

| | | | |
|---|---|---|---|
| integrated circuit | | دائرة كَهْرَبِيّة مُتَكامِلة | |
| parameter | مَحَدِّد | micro processor | مُعالِج |
| plotter | طابِعة رُسوم هندسِيّة | printer | طابِعة |

Miscellaneous

| | | | |
|---|---|---|---|
| bank | مَصْرِف | microscope | مِجْهَر |
| radio | مِذْياع | bus | حافِلة |
| microphone | مِصْوات | speaker, receiver | سَمّاعة |
| periscope | مِقْرَب | radioscope | مِكْشَف |
| pantograph | مِنْساخ | spectroscope | مِطْياف |
| telegram | بَرْقِيّة | telegraph | مِبْرَقة |
| telescope | مِقْراب/مِنْظار | meteograph | مِنْوَأة |
| watt | شَمْعة | stethoscope | مِسْمَع/سَمّاعة |
| acid | حِمْضِيّ | alkaline | قِلْوِيّ |
| sulphuric acid | حِمْض الكِبْريت | typesetting | تَنْضيد |

Medical

| | | | |
|---|---|---|---|
| premature babies | خُدَّج | diabetes | السُكَّرِيّ |
| coagulable | خَثور | cardiac infarction | احتِشاء |
| antigen | مُوَلِّد المُضاد | microbe, bacterium | جُرْثوم |
| bronchitis | التِهاب شُعَبِي | pneumonia | ذاتُ الرِئة |
| tracheotomy | فَتْح القَصَبة الهَوائِيّة | lapratomy | شَقُّ البَطْن |
| aneurysm | أمّ الدَمْ (الشِرْيانِيّة) | ischemia | نَقْص تَرْوِية |
| CAT scan (coaxial tomography) | | طَبَقي مِحْوَري | |
| Magnetic Resonance Imaging (MRI) | | مِرْنان | |
| arterial sclerosis | | تَصَلُّب الشَرايين (العَصيدة الشِرْيانِيّة) | |
| impotence | العُنّة | ulcer | قَرْحة |

| | | | |
|---|---|---|---|
| excretion | الإطراح | metabolism | الاستقلاب |
| mucoid | شِبْه مُخاطي | antibiotic | مُضادّ حَيَوِيّ |
| psychological complex | | | عُقْدة نَفْسِية |

### 2.4.27 *Foreignisms*

Foreignisms are Arabic words and phrases which do not comply with traditionally accepted Arabic usage. Their structure is mostly influenced by either English or French. Basically, they are literal translations of words and phrases.

| | |
|---|---|
| by (when used before the agent in a passive sentence) | مِن قِبَل |
| credibility (this has gained wide circulation) | مِصْداقِيَّة |
| such a report | هكَذا تَقرير (تَقرير كَهذا) |
| to work as a doctor | عَمِلَ كَطَبيب (عَمِلَ طَبيباً) |
| to like s.t. in spite of its taste | أحِبُّهُ على رَغْم طَعْمه (على طعمه) |
| to cover the news of the conference | غَطَّى أنباءَ المُؤتَمَر |
| in the true sense of the word | بكُلِّ مَعْنى الكَلِمَة |
| to play the lute | لعب على َ العود (عَزَفَ) |
| to play a role | لَعِبَ دَوْراً (أدّى/قامَ بـ) |
| to take your time | خُذْ وَقتَك |
| to take the plane | أخَذَ الطائرة (استَقلَّ/ركب) |
| colour blindness | عَمى ألْوان (قَمَر) |
| Dr. so-and-so | دُكْتور فُلان (الدكتور فُلان) |

### 2.4.28 *Blends* (النَحْت)

Blending in Arabic has been recognized since pre-Islamic times. A blend word is made from parts of two or more words. There are hundreds of such words attested in dictionaries, many of which have fallen out of use. With the modern Arabic Renaissance, there was an attempt at creating technical terminology following the practice of European languages of using Greek and Latin words. The blends below are listed with the words from which they are made.

| | | |
|---|---|---|
| هَلَّق (adv.) | هذا الوَقْت | now |
| هَسَّع (adv.) | هذه الساعة | now |
| حَيْعَل (v.) | حَيَّ عَلى | Come to..! |
| حَوْقَل (v.) | لا حَوْلَ ولا قُوَّةَ إلا بالله | to say this phrase |
| بَسْمَل (v.) | بِسْم الله الرحمن الرحيم | to say this phrase |
| كَبَّر (v.) | اللهُ أَكبَر | God is greatest |
| عَبْشَمي (adj.) | عَبْدُ شَمْس | *nisba* derived from this name |
| تَلحَمِيّ (adj.) | بَيْت لَحْم | *nisba* (s.o. coming from this town) |
| هَلَّلة (n.) | لا إلهَ إلاّ الله | no God but Allah |
| كَهْرَطيسِيّ (adj.) | كَهْرَبائي/مَغْنَطيسي | electromagnetic |
| كُهْرَمائِيّ (adj.) | كَهْرَبائي/مائي | hydroelectric |
| حَرْنَوي (adj.) | حَراري/نَوَوي | electronuclear |
| حَلْمَأة (n.) | حَلَّلَ بالماء | hydrolysis |
| فَحْمائيّات (n.) | فَحْمِيّ/مائيّ | carbohydrates |
| رَأسمال | رأس المال | capital |
| عَرْضحال | عَرْض حال | petition |

### 2.4.29 *Arabized words*

Arabic academies resorted to Arabization when translation, derivation, and coining words failed to convey the desired meaning. As noted in Chapter 1, Arabization involves making a foreign word fit into Arabic morphological patterns.

| | | | |
|---|---|---|---|
| fresh | طازَج | stringed instrument | طُنْبور |

| | | | |
|---|---|---|---|
| measure of distance | فَرْسَخ | trench, ditch | خَنْدَق |
| television | تِلْفاز | weight; money | دِرْهَم |
| music | موسيقا | geometry | هَنْدَسة |
| overcoat | بالطو/بانطو/مانطو | antidote | تِرْياق |
| line, queue | طابور | pants, trousers | بِنْطال |
| to apply the breaks | فَرْمَلَ | gasoline, petrol | بَنْزين |

### 2.4.30 *Homophones*

Homophones are words which sound similar, but have different meanings and spellings.

| | | | |
|---|---|---|---|
| case, law suit | دَعْوى | invitation | دَعْوة |
| summits, tops, peaks | ذُرى | corn, maize, durra | ذُرة |
| to take care of, govern | رَعى | to abstain, refrain from | رَعا |
| dream, revelation | رُؤْيا | seeing, sight, vision | رُؤْية |
| to heal, cure | شَفى | edge | شَفا |
| feminine name | لَيْلى | night | لَيْلة |

### 2.4.31 *Homographs*

These are words that look identical, but differ in meaning.

| | | | |
|---|---|---|---|
| income/concern/bearing | دَخْل | conversation/modern | حديث |
| contract/arch/decade | عَقْد | century/horn | قَرْن |
| example/proverb/ideal | مَثَل | currency/criticism | نَقْد |

### 2.4.32 *Personal names*

There exists a wide variety of names; some traditional, others modern. People nowadays prefer to be innovative. It must be noted that some traditional pre-Islamic names are still popular.

a. Traditional male names which are still popular:

| | | | |
|---|---|---|---|
| غَسّان | عَدْنان | مَرْوان | وَليد |
| مُعاوية | زَيْد | عُمَر | أُسامة |
| هِشام | خالِد | كَنْعان | عَمْرو |
| مازِن | إياد | هاني | مُعاذ |
| خَلْدون | عُدَيّ | تَميم | قَيْس |
| سَعْد | لُؤَيّ | نِزار | زِياد |
| نائِل | سُفْيان | عَبْدُ الله⁴ | بَشّار |
| هَيْثَم | حازِم | فَهْد | نُمَيْر |
| مالِك | عَبّاس | خَليل | نَصْر |
| مُحَمَّد | مَحْمود | حاتِم | عَلاء |
| سَعيد | خَليل | بَشير | خَلَف |
| جَعْفَر | حَسَن | حُسَيْن | إبْراهيم |
| نَصْر | دُرَيْد | عِماد | عيسى |
| إسْماعيل | زَكَرِيّا | فارِس | عُقْبة |
| حَسّان | بِشْر | ثابِت | جابِر |
| خَلَف | نَصوح | أُوَيْس | أَيْمَن |
| قُتَيْبة | يوسُف | أَسَد | عَقيل |
| زُهَيْر | عُثْمان | أوْس | يونُس |
| طَلْحة | بِلال | نَوْفَل | هَيْكَل |
| فِراس | ماهِر | نَبيل | سَميح |

b. Some traditional male names are less commonly or rarely used today (this is a subjective judgement). Note the first five names which have a verb form and the numerous names

---

⁴ And similar compound names with عَبْد plus one of the 99 names of God. See section g below.

ending with the feminine marker (*tā' marbūṭa*):

| | | | |
|---|---|---|---|
| يَحْيى | يَشْجُب | جاد | يَشْكُر |
| شَقِرة | رَبيعة | شَيْبة | يَعيش |
| ضُمْرة | جُنْدُب | ضَبّة | جُنادة |
| عَجْرمة | عُبَيْدة | حارثة | طُلَيْحة |
| عَنْترة | قَميئة | مَسْعَدة | عُرْوة |
| حَنْظلة | فَرْوة | مُسَيْلِمة | سَلِمة |
| هُبَيْرة | جَحْش | رفاعة | جِرْوة |
| المُغيرة | ثَعْلَبة | هَذْمة | هَنَّقة |
| كَعْب | عِجْل | الأَعْشى | مُرَّة |
| كُلَيْب | عَبّاد | فيل | الحارِث |

c. Male names typical of the Arabian Gulf area:

| | | | |
|---|---|---|---|
| جَوْعان | حَمْدان | سُلْطان | مُساعد |
| عيد | عَبْد الحُسَيْن | عَبْد الرضا | خَلْفان |
| فَلاح | مُفْلِح | مُتْعِب | فَهْد |
| قَحْطان | عايض | مَكْتوم | زايد |

d. Male names typical of Egypt:

| | | | |
|---|---|---|---|
| مكرم | بَيّومي | محمّدين | حَسَنين |
| صَفْوَت | فَتْحي | سلامة | سَلماوي |
| نافِع | حَنَفي | فكْري | عاطف |
| شْحاتة | عاشور | مَدْكور | شَحْتة |
| عَزّوز | مُتولّي | مَدْبولي | بُرَعي |

e. Typical male Coptic names in Egypt:

| | | | |
|---|---|---|---|
| جورج | أرساني | كيرلس | مينا |
| بُطْرُس | بيشاي | مُرْقُس (ماركو) | جِرجِس (girgis) |

| أثاناسيوس | ميخائيل | كرولوس | شنودة |
|---|---|---|---|
| غُبريال | غالي | أبانوب | نَيْروز |

f. Male names typical of North Africa:

| عَبْد الرَحيم | عَبْد اللالي | لَمَهْدي | لْهادي[5] |
| أنَس | نَجيب | قويدِر | عَبْد الحَيّ |
| بوشْعَيْب | لْمُخْتار | بَهَنَي | دْريس |
| لْمُفَضَّل | صغير | لْخَمّار | بوشْتة |
| لْمَكّي | لْمَدَني | رَحَمون | بوبْكَر |

g. Compound male names made with عَبْد and one of the 99 names of God.

| عبد العزيز | عبد الإله | عبد الرحمن | عبد الهادي |
| عبد الغَفور | عبد الخالق | عبد السَميع | عبد الكَريم |
| عبد السَلام | عبد الرَزّاق | عبد الحَفيظ | عبد الحَقّ |
| عبد المَجيد | عبد القادر | عبد الغَني | عبد الرَحيم |

h. Traditional female names which are still popular:

| فاطمة | لَيْلى | سُعاد | رَباب |
| آمنة | رُقَيّة | زَيْنَب | عائشة |
| أسْماء | يُسَيْرة | سُمَيّة | خَديجة |
| دَعْد | هِنْد | حَفْصة | حَليمة |

i. Modern, popular female names:

| جُمانة | دانة | نِسْرين | حَنين |
| مُزْنة | رَنا | هَنادي | هبة |
| مَيْ | غادة | سَميرة | هالة |
| حَسْناء | هَناء | هِيام | مايا |

---

[5] The *alif* of the article is deleted to reflect actual pronunciation.

| | | | |
|---|---|---|---|
| لين | ليان | دينا | هَيْفاء |
| رانية | نائلة | سيرين | أَسيل |
| رَشا | رولا | نور | دانية |
| عُلا | أماني | ديمة | أَمَل |
| فَرَح | هَديل | رانة | ريم |
| سَمَر | غُصون | مَيْسون | سهام |
| سَناء | رِهام | رَغَد | سَميرة |
| رانية | سَوْسَن | لُجَيْن | ثَناء |
| لَما | ندى | نُهى | سُها |
| وِداد | لَمْيا | فاتن | حَنان |

### j. Female names typical of the Arabian Gulf area:

| | | | |
|---|---|---|---|
| فَرْتونة | أكابِر | مَقْبولة | مُلوك |
| فَيْروز | رَضْوة | كَرْمة | جُوَيْرِيَّة |
| شَمَّة | حصّة | زُليخة | ياسمين |
| مَهْرة | مَيْثة | عَنود | موزة |
| مَزون | عَفْرة | لولُوَة | رَحْمة |
| قْماشة | ساجِدة | فَوْزية | حَسيبة |

### k. Female names typical of North Africa:

| | | | |
|---|---|---|---|
| زَيْنَب | خَدّوجة | خَديجة | عايْشَة |
| إتو | راضْية | عَزيزة | حَبيبة |
| لْعيدية | أُمْ هاني | غَنّو | تامو[6] |
| غيتة | سْعَدية | مْباركة | هَدّة |
| لْبَتول | مارية | مْحْجوبة | فاتِحة |

---

[6] Diminutive of فاطمة

٩

| | | | |
|---|---|---|---|
| زُلِيخة[7] | نزْهة | حْليمة | سْليمة |
| لَكْبِيرة | رَبْحة | عْتيقة | رْحيمو |
| ورْديَّة | لْفَضّة | تاجة | موهو |

1. Typical female Coptic names:

| | | | |
|---|---|---|---|
| إميلي | مَرْيَم | فيبي | ماري |
| روزا | نرمين | دميانا | مارينا |
| نانسي | ڤيڤيان | كريستين | ميرَيم |

## 2.4.33 *Names of traditional clothing*

### The Gulf area

| | |
|---|---|
| man's robe (Gulf) | دشْداشة |
| man's robe (Gulf) | كَنْدورة |
| man's headdress | غُتْرة |
| shoes (Gulf) | نْعال |
| woman's loose outer garment (Gulf) | كَنْدورة |
| woman's head scarf (Gulf) | شيلة |

### Syria

| | |
|---|---|
| man's outer garment | قُنْباز |
| woman's outer gown | مْلاية (مِلاية) |
| man's cloak, gown | عَباية |
| fez (also Egypt, Morocco) | طَرْبوش |
| head cord used to hold down headdress | عقال |
| turban | عَمامة/لَفّة |

---

[7] Muslim and Jewish

159

<u>Egypt</u>

woman's outer gown        مَلاية

man's robe        جَلّابيّة

<u>Morocco</u>

man's outer garment        بُرْنُس

### 2.4.34 *Names of the months of the Gregorian calendar*

In Jordan, Saudi Arabia, and the Gulf, the names of the months of the Gregorian calendar are generally not used, although in most Gulf countries the government is run according to the Gregorian calendar. People in those countries refer to these months generally by numbers (e.g. شَهْر سَبْعة for July).

| North Africa | Egypt | Syria, Lebanon, Iraq |
|---|---|---|
| يَنايِر | يَنايِر | كانون الثاني |
| فِبْرايِر | فِبْرايِر | شُباط |
| مارْس | مارس | آذار |
| أبْريل | أبْريل | نيسان |
| ماي | مايو | أيّار/مايس |
| يونيو | يونيو | حَزيران |
| يوليوز | يوليو | تَمّوز |
| غُشْت | أغُسْطُس | آب |
| شُتَنْبِر | سبْتَمبَر | أيْلول |
| أكْتوبِر | أكْتوبَر | تَشْرين الأوّل |
| نوَنْبِر | نوفَمْبَر | تَشْرين الثاني |
| دُجَنْبِر | ديسَمْبَر | كانون الأوّل |

### 2.4.35 *Names of the Islamic (Hijri) months*

The Prophet Muhammad's emigration from Mecca to Medina at the end of 622 CE marks the beginning of the Islamic calendar.

| | | | |
|---|---|---|---|
| ٢ـ صَفَر | | ١ـ مُحَرَّم | |
| ٤ـ رَبِيع الثاني | | ٣ـ رَبِيع الأوَّل | |
| ٦ـ جُمادى الثانية | | ٥ـ جُمادى الأولى | |
| ٨ـ شَعْبان | | ٧ـ رَجَبْ | |
| ١٠ـ شَوّال | | ٩ـ رَمَضان | |
| ١٢ـ ذو الحِجّة | | ١١ـ ذو القِعْدة | |

### 2.4.36 *Names of Coptic months*

The Coptic calendar is called النَّيْـــروز, and is chiefly used in religious and agricultural contexts It started with the persecution and martyrdom of Christians during the reign of Emperor Diocletian (284-312). Egypt suffered the greatest number of martyrs. Therefore, the year 284 marks the beginning of the Coptic Calendar (عيـد النَّيْـروز). The Coptic months do not correspond to the Gregorian months. September 11th, 2001 coincides with the beginning of the Coptic year 1718. Arabic is used alongside Coptic in church services.

| | | |
|---|---|---|
| ٣ـ هاتور | ٢ـ بابة | ١ـ توت |
| ٦ـ بَرَمْهات | ٥ـ طوبة | ٤ـ كِيَهْك |
| ٩ـ بَشَنْس | ٨ـ بَرْمودة | ٧ـ أمْشير |
| ١٢ـ مِسْري | ١١ـ أبيب | ١٠ـ بَؤونة |
| | | ١٣ـ النَسيء (a five-day month) |

### 2.4.37 *Names of animals, natural phenomena and their sounds*

The categories include animals, birds, and objects.

| **Animals** | Meaning | Sound | Name |
|---|---|---|---|
| | lion | زَئِير | أَسَد |
| | cattle | خُوار | بَقَر |
| | fox | ضُباح | ثَعْلَب |
| | camel, when angry | رُعاء | جَمَل |
| | donkey | نَهيق | حمار |
| | snake | فَحيح | حَيَّة، أفْعى |
| | pig, hog | قُباع | خنْزير |
| | wolf | عُواء | ذِئْب |
| | sheep | ثُغاء | غَنَم |
| | horse, when wanting to be fed | حَمْحَمة | فَرَس |
| | horse | صَهيل | فَرَس |
| | elephant | صأيٌ | فيل |
| | dog | نُباح | كَلْب |
| | cat, when pleased | خَرْخَرة | هرّ، قطّ، بسّ |
| | cat | مُواء | هِرّ، قطّ، بسّ |
| | frog | نَقيق | ضفْدَع |
| **Birds** | bird | تَغْريد | طائِرٌ |
| | dove, pigeon | هَديل | حَمام |
| | sparrow | زَقْزَقة | عُصْفور |
| | hens, chickens | نَقْنقة | دَجاج |
| | rooster | صِياح، زُقاء | ديك |
| | eagle | صَفير | نَسْر |

| | | |
|---|---|---|
| nightingale | عَنْدَلة | عَنْدَليب |
| crow | نَعيق | غُراب |
| **Natural Phenomena** water | خَرير | ماءٌ جارٍ |
| water, when boiling | أزيز | ماء |
| waves | هَدير | مَوج |
| fire | حَسيس | نار |
| bees | دَويّ | نَحْل |
| wail | عَويل | بُكاء |
| thunder | هَزيم، دَويّ | رَعْد |
| trees, when the wind blows | حَفيف | شَجَر |
| **Objects** bell | رَنين | جَرَس |
| grating, scraping noise | جَرْش | حَجَر الطاحون |
| clamour, bellowing of millstone | جَعْجَعة | رَحى |
| pen, door, bed, teeth | قَلَم، باب، سَرير صَرير | |

2.4.38 *Names of towns and the countries where they are located*

| Town | | | | Country | |
|---|---|---|---|---|---|
| Irbid | إرْبد | Amman | عَمّان | Jordan | الأردُن |
| Dubai | دُبَيّ | Abu Dhabi | أبو ظبي | U.A.E | الإمارات |
| | | Manama | المَنامة | Bahrain | البَحْرَين |
| Binzart | بنْزَرْت | Tunis | تونس | Tunisia | تونس |
| Gabes | قابس | Sousa | سوسة | | |
| Constantine | قَسَنْطينة | Algiers | الجَزائر | Algeria | الجَزائر |
| Oran | وَهْران | Tlemsen | تلِمْسان | | |

| | | | | | |
|---|---|---|---|---|---|
| Medina | المدينة | Riyadh, | الرياض | Saudi Ar. | السعودية |
| Jidda | جُدّة | Mecca | مَكّة | | |
| Omdurman | أم دُرمان | Khartoum | الخَرطوم | Sudan | السودان |
| Aleppo | حَلَب | Damascus | دمَشق | Syria | سورية |
| Latakia | اللاذقية | Homs | حمْص | | |
| Marka | ماركا | Mogadisho | مَقَديشو | Somalia | الصومال |
| Kerkouk | كَرْكوك | Baghdad | بَغْداد | Iraq | العِراق |
| Basra | البَصْرة | Mosul | المَوْصِل | | |
| Salala | صَلالة | Muscat | مَسْقَط | Oman | عُمان |
| Jaffa | يافا | Jerusalem | القُدْس | Palestine | فلَسطين |
| | | Doha | الدَوْحة | Qatar | قَطَر |
| Ahmadi | الأحمَدي | Kuwait | الكُوَيْت | Kuwait | الكُوَيْت |
| Beirut | بَيْروت | Tripoli | طرابُلس | Lebanon | لُبنان |
| Tripoli | طرابُلس الغَرب | Benghazi | بنْغازي | Libya | ليبيا |
| Alexandria | الإسكَندَريّة | Cairo | القاهرة | Egypt | مصْر |
| Fez | فاس | Rabat | الرباط | Morocco | المَغرب |
| Tangiers | طَنْجة | Casa Blanca | الدار البَيْضاء | | |
| Nouadhiou | نواذيبو | Nouakchott | نواكشوط | Mauritania | موريتانيا |
| Aden | عَدَن | Sanaa | صَنْعاء | Yemen | اليَمَن |

### 2.4.39 *Names of countries and their official names*

| English Equivalent | Official Name | Name |
|---|---|---|
| Jordan | المَمْلكة الأُرْدُنيّة الهاشميّة | الأُرْدُنّ |
| Emirates | الإمارات العربية المُتَّحَدة | الإمارات |
| Bahrain | مملكة البَحْرَيْن | البَحْرَيْن |

| | | |
|---|---|---|
| Algeria | الجُمهورية الشَعْبية الجَزائِرية الديُمقراطية | الجَزائِر |
| Tunisia | الجُمهورية التونِسية | تونِس |
| Djibouti | جيبوتي | جيبوتي |
| Saudi Arabia | المَمْلكة العَرَبية السُعودية | السُعودية |
| Sudan | جُمهورية السودان الديمقراطية | السودان |
| Syria | الجُمهورية العربية السورية | سورية |
| Somalia | جُمهورية الصومال الديمقراطية | الصومال |
| Iraq | الجُمهورية العِراقية | العِراق |
| Oman | سَلْطَنة عُمان | عُمان |
| Palestine | فلسْطين | فلسْطين |
| Qatar | دَوْلة قَطر | قَطر |
| Kuwait | دَوْلة الكُوَيْت | الكُوَيْت |
| Lebanon | الجُمهورية اللُبْنانية | لُبْنان |
| Libya | الجَماهيرية الليبية الاشتراكية العَظمى | ليبيا |
| Morocco | المَمْلكة المَغْرِبية | المَغْرِب |
| Egypt | جُمهورية مِصْر العربية | مِصْر |
| Mauritania | جُمهورية موريتانيا الإسلامية | موريتانيا |
| Yemen | الجُمْهورية العربية اليَمَنيّة | اليَمَن |
| Germany | ألْمانيا | ألْمانيا |
| USA | الولايات المُتَّحدة الأمريكية | أمريكا |
| Indonesia | جُمْهورية إندونيسيا | إندونيسيا |
| Australia | الكومنولث الأسترالي | أوستراليا |
| Iran | جُمْهورية إيران الإسلامية | إيران |
| Ireland | جُمْهورية إيرلاندا | إيرلاندا |
| Italy | إيطاليا | إيطاليا |
| Pakistan | الجُمْهورية الإسْلاميّة الباكستانية | باكِستان |

165

| United Kingdom | المَمْلَكة المُتَّحدة | بريطانيا |
| Belgium | مَملكة بَلجيكا | بَلجيكا |
| Turkey | الجُمْهورية التُركية | تُركيا |
| South Africa | جَنوب إفريقيا | جَنوب إفريقيا |
| Denmark | مَملكة الدانمارك | الدانمارك |
| Russia | الجُمْهورية الروسية | روسيا |
| Sweden | مَمْلَكة السُوَيْد | السويد |
| China | جُمهورية الصين الشَعبية الديمقراطية | الصين |
| France | الجُمْهورية الفَرَنسيّة | فَرَنْسا |
| Canada | كَنَدا | كَنَدا |
| Korea | جُمهورية كوريا الشعْبيّة الديمقراطية | كوريا |
| Kenya | جُمهورية كينيا | كينيا |
| Hungary | جُمهورية المَجَر | المَجَر |
| Norway | مَمْلَكة النرويج | النرويج |
| Austria | جُمْهورية النمْسا | النمْسا |
| Nigeria | جُمْهورية نَيْجيريا الاتِّحاديّة | نَيْجيريا |
| India | جُمْهورية الهِنْد | الهِنْد |
| Netherlands | مَمْلَكة هولاندا | هولاندا |
| Japan | اليابان | اليابان |
| Greece | الجُمْهورية اليونانية | اليونان |

## 2.4.40 *Names of ethnic and religious groups*

Ethnic and religious groups are listed with the singular of each one in parentheses.

| Spaniards | الأمريكيّون (أمريكيّ) Americans | الإسبان (إسبانيّ) |
| Russians | العَرَب (عَرَبيّ) Arabs | الروس (روسيّ) |

| French | الفَرَنسيون (فَرَنسيّ) | English | الإنْكليز (إنكليزيّ) |
| Chinese | الصينيّون (صينيّ) | Indians | الهُنود (هِنْديّ) |
| Germans | الألْمان (ألْمانيّ) | Japanese | اليابانيّون (يابانيّ) |
| Asians | الآسيَويّون (آسيَويّ) | Africans | الأفارقة (إفْريقيّ) |
| Armenians | الأرْمَن (أرْمَنيّ) | Europeans | الأوروبيّون (أوروبيّ) |
| Christians | النَصارى (نَصْرانيّ) | Muslims | المُسْلمون (مُسْلم) |
| Jews | اليَهود (يَهوديّ) | Christians | المَسيحيّون (مَسيحيّ) |
| Sunni | السنّة (سُنّيّ) | Buddhists | البوذيّون (بوذيّ) |
| Alawi | العَلَويّون (عَلَويّ) | Shiites | الشيعة (شيعيّ) |
| Druze | الدُروز (دُرْزيّ) | Maronites | المَوارنة (مارونيّ) |
| Assyrian | الآشوريون (آشوريّ) | Copts | الأقباط (قبْطيّ) |
| Orthodox | | | الأورثوذُكْس (أرثوذكسيّ) |

### 2.4.41 *Names of continents*

| Europe | أوروبا | Asia | آسيا |
| North America | أمريكا الشَماليّة | Africa | إفريقيا |
| Australia | أسْتراليا | South America | أمريكا الجَنوبيّة |
| | | Antarctica | القُطْب الجَنوبي |

### 2.4.42 *Names of oceans, seas, rivers, and lakes*

| Arctic | المُحيط المُتَجَمِّد الشَمالي | Atlantic Ocean | المُحيط الأطْلَسي |
| Indian Ocean | المُحيط الهِنْدي | Pacific Ocean | المُحيط الهادي |
| South China Sea | | | بَحْر الصين الجَنوبي |
| Mediterranean Sea | | | البَحْر الأبْيَض المُتَوسِّط |
| Red Sea | البحر الأحمَر | Aral Sea | بحر الأرال |
| Black Sea | البحر الأسوَد | Okhotsk Sea | بَحْر أخوتسك |

| Bering Sea | بحر بيرينغ | Yellow Sea | البَحْر الأصفَر |
| Tasman Sea | بَحْر تَسْمان | Baltic Sea | بحر البَلطيق |
| Java Sea | بَحْر جاوة | Timor Sea | بَحْر تيمور |
| North Sea | بحر الشَمال | Siberian Sea | بَحْر سيبيريا |
| Greenland Sea | بحر غرينلاند | Arabian Sea | البحر العَرَبي |
| Caspian Sea | بحر قَزوين | Philippine Sea | بحْر الفليبين |
| Coral Sea | بَحْر المُرْجان | Kara Sea | بَحْر كارا |
| Norwegian Sea | بحر النرويج | Dead Sea | البحر المَيِّت |
| Yellow | النهر الأصفر | Sea of Japan | بحْر اليابان |
| Ohio | نهر أوهايو | Amazon | نهر الأمازون |
| Zambezi | نهر زامبيزي | Danube | نهر الدانوب |
| Seine | نهر السين | Tigris | نهر دجْلة |
| Euphrates | نهر الفُرات | Ganges | نهر الغانج |
| Colorado | نهر كولورادو | Volga | نهر الڤولغا |
| Mississippi | نهر الميسيسيبي | Congo | نهر الكونغو |
| Nile | نَهْر النيل | Mekong | نهر الميكونغ |
| Thames | نهر التيمز | Yangtze | نهر يانغ تسي |
| Lake Erie | بُحَيْرة إيري | Ontario | بُحَيْرة أونتاريو |
| Lake Superior | بُحَيْرة سوبيريور | Tanganyika | بُحَيْرة تانغانيكا |
| Great Salt | البُحَيْرة المالحة العُظمى | Lake Victoria | بُحَيْرة فيكتوريا |
| Nicaragua | بُحَيْرة نيكاراغوا | Lake Michigan | بُحَيْرة ميشيغان |

### 2.4.43 *Other useful geographical terms*

| tropic | مَدار | the equator | خَطّ الاستواء |
| Tropic of Capricorn | مَدار الجَدي | Tropic of Cancer | مَدار السَرَطان |

| | | | | | |
|---|---|---|---|---|---|
| pole | قُطْب | continent | قارّة |

| latitude | خَطّ عَرْض | longitude | خَطّ طول |

### 2.4.44 *Abbreviations*

Arabic is not known for abbreviations. Only a small number of abbreviations exists. Each abbreviation is listed with the full word or term next to it.

| Professor | أُستاذ | أ |
|---|---|---|
| et cetera, and so forth | إلى آخِرِه | إلخ |
| after the birth of Christ, A.D. | بَعدَ الميلاد | ب م |
| telephone | تَلفون | ت |
| Egyptian pound | جنيه مصري | ج م |
| Arab Republic of Egypt | جُمهورية مصر العربية | ج م ع |
| Dr. | دُكْتور | د |
| Kuwaiti dinar | دينار كويتي | د ك |
| Saudi riyal | ريال سُعودي | ر س |
| commercial registration | سِجِلّ تجاري | س ت |
| industrial registration | سِجِلّ صناعي | س ص |
| centimetre | سنْتيمتر | سم |
| street | شارع | ش |
| post office box | صُنْدوق بَريد | ص ب |
| with the Prophet's name | صلّى الله عليه وسلَّم | صلعم (ص) |
| trade mark | علامة تِجارية | ع ت |
| gram | غرام | غ |
| before the birth of Christ, B.C. | قبل الميلاد | ق م |
| kilogram | كيلوغرام | كغ |
| kilometre | كيلومتر | كم |

| litre | لِتْر | ل |
|---|---|---|
| Syrian lira | لَيْرة سوريّة | ل س |
| Lebanese lira | لَيْرة لُبْنانية | ل ل |
| metre | مِتْر | م |
| Common Era, Western calendar, A.D. | ميلاديّ | م |
| milligram | ميليغرام | ملغ |
| millimetre | ميليمتر | ملم |
| telephone | هاتف | هـ |
| Hijri calendar | هِجْريّ | هـ |

### 2.4.45 *Interjections*

Interjections are utterances usually expressing emotion. In Arabic, many of them fall under اسم الفِـعْـل, i.e. nouns with a verbal meaning.

| ugh, pooh | أفٌّ R1 |
|---|---|
| here's the book! take it! | إلَيْكَ الكتاب R3 |
| leave me alone! | إلَيْكَ (عَنِّي) R3 |
| go ahead! | أمامَك R2, 3 |
| amen; answer my prayer | آمين (all register levels) |
| oh, ah (expression of pain) | آه/أوّاه R1, 2/R3 |
| go on! continue talking! | إيهِ R1 |
| enough! | بَسْ R1 |
| calling or driving away animals, especially cats | بسْ بسْ R1 |
| leave alone! let alone! (rare) | بَلْهَ R2 |
| come on! come to..! | حَيَّ (على) R3 |
| take it easy! slowly! take your time! | رُوَيْدَك R3 |

| | |
|---|---|
| what a difference! | شَتَّانَ R3 |
| hush! quiet! silence! | صَهْ R3 |
| deterring a small child from picking up s.t. dirty | كِخ R1 |
| don't move! stay put! | مَكانَك R2, 3 |
| take the book! | هاكَ الكتابَ R2, 3 |
| hush! quiet! silence! | هُس R1 |
| come on! let's go! make haste! quick! | هَيَّا/هَلُمَّ R3 |
| how far! how impossible! I wish it would..! | هَيْهات R3 |
| oh! expressions of admiration | وا/وَيْ R1 |
| alas, unfortunately | واحَسْرَتاه R3، يا لَلْحَسْرة R3، يا حَسْرتي R1 |
| woe unto you | وَيْلَك/وَيْلٌ لَك R3 |
| oh, my God! goodness gracious | يا إلهي/يا الله/يا ربّي R1, 2 |
| I wonder | يا تُرى R2, 3 |
| good heavens! good Lord! | يا سَلام R1 |
| oh, my misfortune! | يا لَلتَعْس R3 |
| what a calamity! | يا لَلشَقاء R3 |
| what a man! | يا لَهُ مِن رَجُل R3 |
| how many, much, often; how many times | يا ما R1 |

### 2.4.46 *Terms of address*

Both written and spoken terms of address are grouped together. They range from Register I through III. Normally, high register is appropriate for writing and for speaking in formal situations.

| | | |
|---|---|---|
| miss so-and-so | R2, 3 | آنِسة فُلانة |
| madam so-and-so | R1 | سِتْ فُلانة |
| madam so-and-so | R2, 3 | سَيِّدة فُلانة |

| | | |
|---|---|---|
| madam (to a stranger) | R1 | أُخْتي |
| madam (to a stranger) | R1 | خالتي |
| madam (acquaintance or stranger) | R1 | مَدام |
| madam (older or high rank, Morocco) | R2, 3 | لالاّ |
| sir (acquaintance or stranger) | R2, 3 | سَيِّد |
| sir (acquaintance or stranger) | R1, 2, 3 | أخي |
| sir (acquaintance or stranger) | R1, 2 | عَمّي |
| addressing a superior (Gulf) | R1, 2 | طال عُمْرَك |
| to a head of state (Syria, Egypt) | R3 | سيادة |
| to a king, majesty | R3 | جَلالة |
| to a head of state (Lebanon) | R3 | فَخامة |
| to a king, my lord | R3 | مولاي |
| to a high-ranking official (your grace) | R3 | سَعادة |
| to a prince, highness | R3 | سُمُوّ |
| to a high-ranking official (Excellency) | R3 | مَعالي |
| to a judge or a religious leader | R2, 3 | سَماحة |
| to religious Muslim leader | R3 | صاحب الفَضيلة |
| to a Christian patriarch | R3 | صاحب الغِبطة |

In letters, there exists a variety of terms used. Here are the most common in opening and concluding a letter:

| | | | |
|---|---|---|---|
| sweetheart | حَبيبي R1 | dear | عَزيزي R2 |
| honourable | المُحتَرَم R2 | dear | أخي R1, 2, 3 |
| cordially | المُشْتاق R2 | mister | السَيِّد R2 |
| sincerely | المُخْلِص R2 | lovingly | المُحِبّ R2 |

### 2.4.47 *Greetings and social niceties*

These are phrases which people exchange constantly. The local spelling is put in parentheses if it significantly differs from the Standard one. The appropriate response is listed after a slash.

| | |
|---|---|
| greetings, hello, hi | السَّلامُ عَلَيْكُم / وعليكم السلام |
| hello | أهْلاً (هَلا) / مَرْحَباً |
| hello | مَرْحَباً / أهْلاً (هَلا) |
| good morning | صَباح الخَيْر (صْبَحْ الخير – المغرب) / صباح النور |
| good morning | صَباح الفُلّ/الياسمين – مِصر / صباح النور |
| good afternoon/evening | مَساء الخَيْر / مساء الخيرات، مساء النور |
| good evening | مَسا الخير (سورية، مصر) / مْسَ الخير (المغرب) |
| goodbye | مَعَ السَّلامة / الله مَعَك |
| goodnight | تُصبِحون على خَيْر / وأنتُم من أهله |
| congratulations | مَبْروك / الله يبارك فيك |
| said after having a bath or haircut | نعيماً / أنعم الله عليك |
| 'happy festivity' and response | كُل عام وأنتُم بِخَيْر / وأنتم بِخَيْر |

### 2.4.48 *Measures*

Metric measures are generally used. Traditional measures are, however, still in use alongside them in some regions.

| | |
|---|---|
| step (about three feet) | خَطوة (خُطْوة) |
| area (900 square metres) | مَرْجَع |
| linear measure (3.55m) and area | قَصَبة |
| length, about 3 feet (Syria, Morocco, Tunisia) | ذِراع (ذراع) |
| weight (2.566 kilograms, Syria, Lebanon) | رَطْل (رْطَل .Mor) |

173

| | |
|---|---|
| length, span of the hand | شِبْر (شِبْر in Morocco and Tunisia) |
| cubic measure | صاع |
| length, width of a finger | إصْبَع (صْبَع Mor. and Tun.) |
| fathom (six feet) | قامة |
| measure for grains (about 15 kilograms) | مُدّ |
| for cereals (Tunisia, 20 litres or kilograms) | قَلْبة (galba) |
| weight, volume (200 centilitres, grams) | اوقيّة (وْقيّة Mor.) |

### 2.4.49 *Currencies*

Several currencies are used in Arab countries. Currencies with even the same name vary widely in value.

| | |
|---|---|
| lira (Syria) $1=50 liras; (Lebanon) $1=1700 liras | لَيْرة |
| dinar (Jordan, Iraq, Bahrain, Libya, Algeria, Tunisia, Kuwait) (exchange rates vary) | دينار |
| riyal (Yemen, Saudi Arabia, Oman, Qatar) | ريال |
| pound, guinea (Egypt, Sudan) | جُنَيْه (جنيه - gindh) |
| dirham (Morocco, the Emirates) | درْهَم |
| ougiya (Mauritania) | اوقيّة (giya) |

### 2.4.50 *Time*

In Modern Standard Arabic ordinal numbers are generally used to tell time, as on the radio and television, whereas in colloquial, casual speech cardinal numbers are used.

| Colloquial | Standard |
|---|---|
| الساعة خَمْسة | الساعةُ الخامسة |
| الساعة خمسة وعَشْرة | الساعةُ الخامسة وعَشْرُ دَقائق |

| | |
|---|---|
| الساعة خَمسة ورُبْع | الساعةُ الخامسة والرُبْع |
| الساعة خَمسة وثُلْث (وْتلت) | الساعةُ الخامسة والثُلْث |
| الساعة خَمسة ونْص | الساعةُ الخامسة والنصْف |
| الساعة خمسة إلا ربع | الساعةُ الخامسة إلا ربعاً |

It is interesting to note that in Morocco a different colloquial system is adopted. The hour is divided into 12 five-minute units each one called قسْم (plural قْسام) for MSA قِسْم، أقْسام. The equivalent of MSA إلا is قَلْ.

| | |
|---|---|
| لْواحدة وقْسِم (lwaḥda w-qsem) | الواحدة وخمس دقائق |
| لْواحدة وقسمَين | الواحدة وعَشْرُ دَقائق |
| لْواحدة ورُبْع | الواحدة والرُبْع |
| لْواحدة وثْلُت | الواحدة والثُلُث |
| لْواحدة وخَمس قْسام | الواحدة والنصْف إلا خمس دقائق |
| لْواحدة ونْص | الواحدة والنصْف |
| لْواحدة وسبْع قْسام | الواحدة والنصْف وخمس دقائق |
| لْواحدة قَلْ ربع | الواحدة إلا ربعاً |
| لْواحدة قَلْ قسمَين | الواحدة إلا عَشر دقائق |
| لْواحدة قَلْ تُلت | الواحدة إلا ثُلُث |
| لْواحدة قَلْ قْسِم | الواحدة إلا خمس دقائق |

### 2.4.51 *Numerals*

Decimals are separated by a comma (tail down). Thousands and millions are not separated from hundreds and tens. A billion (thousand million) is مِليار.

| | |
|---|---|
| خَمسة بالعَشَرة | ٠٫٥ |
| خَمسةٌ وعِشرونَ بالمِئة | ٠٫٢٥ |

| | |
|---|---|
| ثَمانية فاصِلة إثنان وخَمسون/ثمانية وإثنان وخمسون بالمئة | ٨,٥٢ |
| سَبْعٌ وثَلاثون | ٣٧ |
| خَمسُمئة وإثْنان وتسْعون | ٥٩٢ |
| أربعةُ آلاف ومِئَتان وستٌّ وثلاثون | ٤٢٣٦ |
| ستّةُ ملايينٍ وخَمسُمئةِ ألفٍ | ٦٥٠٠٠٠٠ |

# 3  Grammar

## 3.1  What is grammar?

Grammar signifies different things to different people based on their background, experience, and their conception of language in general. For some, it refers to the paradigms and prescriptive, normative rules of correctness found in pedagogical grammars; for others, it is the abstract descriptive rules of a language system found in the discipline of linguistics. It may also refer to the grammar of the psycholinguist, which involves rules of comprehension and production and concepts of processing meaning and form. In this book, grammar is construed as the rules of use, or how people use the language and the norms of usage prescribed in grammar books.

### 3.1.1  *Why are some items listed in the grammar part?*

Some items, such as transition words, are discussed in this part rather than under vocabulary because their use involves changes at a level higher than the word level. Apart from some conjunctions, connectives entail either changes in the phrase or sentence structures or at least require knowledge of the structures. The phrase بمـــا في ذلك 'including', for example, does not cause any change in the structure of the sentence, but it certainly requires knowledge of the structure of the sentence so that the added part after it matches the sentence grammatically.

## 3.2 An outline of Arabic grammar

The following is a graphic illustration of the main components of Arabic grammar as conceived by its native linguists. It may help in creating a conceptual image of the big picture and of how the major components relate to one another. The illustration is based on a simple definition of the essential ingredients of language, the word, representing the three traditional parts of speech in Arabic, namely, particles, nouns (including adjectives), and verbs.

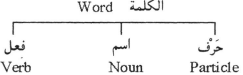

The first category, i.e., حـرف, includes particles and prepositions. In other words, this category comprises all that is not noun or verb. The second category is that of the noun اسم. This includes the traditional Western categories of noun and adjective. Unlike some English nouns and adjectives, Arabic nouns and adjectives are distinguished by function rather than form. Thus, a word like جَـــــيـل can either be a noun or an adjective out of its sentence context. Examine these two sentences where جَـمـيـل functions as noun and adjective.

| *The weather is beautiful.* (n.) | الطقسُ جميلٌ. |
| *I like beautiful weather.* (adj.) | أحب الطقسَ الجميلَ. |

The diagram shows the different types of nouns. Mainly, nouns are either derived or underived. Derived nouns are either fully declinable (known as triptotes in Western grammars of Arabic) and partially declinable (known as diptotes in Western grammars of Arabic). Underived nouns can be both declinable and indeclinable.

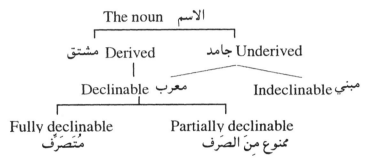

The majority of Arabic verbs are based on and derived from the triliteral root, that is, a basic form which is composed of three letters (also known as radicals). These may be all consonants (e.g., كتب *to write*), a combination of two consonants and a long vowel (e.g., قال *to say*), a consonant, a semi-vowel, and a vowel (e.g., لوى *to twist*), or some other combination. A verb may be uninflected (مبني) or inflected (مُعرَب). All categories below are for inflected verbs. See Indeclinable verbs below (3.3.14).

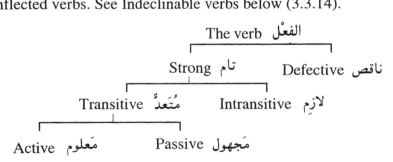

Verbs may be viewed according to their tense and form. Arabic distinguishes two tenses: perfect (الماضي) which is most basically used for completed action, and imperfect (المضارع) which is most basically used for action not yet complete. Future time is expressed by the imperfect plus one of two future markers, سَوفَ and ـسَ. The imperative is also considered a tense.

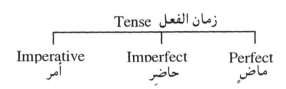

If the root of the verb contains no long vowels or semi-vowels, it is called sound (صـــحـــيـــح) and if contains a vowel or one or two semi-vowels, it is called weak (مُـــعـــتَل). The sound verb, as the chart shows, can be hamzated مَـهـمـوز (i.e., containing a *hamza* in either the initial, medial, or final positions: أخذ، سـأل، بدأ), doubled مُضاعَف (i.e. containing two identical consonants geminated with a *shadda*: جَرّ *to pull*), or sound سـالِم (i.e., composed of consonants only: دَفَع *to push*). If a weak verb contains a semi-vowel and a vowel separated by a consonant (e.g., وَقَى *to protect*), it is called لفيف مَفروق. If the vowel and semi-vowel are contiguous, it is called لفيف مقرون (e.g., طوى *to fold*).

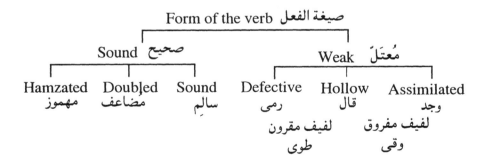

180

## 3.3    Grammatical categories

This book is concerned with both prescriptive and descriptive aspects of grammar. The former is gleaned from grammar books and the latter culled from observations of language in use, and include linguistic deviations made by native and non-native users of Arabic. Not all grammatical categories are included; only those that pose the greatest confusion to learners are discussed.

<u>Important Note</u>: The grammatical categories discussed below may also be found in other Arabic grammar books and textbooks (see Abboud et al. 1968; Alosh 2000; Dickens and Watson 1998; Schulz, Krahl, and Reuschel 2002). These works deal with these categories in varying degrees of brevity and length and provide adequate practice through well-designed exercises.

### 3.3.1 *The particles* الحروف

There are two kinds of حرف, (a) the letters which make up words, and (b) the particles. The letters fall into two ordering systems, one used in dictionaries, and another used for numbering.

A.    Letters of the alphabet are used for ordering dictionary entries. There are 28 of them with the *hamza* and *alif* counting as one.

ء ا ب ت ث ج ح خ د ذ ر ز س ش ص ض ط ظ ع غ ف ق ك ل م ن ه و ي

To the above, two variants may be added, *tā' marbūṭa* ة (تاء مربوطة) a t-variant whose position is restricted to word-final position, and *alif maqṣūra* ى which is also restricted to the final position.

B. The 28 letters used for numbering can be grouped into meaningless words for ease of memorization:

أَبْجَد هَوَّز حِطّي كَلَمُن سَعْفَص قُرِشَت ثَخَذ ضَظَغ

181

The particles are entities which acquire a complete meaning together with a following noun or a verb. For example, the preposition في may be translated into English as *in, on, at, during, among, by, concerning,* depending on the following word, e.g.

*I forgot my coat in my office.*  .نسيت معطفي في مكتبي

*I live on Ibn Khaldoun Street.*  .أسكن في شارع ابن خلدون

*I'll see you at nine o'clock.*  .سأراك في الساعة التاسعة

*He doesn't work in the summer.*  .لا يعمل في الصيف

*He was among a group of his peers.*  .كان في جماعة من أقرانه

*I consulted her concerning this issue.*  .استشرتها في هذه المسألة

The particles are of two types, those that affect the form of the nouns and verbs they govern (e.g. prepositions, particles which take subjunctive or jussive word) and those that do not (e.g. conjunctions). The total number of particles is 80. They are discussed further with nouns and verbs. A few examples of particles that affect the structure of the following word follow.

*She cut the apple with a knife.*  .قطعَت التُفّاحةَ بالسكّين  ب

حَتّى ركبَ الحافلةَ حتّى لا يتأخَّرَ.

*He took the bus in order not to be late.*

لا تَنس مَوعدَ الطبيب.  لا

*Don't forget the doctor's appointment.*

*I arrived here two days ago.*  .وصلتُ إلى هنا منذ يومين  مُنذُ

*Today is the first day of winter.*  .إنَّ اليومَ أوّلُ أيّام الشتاء  إنَّ

(for emphasis; does not translate)

*This is wonderful, Abu Lou'ai!*  .هذا رائعٌ يا أبا لُؤَيّ  يا

*I did not see the plane land.*  .لم أرَ الطائرةَ وهي تهْبطُ  لَمْ

دفع أجْرَ الطبيبَ من ماله الخاص.  مِنْ

*He paid the doctor out of his own pocket.*

Among the particles that do not affect the form of the following word are these two.

أوْ    سَأراكِ على زاوية الشارع أو في المَقهى المجاور.

*I'll meet you at the street corner or in the nearby café.*

وَ    تختمُ طعامَها بالحلوى وَالفواكه.

*She has dessert and fruits after meals.*

### 3.3.2 *The noun* الاسم: *form and type*

Remember that the noun category includes adjectives. An attributive adjective follows a noun and agrees with it in gender, number, definiteness, and case, e.g.

| | |
|---|---|
| *This is a tall man.* | هذا رجلٌ طويلٌ. |
| *I know two tall men.* | أعرف رجلين طويلين. |
| *Those are tall men.* | هؤلاء رجالٌ طوالٌ. |

However, non-rational (i.e., non-human) plurals usually take feminine singular adjectives regardless of the gender of the noun, e.g.

| | |
|---|---|
| *new books* (masculine) | كُتبٌ جديدة. |
| *new cars* (feminine) | سياراتٌ جديدة |

a. <u>Form</u>: A noun may be مُجَرَّد 'basic' or مَـزيد 'increased'. In the latter case, one or more letters are added to it.

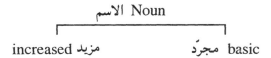

The basic noun form may be triliteral (the vast majority), that is, consisting of three basic root letters, such as رَجُل; quadriliteral (four basic root letters), such as دِرْهَم 'currency unit'; or quinquiliteral (five basic root letters), such as سَفَرْجَل 'quince'.

The increased noun may be increased by one letter (*alif* in حصان 'horse' from the root حصن), two letters (م+ا in مِصْباح 'lamp' from صبح), three letters (ا+ت+ا in اخْتِبار 'test' from خبر), or four letters (ا+س+ت+ا in اسْتِفهام 'query' فهم).

b. Type: A noun is either جـامـد 'static, underived' or مُـشـتَـقّ 'derived'. The static noun includes nouns which are not derived from verbs, such as بَيْت، دِرهَم, as well as verbal nouns derived from basic triliteral verbs, such as خَوْف 'fear'.

### 3.3.3 *Derived nouns* (المشتق)

Derived nouns are formed from verbs (e.g. from علم you get *educated* مُتَعَلِّم, *scholar* عالِم, *inquiry* استعلام). There are ten derived types of noun for each verb form I-X. The following table lists the ten types for each verb form. The list below the table provides more details. Arabic grammars use patterns to represent the various derivations, where the ف stands for the first letter of the root, ع stands for the second, and ل represents the last letter. All other letters in the pattern are added. For instance, مُـفَـعِّل is the pattern for the active participle of verb form II. Here the initial م is a prefix and the letter ع is doubled. It rhymes with active participles on the same pattern such as مُحَـرِّك (engine), مُـدَرِّس (teacher), and مُكَيِّف (air conditioner).

1. Verbal nouns (المصدَر) derived from increased verbs. The Roman numerals on the right refer to pattern numbers I-X. More on this under *Derivation* (3.4) below.

| | | |
|---|---|---|
| *I like the beauty of the countryside.* | يعجبني جمال الريف. | I |
| | هَمُّه الأول تَجميلُ المدينة. | II |
| *His major concern is beautifying the city.* | | |

كانت زراعةُ البَقولِ تَجرِبةً ناجحة.

*Planting legumes was a successful experiment.*

أعجبَني التَجْوالُ في شوارعِ باريس.

*I liked walking around the streets of Paris.*

| Verbal noun | Active Participle | Passive Participle | Adjective | Intensive forms |
|---|---|---|---|---|
| فِعل، فعالة،... | فاعِل | مَفعول | فَعيل/فَعلان | فَعّال/فَعّالة |
| Comparative/ Superlative | Noun of place | Noun of time | Noun of instrument | m- prefix verbal noun |
| أفعَل | مَفعَل | مَفعِل | مِفعَل/فَعّال.. | مَفعَل |

III   كان شراؤه الشركة مُجازَفةً ماليةً كبيرة.

*His purchase of the company was a great financial risk.*

لا تدخُلْ في جِدالٍ لا طائلَ منه.

*Do not engage in a useless argument.*

IV   إضرابُ العُمّالِ أثّر في الاقتصادِ سَلبياً.

*The workers' strike affected the economy negatively.*

V   ننتظر تَغَيُّرَ سياسةِ الحُكومة.

*We are waiting for government policies to change.*

VI   أعلن استقالتَه تجنُّباً للفَضيحة.

*He announced his resignation to avoid scandal.*

VII   أحدث انشِطارُ الذَرَّةِ ثورةً في العلوم.

*Atomic fission caused a revolution in science.*

VIII   يخشى المُرَبّون انتِشارَ المُخَدِّراتِ في المدارس.

*Educators dread the spread of drugs in schools.*

IX   أدّت الزيادة في الاستيرادِ إلى اختلالِ الميزانِ التجاري.

*The increase in imports has led to an unfavourable trade balance.*

X نالَ المُحاضرُ استحسانَ الجُمهور.

*The lecturer won the appreciation of the audience.*

2. Active participle اسم الفاعل (كاتب، مُنَسِّق، مُتَعاون، مُصلح، مُسْتَشرق)

3. Passive participle اسم المفعول (مكتوب، مُخَرَّب، مُنْطَلَق، مُسْتَشْفىً)

4. Adjective الصفة المشبهة (كسلان, جميل)

5. Intensive form أمثلة المُبالغة (كذّاب) (علّامة)

6. Comparative/superlative of adjective اسم التفضيل (أطوَل)

7. Noun of place اسم المكان (مكتَب)

8. Noun of time اسم الزمان (مَوعد)

9. Noun of instrument اسم الآلة (مفتاح)

10. Verbal noun with *m-* prefix المصدر الميمي (مَشهَد)

### 3.3.4 *Noun inflection*

Most nouns show changes on their ends by diacritics or letters which reflect their case. These include the three short and long vowels. A declinable noun (مُتَصَرِّف), known as a triptote in Western grammars, shows all inflections (رفع، نصب، جـــر), but a partially declinable noun (ممنوع من الصـرف 'diptote') shows *damma* ـُ for the nominative and *fatha* ـَ for both the accusative and genitive. Although indefinite, a diptote does not show تَنوين. However, when the definite article is prefixed to it or it is added to another noun, forming an *idāfa* phrase (examples 7 and 8 below), it is no longer partially declinable. Static nouns are either declinable or indeclinable, but all derived nouns are declinable. Examples of declinable nouns in all cases follow.

١. هذا ولدٌ في الحديقة.

٢. أرى ولداً في الحديقة.

٣. أنظرُ إلى ولدٍ في الحديقة.

<u>Partially declinable nouns</u> (ممنوع من الصـرف). Partially declinable nouns include names ending with ـان, non-Arabic names,

compound names, feminine names, plurals patterned after مَفـاعِل and مَفاعيل, and nouns with the patterns أفعَل and فَعلان.

بُشْرى، صَحراء، مَساجِد، مَصابيح، رُباع، جَوْعان، أسوَد، زُحَل،

إبراهيم، مَريَم، أسامة، هِند، بَعْلَبَك، يَزيد، أحمَد، عَدنان

٤- دِمشقُ أقدم مدينة مأهولةَ باستمرار في العالم.

٥- زرتُ دمشقَ في الصيف الفائت.

٦- مررتُ بدمشقَ في طريقي إلى بيروتَ.

Note that partially declinable plurals (e.g., مـدارس) become fully declinable when definite.

٧- درس في مَدارسَ حُكوميةٍ. (ممنوع من الصرف)

٨- درس في المَدارِسِ الحُكوميةِ. /درس في مدارسٍ الحكومةِ. (مُنصرِف)

Note also that indeclinable nouns such as ألمانيـا and فـرنسـا do not show any changes according to case.

### 3.3.5 *Gender of nouns*

There are two genders in Arabic, masculine and feminine. The masculine is not marked. It is of two types: natural (حقـيقي), e.g. رَجُل، أسَد، وَلَد and non-natural (معنوي), e.g. باب، قَمَر.

The three feminine markers are suffixes: ة, ى, and ـاء e.g. لُعبة, سَلْمى, حَـسْناء. However, there are some masculine nouns which have a feminine marker, e.g. زَكَرِيّا، مُعاوِية، مَشفى. Similarly, some feminine nouns look masculine such as دار and سُـعـاد because they do not display a feminine marker (see the list below). Here are some guidelines to help the reader identify feminine nouns.

a. Nouns that are intrinsically feminine: أُخْت, أُم.

b. Personal names of females: مَريَم, مَيْسون.

c. Names of towns, tribes, and the vast majority of countries: الشـام, قُـرَيْش, بَغـداد, تونس. The exception among names of countries are those which begin with the definite article (e.g. العِـراق، الأردُنّ، اليَـمَن، السـودان، المغـرب). They are normally masculine. There is one exception which is masculine and does not have the article: لُبنان. A few non-Arab country names with الـ are feminine (e.g., النرويج، الهند).

d. Names of organs that come in pairs: يَد، عَيْن.

• Unmarked nouns which are feminine.

| | | | |
|---|---|---|---|
| leg | ساق | mill | طاحون |
| thigh | فَخذ | well | بِئْر |
| earth, ground | أرْض | pelvis | وِرْك |
| hare, rabbit | أرْنَب | finger, toe | إصْبَع |
| fire | نار | hell | جَحيم |
| bucket | دلْو | war | حَرْب |
| hand mill | رَحىً | house | دار |
| hyena | ضَبْع | sun | شَمْس |
| butt, stub | عَقب | stick | عَصا |
| celestial body | فَلَك | axe, hatchet | فأس |
| wind | ريح | glass, goblet | كأس |
| servant | خادم[1] | shoe | نَعْل |
| pregnant | حامل | spirit, self | نَفْس |

• Nouns which may be masculine and feminine.

| | | | |
|---|---|---|---|
| thumb | إبْهام | armpit | إبْط |
| generous, freehanded | مِعْطاء | belly | بَطْن |
| condition, circumstance | حال | chameleon | حِرْباء |
| wine | خَمْر | shop, store | حانوت |

---

[1] This is also used as a masculine noun as in خادم الحرَمَين (i.e., the King of Saudi Arabia).

188

| | | | |
|---|---|---|---|
| gold | ذَهَب | armour, shield | دِرْع |
| knife | سكّين | trousers, pants | سروال |
| soul, spirit, psyche | نَفْس | ladder, scale | سُلَّم |
| finger | إصبَع | market | سوق |
| road, way | طَريق | buttocks, posterior | عَجُز |
| upper arm | عَضُد | bride, groom | عَروس |
| single, bachelor | عَزَب | old man or woman | عَجوز |
| scorpion | عَقْرَب | eagle | عُقاب |
| spider | عَنْكَبوت | neck | عُنُق |
| horse, mare | فَرَس | paradise | فِرْدَوْس |
| leopard | فَهْد | ship, vessel | فُلْك |
| back, reverse | قَفا | cooking pot | قِدْر |
| cattle | بَقَر | pigeons | حَمام |
| convoy, riders | رَكْب | clouds | سَحاب |
| human being | بَشَر | article of clothing | إزار |
| shop, store | دُكّان | path | صراط |
| injured person | جَريح | murdered person | قَتيل |
| lactiferous, milk cow | حَلوب | gluttonous | أكول |

• Nouns for people and animals based on gender (see 3.3.5).

| | Feminine | | Masculine |
|---|---|---|---|
| woman | امرَأة | man | رَجُل |
| mother | أُم | father | أب |
| wife | زَوْجة | husband | بَعْل |
| daughter-in-law | كَنّة | son-in-law | صِهْر |
| girl | بِنْت | boy | وَلَد |

| | | | |
|---|---|---|---|
| *hen* | دَجاجة | *cock, rooster* | ديك |
| *she-camel* | ناقة | *camel* | جمل |
| *cow* | بَقَرة | *bull, ox* | ثَوْر |
| *lioness* | لَبْوة، لَبُؤة | *lion* | أَسَد |
| *mare* | فَرَس | *horse* | حِصان |
| *female hyena* | جَعار | *hyena* | ضَبُع |

Nouns and adjectives used only with reference to females are without ة if they signify an action or a state, e.g.,

| | | | |
|---|---|---|---|
| suckling mother | مُرضِع | barren, childless | عاقِر |
| spinster, unmarried | عانِس | having large breasts | ناهِد |
| menstruating | حائِض | pregnant | حامِل |
| divorced | طالِق | with no head cover | حاسِر |

But all the above nouns would take ة when the state or action is described as beginning or in progress (e.g., هي حائضة).

### 3.3.6 *Uses of the feminine marker* tā' marbūṭa ة

1. Forming feminine nouns by suffixing a *tā' marbūṭa* to a masculine noun or adjective, e.g. رحيم: رحيمة.
2. Indicating the singular of a collective noun, e.g. تُفّاح: تُفّاحة. Here, the ة has a double function; it makes the noun singular and feminine.

### 3.3.7 *Cases of the noun*

There are three cases: رَفْع، نَصْب، جَرّ. The nominative (رفع) is marked by *ḍamma*, ا, and و for the dual and sound plural, respectively (المُعلِّمُ، مُعلِّمٌ، مُعلِّمانِ، مُعلِّمونَ). The accusative (منصوب) is marked by *fatḥa*, ي for both the dual and sound plural (المُعلِّمَ، مُعلِّماً، مُعلِّمَيْنِ، مُعلِّمين). The genitive (جَرّ) is marked with *kasra*, double *kasra*, ي

for both the dual and sound plural (المُعلَم، مُعلَمٍ، مُعلَمَيْن، مُعلَمين).

<u>Note on the use of 'agent' and 'subject'</u>: In Arabic grammatical terminology, the subject of a nominal sentence is called مُبتَدأ and the subject of a verbal sentence فاعل. However, the فاعل in some sentences with certain verbs does not correspond to 'agent' in Western terms because it does not indicate an action, e.g.

*Ahmed resembles his father.*     يُشبه أحمدُ أباه.

In this book, 'agent' will be used to express the notion of فـــاعل, and 'subject' to express that of مـــبــتــدأ. The term 'agent' will, therefore, represent the notion of فـــاعـل of a verbal (rather than nominal) active (rather than passive) sentence.

### 3.3.7.1 A noun is nominative (مَرفوع) if it is:

1.  The agent فـــاعـل of a verbal sentence. It may be a noun (الرجل), a noun phrase (هذا الرجل), an independent pronoun (هو), an attached pronoun (ه), or a covert pronoun.

    *The president resigned.*     استقالَ الرئيسُ.

    وقّع البَلَدان اتِّفاقيةً تَعاون.

    *The two countries signed a cooperation agreement.*

    *The engineers have built a dam.*     بنى المهندسون سداً.

2.  The subject or predicate of a sentence (مُبتَدأ/خَبَر):

    *The weather is fine today.*     الطقسُ صَحْوٌ اليومَ.

    الكتابان غيرُ مَوجودِين بالمكتبة.

    *The two books are not in the library.*

    *The truck drivers are educated.*     سائقو الشاحنات متعلِّمون.[2]

    *Is there anybody at home?*     هل أحَدٌ في البيتِ؟

---

[2] Note that the ن in سائقون is deleted to mark the word as the first term of the *iḍāfa* structure.

3. The subject in a passive sentence (deputy agent نائب فاعل):

يُقبَلُ الطلابُ حَسَبَ علاماتِهم.

*Students are admitted according to their scores.*

4. The subject of a sentence introduced by a member of the كان set (أخَوات كان) (see Auxiliaries 3.4.1).

| | |
|---|---|
| *The weather has turned cold.* | صار الطقسُ بارداً. |
| *The two twins are not identical.* | ليس التوأمانِ مُتَماثلَين. |
| *The managers were in a meeting.* | كان المديرونَ مُجتَمعينَ. |

5. The predicate of a sentence introduced by a member of the إنَّ set (أخَوات إن) (see Auxiliaries 3.4.1).

| | |
|---|---|
| *The world is small.* | إنَّ العالَمَ صغيرٌ. |
| *The two men look as if they were brothers.* | كأنَّ الرجُلَين أخَوانِ. |
| *Perhaps the men are asleep.* | لعلَّ الرجالَ نائمونَ. |

3.3.7.2 A noun is accusative (منصوب) if it is:

3.3.7.2.1 The subject of a sentence introduced by a member of the إنَّ set (أخَوات إن):

لَيْتَ المدرسةَ أقربُ إلى دارِنا.

*I wish the school were closer to our house.*

3.3.7.2.2 The predicate of a sentence introduced by a member of the كان set (أخَوات كان):

| | |
|---|---|
| *The problem is still existing.* | لا تزالُ المُشكلةُ قائمةً. |

3.3.7.2.3 The object of a verb. There are several types of objects:

a. The direct object (مفعول به):

| | |
|---|---|
| *Ahmed has bought a car.* | اشترى أحمدُ سيّارةً. |

b. The indirect object (مفعول به ثان). There are two types of verbs which can have two objects. The first type includes

many verbs such as: ،كَسـا، أعطى، وَهَب، سـقى، زوّد، أطعم، أسْكن
.أنْسى حبّب، ملأ، سأل، جزى، سمّى، زوّج، كال، لقّن

| | |
|---|---|
| *He named his son Khalid.* | سمّى ابنَه خالداً. |
| *He gave the student a pen.* | أعطى الطالبةَ قلماً. |
| *The poet recited a poem to the audience.* | أنشد الشاعرُ الجُمهورَ قصيدةً. |
| *God gave the couple a baby.* | رزق اللهُ الزوجينِ طفلاً. |
| *Hala watered the plants.* | سَقَتْ هالةُ النباتاتِ ماءً. |
| *Thank you! (lit. May God reward you.)* | جَزاكَ اللهُ خَيراً. |
| *She brought him double retaliation* | كالت له الصاعَ صاعَين. |
| *I asked the teacher a question.* | سألتُ الأستاذَ سؤالاً. |
| *God gave us intellect.* | وَهَبنا اللهُ عقلاً. |

- Note: The suffix نا in وَهَبنا is the indirect object.

The other type includes the so-called 'verbs of the heart'
(أفعال القلوب), thus named because they have to do with certainty, doubt, and the like. They normally introduce a nominal sentence and change its subject and predicate into objects. The first sentence below is originally made up of two nominative nouns (subject and predicate) المسألةُ سهلة. Here are some of these verbs: ظنّ، خال، حَسِبَ، جـعل، عـدّ، رأى، علم، وجـد، ألفى،
.درى،تعلم، صيّر، ترك، غادر، اتّخذ

| | |
|---|---|
| *I found it a simple matter.* | وجدتُ المسألةَ سهلةً. |
| *We found the relations severed.* | ألفينا العلاقاتِ مَقطوعةً. |
| *He left the door open.* | ترك البابَ مفتوحاً. |
| *I thought your friend was loyal.* | حَسِبتُ صاحبَكَ وفيّاً. |

- Note that the agent and direct object can be pronouns attached to the same verb ني (personal pronouns 3.3.10).

| | |
|---|---|
| *I realized I was early.* | رأيتُني مُبكّراً. |

From a Western grammar perspective, the three object types below look like adverbs.

    c. The absolute object (المفعول المُطلَق) is used for emphasis.

*I studied the report closely.*        درستُ التَقريرَ <u>دراسةً دقيقةً</u>.

    d. The object of purpose (المفـعـول لأجله) serves the general meaning 'for the purpose of'.

*He was jailed in order to enforce the law.*    سُجن <u>تطبيقاً</u> للقانون.

قدّمنا له جائزةً <u>تقديراً</u> لعمله.

*We gave him an award in recognition of his work.*

زَيّنا الدارَ <u>احتِفالاً</u> بالعيد.

*We decorated the house in celebration of the Eid.*

    e. The object of accompaniment (المفعول معه): This requires the use of the particle وَ 'with, along, at, during' before it. This is an old usage and is rarely encountered in Modern Standard Arabic.

*I walked along the river.*        مَشيتُ <u>والنَهرَ</u>.

*We arrived in the city during the day.*    وصلنا المدينةَ <u>والنهارَ</u>.

3.3.7.2.4 **Adverb of time** ظـرف زمــان. This refers to the time when the action occurred, and is considered an object (مفعول فيه) in Arabic grammar. Adverbs of time and place are considered 'vessels' (i.e. ظرف pl. ظروف) *within* which an action takes place, hence the term مفعول فيه. Thus, if the adverb does not allow في (e.g. صباحاً= في الصبـاح), then it is regarded as a regular object, not an adverb.

*I lived for one year in Cambridge.*    سكنتُ <u>سنةً</u> في كيمبردج.

*We set out in the morning.*    انطلقنا منَ الدارِ <u>صباحاً</u>.

*Her flight arrived in the evening.*    وصلتْ طائرتُها <u>مساءً</u>.

Adverbs are variable (مُعرَبة) and invariable (مَبنيّة). Variable adverbs are either specific (محدودة) or non-specific (مُبهَمة). The

هُنَيْهة، لَحْظة، دَقيقة، ساعة، يوم أسبوع، شَهْر، فَصْل سنة، عام، former include قَرْن، صَباح، مَساء، ظُهْر، عَصْر، لَيْل، أربع سنوات، آذار .Non-specific adverbs include: حين، عندَ، وقت، دَهْر، زَمـان، أبَداً .Both types are accusative (منصوب). Note that some adverbs stand by themselves as single-word adverbs (e.g. الآنَ، أمس، قَطّ) and others as an adverbial phrase head (e.g. منذُ، نَحـوَ). The latter adverbial items form a genitive structure with the following noun as in these examples:

A. Demonstratives:

*I arrived in the afternoon.* وَصَلتُ بعدَ الظهرِ.

B. Verbal nouns:

*I set out at sunrise.* سافَرتُ طُلوعَ الشمسِ.

C. Partitives:

*I walked all day.* سِرتُ كُلَّ النَهارِ.

D. Numbers:

*I read for three hours.* قرأتُ ثلاثَ ساعاتٍ.

Invariable forms are regarded as adverbs of time in Arabic grammar although most of them look to the reader like subordinating conjunctions. The following examples are classified according to adverbial heads (إذا through بينمـا) and single-word adverbs (الآنَ to the end).

Conditional

إذا    *If you work, you make money.*    إذا عملتَ تكسبُ.

Past time

إذْ    *Do you remember school days?* أتذكُرُ إذْ كُنّا في المدرسة؟

(*lit. when we were at school*)

Future time

إذْ    ستُسَرُّ إذْ ترى مَن في الدارِ.

*You'll be pleased to know who's in the house.*

Past and present time

لَمّا    صَفَّقَ الحاضرن لَّا دخل الرئيسُ.

*The audience applauded when the President entered.*

Duration in the past

رَيْثَما    انتَظرتُها رِيثَما أنهت الرسالة.

*I waited for her till she finished the letter.*

A point in the past (with v.)

مُنْذُ    ما رأيتُه مَنذُ صار طبيباً.

*I haven't seen him since he became a doctor.*

A point in the past (with n.)

مُنْذُ    ما رأيتُه مُنذُ شهرِ نيسان..    *I haven't seen him since April.*

Past occurrence

بَيْنَما    دخلتُ الدارَ بينما كان الأطفالُ نياماً.

*I walked in while the children were asleep.*

Present time

الآنَ    سَوسَنُ نائمةٌ الآنَ.    *Sawsan is sleeping now.*

Past time (with a negative)

قَطُّ    لَم أقابِلْهُ قَطُّ.    *I have never met him.*

Past and present time (question)

مَتى    مَتى وصَلتِ؟    *When did she arrive?*

Reference to the day before today

أمْسِ    زُرتُها أمْسِ.    *I paid her a visit yesterday.*

Past/present

كَيْفَ    كَيفَ أنتَ؟/كيف حالُ خالد؟/كيف أتى خالدُ؟

*How are you?/How's Khaled?/How did Khaled come?*

3.3.7.2.5 Adverb of place ظرف مكان. This refers to the place where an action occurs. It is also considered an object. Adverbs of place are divided into variable and invariable

adverbs. Variable adverbs are subdivided into specific such as بيت، مدينة، بلد، جبل، بحر، (محدودة), and non-specific adverbs such as أمام، وراء، يمين، يسار، فوق، تحت، عند، (مبهمة)
غرب، شرق، جهة، متر، ميل، مكان، إزاء، حذاء، خلال، قُرب، نحو، حَول، بدل.

| | |
|---|---|
| سافرنا إلى حَلَبَ بَرّاً. | *We travelled to Aleppo by land.* |
| انعطِفْ يميناً عند شارعِ الفَرَزدَق. | *Turn right at Farazdaq Street.* |
| قطعتُ ميلَينِ في ساعة. | *I walked two miles in one hour.* |
| وقفتُ تحتَ المَظَلَّة. | *I stood under the awning.* |

| | | |
|---|---|---|
| ميل | سرتُ ميلاً. | *I walked for a mile.* |
| أرض | رَماهُ أرْضاً. | *He tossed it on the floor.* |
| جانب | طَرَحَهُ جانباً. | *He set it aside.* |
| قُرْبَ | سكنَتْ قُربَ الجامعة. | *She lived near the university.* |
| مَكان | عملتُ مَكانَ زَميلي. | *I substituted for my colleague.* |

| | |
|---|---|
| نَحْوَ | تَوَجَّهَ الرُّكّابُ نَحوَ الطائرة. |

*The passengers headed toward the aircraft.*

| | |
|---|---|
| بَدَلَ | زارَتْنا سَلمى بَدَلَ ذهابها إلى السوق. |

*Salma came to see us instead of going shopping.*

| | |
|---|---|
| حَوْلَ | طافَ الحُجّاجُ حَولَ الكَعبة. |

*The pilgrims walked around the Kaʿba.*

| | |
|---|---|
| خِلالَ | جُلنا خلالَ أروقة المُتحَف. |

*We walked through the halls of the museum.*

- Another type of ظرف مكان is the derived noun اسم مكان. It can only be ظرف مكان if it accompanies the verb from which it is derived. However, it is a regular noun rather than a verbal noun.

| | |
|---|---|
| ذهبَ مَذهَبَ أستاذه. | *He followed his teacher's view.* |
| عَرَضَ رأيَهُ مَعرِضَ الخَبير. | |

*He presented his opinion like an expert.*

- Invariable adverbs of place: These do not change in form.

*This is Damascus. (i.e. broadcasting from)* هُنا دمَشق.

*Go back to where you came from.* ارجعي من حَيْثُ أتَيْت.

ثَمَّةَ فارقٌ بين الأولاد والبَنات.

*There is a difference between boys and girls.*

*From there we moved to Rabat.* ومن ثَمَّ انتقلنا إلى الرباط.

أتعرفينَ أَينَ دُفِنَ صلاحُ الدين؟

*Do you know where Saladin was buried?*

*Where do you get that?* أنّى (من أينَ) لكَ هذا؟[3]

*Wherever he goes, he finds work.* أنّى يذهب يجد عملاً.

*When did you arrive?* أنّى (متى) وصلت؟

*How can one go to sleep!* أنّى (كيف) لعين أَنْ تنام!

- Some readers might view some adverbs of time and place as prepositions due either to the use of prepositions in their translation or to how the following noun is affected by them. The noun in the third sentence below, for example, might look like the object of عند, given its genitive case. In Arabic grammar, however, these adverbs function as مـضـاف (first term of the *iḍāfa*) and the following noun as مضاف إليه, or the second term.

*one time, once; one day* ذاتَ مَرَّةٍ، ذاتَ يَومٍ

*to the right* ذاتَ اليَمين

*at sunset* عندَ المَغرب

*at the barber's* عندَ الحَلاّق

*I have a car.* عندي سَيّارةٌ.

*at/upon their arrival (same as عند, but RIII)* لَدى قُدومِهِم

*Your letter is at the director's desk.* كتابُكَ لَدى المُدير.

*He has two brothers.* لَدَيْه أخَوان.

---

[3] This adverb is rare in Modern Standard Arabic and sounds archaic.

وصلنا القاهرةَ مَعَ عيد الفطْر.

*We arrived in Cairo at the feast following Ramadan.*

*We are with this group.*     نحن مَعَ هذه الجَماعة.

*between five and six o'clock*    بَيْنَ الساعة الخامسة والسادسة

*between two cities*     بَيْنَ مَدينتين

*before noon*     قَبْلَ الظُهْر

*before our street*     قَبْلَ شارعنا

*after the vacation*     بَعْدَ الإجازَة

*after (you pass) the park*     بَعْدَ الحَديقة

3.3.7.2.6 The subject of لا, which negates the whole class of a noun in the sentence, is an accusative noun:

*We have no hope.*     لا أَمَلَ لنا.

*He is fine; there is nothing wrong with him.*     لا بأسَ به.

*There is no God but Allah.*     لا إلهَ إلاّ الله.

*You must have patience.*     لا بُدَّ لكَ منَ الصبْر.

*There is no use antagonizing them.*     لا فائدةَ من مُعاداتهم.

*It's unavoidable.*     لا مَناصَ منه.

*There's no doubt about that.*     لا شَكَّ في ذلك.

*There is no way out of this.*     لا مَفَرَّ من ذلك.

3.3.7.2.7 Adverb of manner, or circumstantial adverb الحـال. This describes the state of the agent when the action is being performed. Generally, it has the form of the active participle (اسم فـاعل), but it can also be a substantive noun اسم, passive participle اسم مـفعـول, adjective صفـة مشبهـة, and verbal noun مصدر as well.

*She was sitting in the first row.*     كانت جالسةً في الصفّ الأوّل.

*He walked fast toward his daughter.*     مشى مُسرعاً نحو ابنته.

199

| | |
|---|---|
| *I responded to his letter in writing.* | رددتُ على رسالته كتابةً. |
| *The army returned defeated.* | رجع الجَيشُ مَهزوماً. |
| *They walked hand in hand.* | سارتا يَداً بِيَد. |
| *They walked in one by one.* | دخلوا فَرْداً فَرْداً. |
| *Man was created weak.* | خُلِقَ الإنسانُ ضَعيفاً. |

3.3.7.2.8 Specification التمييز. This is an indefinite noun which is used to explain or specify another noun or phrase.

| | |
|---|---|
| *I bought eleven books.* | اشتريتُ أحَدَ عَشَرَ كتاباً. |
| *How many brothers do you have?* | كم أخاً عندك؟ |
| *I have as much money as you have.* | عندي مثلُ ما عندكَ مالاً. |
| *The garden was full of flowers.* | امتلأت الحديقةُ زُهوراً. |
| *He is taller than his brother.* | هو أطولُ من أخيه قامةً. |
| *I have a number of friends.* | لديَّ كَذا وكذا صديقاً. |

3.3.7.2.9 Exception الاسـتـثـنـاء. The excepted noun is indicated by the use of إلا and other members of the إلا set (عدا، سوى). Note that in affirmative sentences, the noun after إلا must be in the accusative (منصـوب). In negative sentences, the noun in question takes the case consistent with its general syntactic state in the sentence.

| | |
|---|---|
| *Everyone has left except one.* | غادر الجميعُ إلا واحداً منهم. |
| *All came except Samer.* | حضر الجميعُ ما عدا سامراً. |
| *They swam except the youngest one.* | سبحَوا سوى أصغرِهم. |
| *No one came except Khalid.* | ما حضر أحدٌ إلا خالدُ. |
| *I saw no one except Khalid.* | ما رأيتُ أحداً إلا خالداً. |
| *I wrote to no one except Khalid.* | ما كتبتُ إلى أحدٍ إلا خالدٍ. |

For additional information about exception, see 3.22.

3.3.7.3 The genitive مَجْرور: A noun is genitive (مَجْرور) if it is:

1. The object of a preposition (see *Prepositions*, section 3.6). This case is marked by a *kasra* and ـِ for dual and sound plurals. Adjectives modifying genitive nouns are also genitive.

   *at the American University*      في الجامِعةِ الأَمِريكيّةِ

   *at an American university*      في جامِعةٍ أَمِريكيّةٍ

   *at two universities*      في جامِعتَيْنِ

   *to university students*      إلى الجامِعيّينَ

2. The modifying element of an *iḍāfa* structure (مُضاف إليه).

   *president of the American University*   رَئيسُ الجامِعةِ الأَمِريكيّةِ

   *president of an American university*    رَئيسُ جامِعةٍ أَمِريكيّةٍ

   *(the two) presidents of the two universities*   رَئيسا الجامِعتَيْنِ

   *the first of the  university students*   أَوَّلُ الجامِعيّينَ

For additional information on this topic, see section 3.23.


3.3.8    *Number* المُفرَد والمُثنّى والجَمْع

The Arabic language distinguishes three numbers: singular (one), dual (two), and plural (three or more). There is also a class of nouns called collective nouns. A collective singular noun refers to groups of certain animals, plants, and objects such as تُفّـاح *apples,* قَمح *wheat,* شَجَر *trees,* جَمَر *embers,* and حَجَر *stones.* Suffixing a ة indicates a single example of that noun (e.g., تفاحة 'an apple,' جمرة 'an ember').

Conversely, the ة can act not as a singulative as above, but as a plural marker for certain nouns, e.g.

|  |  |  |  |
|---|---|---|---|
| snipers قَنّاصة | | sniper قَنّاص | |
| camel riders هَجّانة | | camel rider هَجّان | |

***Dual*** nominative nouns are formed by the suffix ان.

وَلَد: وَلَدان *boy*     قِطَّة: قِطَّتان *cat*

Note that if the singular noun ends with a ة, it changes to a regular ت before the suffix is added.

The suffix ـَيْن is added to accusative and genitive nouns.

وَلَد: وَلَدَيْن     قِطَّة: قِطَّتَيْن

Nouns ending in an *alif* which is originally a *wāw* in the root; the *wāw* is restored before ان is added.

عَصا: عَصَوان *stick*     رِبا: رِبَوان *interest, usury*

But if the final *alif* is *maqṣūra*, it changes to ي before the dual marker is added.

هُدى: هُدَيان *girl's name*     فَتى: فَتَيان *young man*

In quadriliteral and quinquiliteral nouns with the same ending, a *yā'* is added before the dual ending.

حُبْلى: حُبْلَيان *pregnant*     مَصْطَفى: مُصْطَفَيان *name*

Nouns ending with the feminine marker اء take a و before the suffix.

حَسْناء: حَسْناوان *girl's name*     حَرْباء: حَرْباوان *chameleon*

The final ي deleted in some nouns is restored before ان. (See Defective nouns 3.3.45.)

مُحامٍ: مُحاميان *lawyer*     قاضٍ: قاضيان *judge*

The dropped و in the five nouns (أبو، أخو، حَمو، فو، ذو) is restored before adding ان.

أخٌ: أخَوان *brother*     أبٌ: أبَوان *father*

***Plurals*** are of three major types:

3.3.8.1. Sound masculine plural. This plural is called sound because it is formed by suffixing ون (nominative) or ين (accusative and genitive) to it without any internal changes. This process applies to nouns and adjectives except nouns of the pattern أَفْعَل and compound nouns. Note that the ن in the plural suffixes is dropped if the plural is *muḍāf* مُضاف, e.g.,

مُدَرِّسو العربية (nominative) *teachers of Arabic*

إلى مدرّسي العربية (genitive)

The sound masculine plural is formed from singular masculine rational nouns on the patterns مُفعِل، مُفاعِل، فَعّال، فاعِل, e.g.

| | |
|---|---|
| كاتب: كاتبون  *writer, scribe* | مُحَمَّد: مُحَمَّدون *name* |
| مُرْسَل: مُرْسَلون *messenger* | مُراسِل: مُراسلون *reporter* |
| خَيّاط: خَيّاطون *tailor* | زَيْد: زَيْدون *name* |
| عَدّاء: عَدّاؤون *runner* | أَعْلى: أَعْلَوْن *most sublime* |
| مُصْطَفى: مُصْطَفَوْن *name* | قاض: قاضون *judge* |
| سوريّ: سوريّون *Syrian* | قارِئ: قارِئون *reader* |
| عابد: عابدون *worshipper* | مُدْمِن: مُدمِنون *addict* |
| خَبّاز: خَبّازون *baker* | مئة: مئون *hundred* (rare) |
| عنيف: عَنيفون *violent* | كثير: كثيرون *numerous* |

It might be worth noting that some of these nouns also have other plural forms such as كاتب/كُتّاب، قارِئ/قُرّاء، مئة/مئات.

Other nouns deviate slightly from the rules in terms of internal sound change, but they are considered sound plurals, e.g.

| | |
|---|---|
| أرْض: أرَضون *earth* (rare) | سَنة: سنون *year* |
| ذو: ذوو *possessors of* | أهْل: أهْلون *folks, family* |
| ثلاثة: ثلاثون *thirty* | ابن: بَنون *son* |

Most relative adjectives are made plural by suffixing ون / ين except a few that are broken plurals (see 3 below), e.g.

فارسيّ: فُرْس Persian    أَجْنَبِيّ: أجانب foreigner

حَبَشيّ: أحْباش Ethiopian    نَصْرانيّ: نَصارى Christian

A few relative adjectives have plural forms that are the singular minus the *nisba* ending, e.g.

عَرَبيّ: عَرَب Arabs    يَهوديّ: يَهود Jews

روميّ: روم Greeks    بَرْبَريّ: بَرْبَر Berbers

3.3.8.2. <u>Sound feminine plural</u>. This is formed by adding ات to feminine nouns; اتُ for the nominative and ات for both the accusative and genitive. This applies to the following cases.

* Feminine names with no feminine markers:

سُعاد: سُعادات    دَعْد: دَعْدات

هِنْد: هِنْدات    مَيْسون: مَيْسونات

زَيْنَب: زَيْنَبات    لَميس: لَميسات

* Some nouns and adjectives ending with *tā' marbūṭa*. Note the deletion of ة when the plural suffix ات is added.

شَجَرة: شَجَرات    سَيَّارة: سَيَّارات

مُرْضِعة: مُرْضِعات    سَليمة: سَليمات

Note that not all nouns ending in ة have sound feminine plurals. Some examples:

صورة: صُوَر picture    فِكْرة: فِكَر thought

عِبْرة: عِبَر lesson, example    جُمْلة: جُمَل sentence

* Masculine nouns ending with *tā' marbūṭa*:

طَلْحة: طَلْحات name    قُتَيْبة: قُتَيْبات name

* Masculine adjectives modifying non-rational (inanimate) plural nouns may take ات, but these have virtually fallen out of use in Modern Standard Arabic:

جَبَل شاهِق: جِبال شاهِقات high mountains

يَوْم: أَيَّامٌ مَعدودات *a few days*

- Verbal nouns of four or more letters:

  إجْراء: إجْراءات *procedure*     إصلاح: إصلاحات *repair*

  تَرميم: ترميمات *renovation*     تَدريب: تدريبات *drill*

  نَشاط: نَشاطات *activity*     استِعداد: استعدادات *preparation*

- Active participles referring to non-humans:

  مُقاوِم: مُقاومات *resistor*     مُفاعِل: مُفاعلات *reactor*

- A few masculine nouns:

  نداء: نداءات *call*     سِجلّ: سجلّات *record*

  حَمّام: حَمّامات *bathroom*     صَمّام: صَمّامات *valve*

- Diminutives of non-rational nouns:

  دُرَيْهم: دُرَيْهمات *penny*     كُتَيِّب: كُتَيِّبات *booklet*

  جُبَيْل: جُبَيْلات *small mountain*     سُوَيْعة: سُوَيْعات *a short while*

- Nouns ending with the feminine marker *alif*. Note the insertion of و before the ending:

  صَحْراء: صَحْراوات *desert*     حَسْناء: حَسْناوات *beautiful*

- Nouns ending with the feminine marker *alif maqṣūra*. The final *alif* changes to ي.

  حُمّى: حُمّيات *fever*     ذكْرى: ذكْرَيات *remembrance*

  مُسْتَشْفى: مُسْتَشْفَيات *hospital*     هُدى: هُدَيات *f. name*

- Foreign nouns:

  راديو: راديوات/راديوهات *radio*     تلفزيون: تلفزيونات *television*

  إصْطَبْل: إصْطَبْلات *stable*     سُرادِق: سُرادِقات *pavilion*

Note the following:

a. Nouns ending with ة preceded by an *alif* are made plural by dropping the ة, reverting the *alif* to its underlying form, either و or ي, and adding ات, unless this would result in two consecutive ي s. In this case, the second ي is changed to و.

صَلاة: صَلَوات *prayer*    فَتاة: فَتَيات *young woman*

حَياة: حَيَوات *life*

b. Feminine plurals ending with ات do not show the accusative
marker fatḥa فتحة. The accusative and genitive are marked
with a *kasra*, e.g.

شاهدنا مُبارَيات كُرة القَدَم على التلفاز.

*We watched the football games on television.*

3.3.8.3 Broken plural. This is called broken because it is the
result of internal changes in the noun rather than the addition
of a suffix. Adjectives modifying non-rational plural nouns
take feminine singular adjectives regardless of their gender,
e.g.,

كِتاب ثَمين: كُتُب ثَمينة.    *precious book*

جامعة خاصّة: جامعات خاصّة    *private university*

Grammarians have tried to systematize this process by specifying a number of patterns, but they are so numerous and
exceptions so abundant that the student is better off looking
up the plural of particular nouns. The nouns are grouped
below according to the most common of these patterns, each
listed before a group. Please note that many nouns have more
than one plural. If a noun has more than one plural form, the
more common one is listed first.

أَفْعُل

| | | |
|---|---|---|
| *ceiling* سَقْف: أَسْقُف | *soul, spirit* نَفْس: أَنْفُس/نُفوس | |
| *leg* رِجْل: أَرْجُل | *share of a stock* سَهْم: أَسْهُم | |
| *oath* يَمين: أَيْمُن | *arm* ذِراع: أَذْرُع | |

أَفْعال

| | |
|---|---|
| *liver* كَبِد: أَكْباد | *neck* عُنُق: أَعْناق |

| | | | |
|---|---|---|---|
| paternal uncle | عَمّ: أَعْمام | dress, garment | ثَوْب: أَثْواب |
| door | باب: أَبْواب | maternal uncle | خال: أَخْوال |
| colour | لَوْن: أَلْوان | turn, role | دَوْر: أَدْوار |
| species | جِنْس: أَجْناس | load, cargo | حِمْل: أَحْمال |

**أَفْعِلة**

| | | | |
|---|---|---|---|
| loaf | رَغيف: أَرْغِفة | food | طَعام: أَطْعِمة |
| alley | زُقاق: أَزِقّة | pole | عَمود: أَعْمِدة، عُمُد |
| ray | شُعاع: أَشِعّة | rein, bridle | زِمام: أَزِمّة |
| bandage, bond | رِباط: أَرْبِطة | lamb | خَروف: خِرْفان، أَخْرِفة |

**فِعْلة**

| | | | |
|---|---|---|---|
| boy | صَبيّ: صِبْية | young man | فَتى: فِتْية |
| scoundrel | سافِل: سِفْلة | boy | غُلام: غِلْمان، غِلْمة |

**فُعْل**

| | | | |
|---|---|---|---|
| green | أَخْضَر: خُضْر | red | أَحْمَر: حُمْر |
| yellow | أَصْفَر: صُفْر | lame | أَعْرَج: عُرْج |
| white | بَيْضاء: بيض | slender | هَيْفاء: هيف |

**فُعُل**

| | | | |
|---|---|---|---|
| book | كِتاب: كُتُب | patient | صَبور: صُبُر |
| bed | سَرير: أَسِرّة، سُرُر | pole | عَمود: أَعْمِدة، عُمُد |
| arm | ذِراع: أَذْرِعة، ذُرُع | newspaper | صَحيفة: صُحُف |
| city, town | مَدينة: مُدُن | lion | أَسَد: أُسود، أُسْد، آساد |

**فُعَل**

| | | | |
|---|---|---|---|
| excuse, proof | حُجّة: حُجَج | room | غُرْفة: غُرَف |
| greatest | عُظْمى: عُظَم | pocketknife | مُدْية: مُدىً |
| knee | رُكْبة: رُكَب | picture | صورة: صُوَر |

**فعَل**

| | | | |
|---|---|---|---|
| قِطْعة: قِطَع | *piece* | حجّة: حجَج | *pilgrimage* |
| فقْرة: فقَر | *item, paragraph* | لِحْية: لِحى | *beard* |

**فُعَلة**

| | | | |
|---|---|---|---|
| قاضٍ: قُضاة | *judge* | غازٍ: غُزاة | *invader* |
| رامٍ: رُماة | *shooter, rifleman* | عادٍ: عُداة | *enemy* |

**فَعْلى**

| | | | |
|---|---|---|---|
| مَريض: مَرْضى | *patient* | جَريح: جَرْحى | *wounded* |
| قَتيل: قَتْلى | *casualty, killed* | أَسير: أَسْرى | *prisoner of war* |

**فعَلة**

| | | | |
|---|---|---|---|
| دُبّ: دِبَبة | *bear* | هِرّ: هِرَرة | *cat* |
| قِرْد: قِرَدة | *monkey* | فيل: فِيَلة | *elephant* |

**فُعَّل**

| | | | |
|---|---|---|---|
| راكع: رُكَّع | *kneeler* | ساجد: سُجَّد | *one prostrate* |
| صائم: صائمون صُوَّم | *faster* | نائم: نُوَّم | *sleeper* |

**فُعَّال**

| | | | |
|---|---|---|---|
| كاتب: كُتّاب | *writer* | قائد: قُوّاد | *leader, commander* |
| تاجِر، تُجّار | *merchants* | راكِب: رُكّاب | *passenger* |

**فعال**

| | | | |
|---|---|---|---|
| كَعْب: كعاب | *heel* | ثَوْب: ثياب | *garment* |
| صَعْب: صعاب | *difficulty* | ضَخْم: ضخام | *huge* |
| جَنّة: جِنان | *paradise* | رَقَبة: رقاب | *neck* |
| دار: ديار | *residence* | جَمَل: جِمال | *camel* |
| جَبَل: جبال | *mountain* | ثَمَرة: ثمار | *fruit* |
| ذِئْب: ذئاب | *wolf* | ظِلّ: ظِلال | *shade, shadow* |

| | | | |
|---|---|---|---|
| *tall one* | طَوِيل: طِوال | *spear* | رُمْح: رِماح |
| *thirsty one* | عَطْشان: عِطاش | *generous one* | كَرِيم: كِرام |
| *arrow* | نَبْل: نِبال | *bowl* | قَصْعة: قِصاع |
| *sheep, lamb* | خَروف: خِرْفان | *rope* | حَبْل: حِبال، أَحْبُل، أَحْبال |

فُعول

| | | | |
|---|---|---|---|
| *heart* | قَلْب: قُلوب | *tiger, leopard* | نَمِر: نُمور |
| *soldier* | جُنْد: جُنود | *lion* | لَيْث: لُيوث |
| *path* | دَرْب: دُروب | *spirit* | نَفْس: نُفوس |

فَعْلان

| | | | |
|---|---|---|---|
| *crow* | غُراب: غِرْبان | *boy* | غُلام: غِلْمان |
| *whale, fish* | حوت: حيتان | *rat* | جُرْذ (جُرَذ): جِرْذان |
| *crown* | تاج: تيجان | *stick, twig* | عود: عيدان |
| *fire* | نار: نيران | *neighbour* | جار: جيران |

فُعْلان

| | | | |
|---|---|---|---|
| *lamb* | حَمَل: حُمْلان | *stick, rod* | قَضِيب: قُضْبان |
| *procession* | رَكْب: رُكْبان | *back* | ظَهْر: ظُهْران |

فُعَلاء

| | | | |
|---|---|---|---|
| *generous one* | كَرِيم: كُرَماء | *poet* | شاعِر: شُعَراء |
| *witty one* | ظَرِيف: ظُرَفاء | *great one* | عَظِيم: عُظَماء |
| *companion* | جَلِيس: جُلَساء | *stingy one* | بَخِيل: بُخَلاء |
| *ignorant one* | جاهِل: جُهَلاء | *scholar* | عالِم: عُلَماء |

أَفْعِلاء

| | | | |
|---|---|---|---|
| *intimate friend* | خَلِيل: أَخِلّاء | *abject one* | ذَلِيل: أَذِلّاء |
| *firm one* | شَدِيد: أَشِدّاء | *dear one* | عَزِيز: أَعِزّاء |
| *guardian* | وَصِيّ: أَوْصِياء | *prophet* | نَبِيّ: أَنْبِياء |

In addition to the above plural patterns, there are 19 others which can be classified under two general patterns: مَفَاعِل and مَفاعِيل. These are the so-called 'plural of plural' patterns جمع الجَمع. They are thus named because in Arabic there are nouns that have a plural and another one that structurally looks like a plural of the first plural, such as the following:

| | | | |
|---|---|---|---|
| *club* | ناد: أَنْدية (نَواد) | *flower* | زَهْر: أَزْهار: أَزاهير |
| *establishment* | بَيْت بيوت بُيوتات | *finger nail* | ظفْر: أَظافِر: أَظافير |
| *master* | سَيِّد: سادة: سادات | *man* | رَجُل: رِجال: رِجالات |

The condition for using these patterns is that the noun must have four letters, not counting the *tā' marbūṭa* if there is one; or it may have as the fourth letter either *ā* or *ī*.

| | | | |
|---|---|---|---|
| *depot, crop* | حاصِل: حَواصِل | *penny* | دِرْهَم: دَراهِم |
| *fingertip* | أُنْمُلة: أنامِل | *method* | أُسْلوب: أَساليب |
| *praise of God* | تَسْبيح: تَسابيح | *experiment* | تَجْرِبة: تَجارِب |
| *lantern* | مِصْباح: مَصابيح | *mosque* | مَسْجِد: مَساجِد |
| *treaty, pact* | ميثاق: مَواثيق | *mosque* | جامِع: جَوامِع |
| *ring* | خاتَم: خَواتِم | *water spring* | يَنْبوع: يَنابيع |
| *precedent* | سابِقة: سَوابِق | *world* | عالَم: عَوالِم |
| *virgin* | عَذْراء: عَذارى | *mill* | طاحون: طَواحين |
| *chair* | كُرْسيّ: كَراسٍ (الكَراسي) | *drunken* | سَكْران: سُكارى |

Quadriliteral nouns made plural on the pattern مَفاعِل:

| | | | |
|---|---|---|---|
| *playground* | مَلْعَب: مَلاعِب | *school* | مَدْرَسة: مَدارِس |
| *exit* | مَخْرَج: مَخارِج | *academy* | مَجْمَع: مَجامِع |

Quadriliteral nouns made plural on the pattern مَفاعيل:

| | | | |
|---|---|---|---|
| *plough* | مِحْراث: مَحاريث | *key* | مِفْتاح: مَفاتيح |
| *demented one* | مَجْنون: مَجانين | *cursed one* | مَلْعون: مَلاعين |

Quadriliteral nouns made plural on the pattern فَعالِل:

essence, gem جَوْهَر: جَواهِر    schedule, stream جَدْوَل: جَداوِل

ointment مَرْهَم: مَراهِم    cupboard, closet خِزانة: خَزائِن

Quadriliteral nouns made plural on the pattern فَعاليل:

barrel بِرْميل: بَراميل    gown جِلْباب: جَلابيب

sparrow عُصْفور: عَصافير    dinar (currency) دينار: دَنانير

Quadriliteral nouns made plural on the pattern تَفاعيل:

solo recital تَقْسيم: تَقاسيم    recitation, hymn تَرْتيل: تَراتيل

design تَصْميم: تَصاميم    detail تَفْصيل: تَفاصيل

### 3.3.9 *Broken plurals of adjectives*

Remember that in Arabic adjectives are technically nouns. The following are some examples.

difficulty صَعْب: صِعاب    impure جُنُب: أجْناب

athlete, hero بَطَل: أبْطال    enemy عَدوّ: أعْدا ء

coward جَبان: جُبَنا ء    honourable شَريف: أشْراف

friend صَديق: أصْدِقا ء    menstruating (f.) حائِض: حَوائِض

ignorant جاهِل جُهّال جُهَلا ء جَهَلة    grander أكْبَر: أكابِر

blind أعْمى: عُمْي/عُمْيان    thirsty عَطْشى: عِطاش

girlfriend صاحِبة: صَواحِب    pregnant حامِل: حَوامِل

alert يَقِظ: أيْقاظ    unarmed أعْزَل: عُزَّل

### 3.3.10 *Nouns that are plural in English, singular in Arabic*

Note that most of these nouns can be preceded by 'pair of'.

pants سِرْوال    (pair of) shoes حِذا ء

trousers سِرْوال، بِنْطال    (pair of) pliers كَمّاشة

| | | | |
|---|---|---|---|
| *shorts* | سِرْوال قَصير | *pyjamas* | بيجاما |
| *tweezers, tongs* | ملقَط | *underpants* | لِباس |

There are a number of singular abstract nouns in Arabic which look plural in English.

| | | | |
|---|---|---|---|
| *optics* | (علم) الضَوْء | *diabetes* | السُكَّريّ |
| *dialectics* | الجَدَليّة | *physics* | الفيزياء |
| *linguistics* | علم اللُغة | *politics* | السياسة |
| *gymnastics* | رياضة بدنية | *statistics* | (علم) الإحْصاء |

### 3.3.11 *Personal pronouns* الضَمائِر

There are two types of personal pronouns, overt (ضَــمـــيـــر بارِز) and covert (also known as implied ضَمير مُسْتَتِر). Overt pronouns are either attached (suffixes) (مُتَّصِل) or independent (ضَمير مُنْفَصِل).

Independent pronouns have two cases only, nominative (رَفْع) and accusative (نَصْب). On the other hand, attached pronouns show three cases: nominative, accusative, and genitive (جَرّ). The chart and table below illustrates this graphically. Note that nominative and accusative attached pronouns are suffixed to verbs and the genitive pronouns are suffixed to nouns, auxiliaries (كان), particles (إنّ), and prepositions.

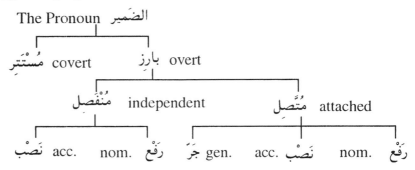

212

3.3.11.1 Covert (hidden, implied) pronouns الضَمير المُستَتِر

Covert pronouns always stand for a nominative noun which occurs either as an agent (فاعل) or deputy agent in a passive sentence (نائب فاعل) in past, present, and imperative, e.g.

With the perfect | مع الماضي

هالة حَلَمَتْ بسيّارة جديدة.

هالة (مبتدأ)/حلَمَتْ (ماض)/هي (فاعل)

أستاذُنا شَرَحَ الدرسَ.

أستاذُنا (مبتدأ)/شرح (فعل ماض)/هو (فاعل)

الوَعْدُ نُسِيَ.

الوعد (مبتدأ)/نُسي (فعل ماض مبني للمجهول)/هو (نائب فاعل)

With the imperfect | مع المضارع

أحبُّ السباحةَ. | أحبّ (فعل مضارع)/أنا (فاعل)/السباحةَ (مفعول به)

ندرسُ العربيةَ. | ندرسُ (فعل مضارع)/نحن (فاعل)/العربيةَ (مفعول به)

لا تنسَ واجبَك. | لا تنسَ (فعل مضارع)/أنت (فاعل)/واجبَك (مفعول)

الاقتصادُ ينمو. | الاقتصادُ (مبتدأ)/ينمو (فعل مضارع)/هو (فاعل)

الطائرةُ وصَلَتْ. | الطائرةُ (مبتدأ)/وصلتْ (فعل مضارع/هي (فاعل)

With the imperative | مع الأمر

اسمَعْني. | اسمَعْ (فعل أمر)/أنتَ (فاعل)/ني (مفعول به)

In traditional Arabic grammar, covert pronouns are also said to occur in the following positions:

1.  Verbs of exception (e.g. *Everything is easy except grammar.* كلُّ شيءٍ ما عدا النحوَ سَهْلٌ). The covert pronoun here is هو, and is coreferential with the noun being excepted (i.e., النحو).

2.  Expressions of wonder (التـعـجُّب) (e.g. *What a long way!* ما أطوَلَ الطريق!). The covert pronoun هي is considered to be the subject of the verb of wonder أطول.

3.  Some nouns with a verbal force (اسم الفعل See) .(بَسّ (أنت)). (See اسم الفعل
    Nouns with a verbal force 3.20.)

### 3.3.11.2 Independent and attached pronouns الضمير البارز

- Independent nominative pronouns ضَمائِر الرَفع المُنفَصِلة

  أنا   نَحْنُ   أنتَ   أنتِ   أنتُما   أنتُم   أنتُنَّ   هُوَ   هِيَ   هُما   هُم   هُنَّ

- Independent accusative pronouns ضَمائِر النَصب المُنفَصِلة

  إيّايَ   إيّانا   إيّاكَ   إيّاكِ   إيّاكُما   إيّاكُم   إيّاكُنَّ   إيّاهُ   إيّاها   إيّاهُما   إيّاهُم   إيّاهُنَّ

  These pronouns consist of إيّا, the base pronoun, plus the attached pronouns. They serve as direct objects of verbs, especially when the object is preposed, e.g.

  إيّاكَ والقِمار! *Beware of gambling.*

  إيّاكم أن تتأخروا! *Take care not to be late.*

  إيّاكَ نعبدُ. *We Thee worship.*

  They are also used as the second of two object pronouns, e.g.

  كاتبته وإيّاها. *I corresponded with them both (lit. I corresponded with him and her.)*

- Attached nominative pronouns ضَمائِر الرَفع المُتَّصِلة

  They are suffixed to perfect verbs and prefixed to the imperfect. They function as agents and, thus, they can be regarded as nominative.

  كَتَبْتُ كَتَبْنا كَتَبْتَ كَتَبْتِ كَتَبْتُما كَتَبْتُم كَتَبْتُنَّ كَتَبَ كَتَبَتْ كَتَبا كَتَبَتا كَتَبوا كَتَبْنَ

  تُ   نا   تَ   تِ   تُ   تُ   تُ   َ   ـَ   ا   ا   و   نَ

  أكتُبُ نكتُبُ تَكتُبُ تكتُبينَ تَكتُبا تَكتُبونَ يَكتُبُ تَكتُبُ يَكتُبْنَ تَكتُبانِ يكتُبانِ يكتُبونَ يكتُبْنَ

  أ   ن   ت   ي   ت

  The attached nominative pronouns can be combined in one word for ease of memorization (أنَيْتُ).

- Attached accusative pronouns ضَمائِر النَصب المُتَّصِلة

  These are suffixed to perfect, imperfect, and imperative verbs and function as direct objects. They are also suffixed to particles (إنّ set) and function as subject. Pronouns in this position are equivalent to object nouns in the accusative case. As such, these pronouns may themselves be described as being in the accusative.

عَلَّمَني عَلَّمَنا عَلَّمَكَ عَلَّمَكِ عَلَّمَكُما عَلَّمَكُم عَلَّمَكُنَّ عَلَّمَهُ عَلَّمَها عَلَّمَهُما عَلَّمَهُم عَلَّمَهُنَّ

عَلَّمْني عَلَّمْنا عَلَّمْهُ عَلَّمْها عَلَّمْهُما عَلَّمْهَم عَلَّمْهُنَّ

إنَّني إنَّا إنَّكَ إنَّكِ إنَّكُما إنَّكُم إنَّكُنَّ إنَّهُ إنَّها إنَّهُما إنَّهُم إنَّهُنَّ

ي نا كَ كِ كُما كُم كُنَّ هُ ها هُما هُم هُنَّ

• Attached genitive pronouns ضَمائِر الجَرِّ المُتَّصِلة

These are suffixed to nouns, adverbs, and prepositions. They form *iḍāfa* structures with nouns and adverbs. Being the second term of the structure, they are equivalent to nouns in the genitive, and may themselves be described as being in the genitive.

والدي والدُنا والدُكَ والدُكِ والدُكُما والدُكُم والدُكُنَّ والدُهُ والدُها والدُهُما والدُهُم والدُهُنَّ

عِنْدي عِنْدَنا عِنْدَكَ عِنْدَكِ عِنْدَكُما عِنْدَكُم عِنْدَكُنَّ عِنْدَهُ عِنْدَها عِنْدَهُما عِنْدَهُم عِنْدَهُنَّ

مِنّي مِنّا مِنْكَ مِنْكِ مِنْكُما مِنْكُم مِنْكُنَّ مِنْهُ مِنْها مِنْهُما مِنْهُم مِنْهُنَّ

ي نا كَ كِ كُما كُم كُنَّ هُ ها هُما هُم هُنَّ

Notes: (1) In the prepositions إلى and على, the ى changes to ي when a pronoun is suffixed (e.g. عَلَيْنا، إلَيْهِ). (2) The *ḍamma* in the pronoun هُ changes to *kasra* in ه when suffixed to بِ, في, إلى (e.g. بِهِ، فيهِ، هما، هم). (3) One verb may take a nominative pronoun and an accusative pronoun at the same time (e.g. أعطَيْتُهُ الكِتابَ 'I gave him the book').

Nominative (1-4), accusative (5-8), and genitive (9-10) attached pronouns (ضَمائِر مُتَّصِلة):

| | |
|---|---|
| *You are the leader.* | ١ـ أنتَ الزَعيمُ. |
| *She/it is the best.* | ٢ـ هِيَ الأفضَلَ. |

| | |
|---|---|
| *Call for equity!* | ٣ـ طالبوا بالمُساواة. |
| *They were late coming.* | ٤ـ تأخَّرْنَ بالوُصول. |
| *Thee do we worship.* | ٥ـ إيَّاكَ نَعبُدُ. |
| *Give it to me!* | ٦ـ أعطِني إيّاهُ. |
| *He is like my brother.* | ٧ـ كَأنَّهُ أخي. |
| *He may be angry.* | ٨ـ لعلَّهُ غاضبٌ. |
| *My computer is new.* | ٩ـ حاسوبي جديد. |
| *We trust in Him.* | ١٠ـ عَلَيْهِ تَوَكَّلنا. |

### 3.3.12 *Verb conjugation* تَصريف الفعل

Conjugating a verb entails adding affixes to the verb form. These affixes are suffixes in the perfect, and prefixes and suffixes in the imperfect and imperative. The different prefixes and suffixes attached to a verb vary according to person, number, and gender. Examine the affixes added to the root لعب in the perfect, imperfect (indicative, subjunctive, jussive), and imperative, respectively.

| أنا | نَحْنُ | أنتَ | أنتِ | أنتُما | أنتُم | أنتُنَّ | هُوَ | هِيَ | هُما | هُما | هُم | هُنَّ |
|---|---|---|---|---|---|---|---|---|---|---|---|---|
| لَعِبْتُ | لَعِبْنا | لَعِبْتَ | لَعِبْتِ | لَعِبْتُما | لَعِبْتُم | لَعِبْتُنَّ | لَعِبَ | لَعِبَتْ | لَعِبا | لَعِبَتا | لَعِبوا | لَعِبْنَ |
| ألعَبُ | نَلعَبُ | تَلعَبُ | تَلعَبينَ | تَلعَبان | تَلعَبونَ | تَلعَبْنَ | يَلعَبُ | تَلعَبُ | يَلعَبان | تَلعَبان | يَلعَبونَ | يَلعَبْنَ |
| ألعَبَ | نَلعَبَ | تَلعَبَ | تَلعَبي | تَلعَبا | تَلعَبوا | تَلعَبْنَ | يَلعَبَ | تَلعَبَ | يَلعَبا | تَلعَبا | يَلعَبوا | يَلعَبْنَ |
| ألعَبْ | نَلعَبْ | تَلعَبْ | تَلعَبي | تَلعَبا | تَلعَبوا | تَلعَبْنَ | يَلعَبْ | تَلعَبْ | يَلعَبا | تَلعَبا | يَلعَبوا | يَلعَبْنَ |
| | | العَبْ | العَبي | العَبا | العَبوا | العَبْنَ | | | | | | |

Note that the conjugations of the two moods of the imperfect, the subjunctive and jussive, are very similar. The singular forms have *fatḥa* on their ends in the subjunctive, whereas they have a *sukūn* in the jussive. Compare also how these two moods differ from the indicative. In the subjunctive and jussive, the *ḍamma* changes to *fatha* and *sukūn*, respectively, and the final ن is deleted, but not in the feminine plurals. The bottom line shows the conjugation of the imperative, which is restricted only to the second person. (See conjugation tables of various verb forms in Appendix 3 and Appendix 4 for conjugations of all verb forms.)

### 3.3.13 *The verb* الفعل

Verbs have three tenses: perfect, imperfect, and imperative (ماض، مُضارِع، أمر). They also have three times: past, present, and future (ماض، مُضارِع، مُسْتَقبَل). Nonetheless, perfect and imperfect verbs may not necessarily refer to past and present.

### 3.3.13.1 Perfect tense الماضي

This refers most basically to a state or action which took place at some time before the present moment, e.g. كَتَبَ، كَبُرَ. Past time may be divided into three aspects:

a.  Perfect: The action is completed in the past with no relationship to another action. This is similar to the English past tense 'did' and present perfect 'to have done'.

*The mail has arrived.* وصَلَ البَريدُ.

*The elections came to an end.* انتَهَتِ الانتخاباتُ.

*The patient died at midnight.* ماتَ المَريضُ في مُنتَصَفِ الليلِ.

b.  Perfective: The action happens in the past before another action which also takes place in the past. It is used after قَد and is similar to the past perfect in English. (See section 3.3.13.4 on compound tenses below.)

لَمّا وصلنا إلى المطار كانَتِ الطائرةُ قَد أقلَعَت.

*When we got to the airport, the flight had departed.*

*I had expected that.* كنتُ قَدْ توقَّعتُ ذلك.

c. <u>Progressive</u>: The action took place when another action occurred. The auxiliary verb كان precedes an imperfect verb.

*I was eating when they came in.* كنتُ آكلُ حينَ دَخَلوا.

ماذا كُنتَ تفعل لَّما دَقَّ جَرَسُ الهاتف؟

*What were you doing when the phone rang?*

A perfect verb may also signify <u>present</u> time in so-called performative verbs (i.e. where the uttering of the verb is an intrinsic part of the performance of the action), e.g.

*I hereby sell you the car.* بعتُكَ السيّارةَ.

*I give you my daughter in marriage.* زوّجتُكَ ابنتي.

A perfect verb refers to <u>future</u> time if:

a. It involves a supplication, eulogy, or request, e.g.

*May God forgive you.* غَفَرَ اللهُ لَك.

*May God bless his soul.* رَحمَهُ الله.

*Thank you (lit. May your hands be safe).* سَلَمَتْ يَداك.

*Thank you (lit. May God reward you).* جَزاكَ اللهُ خَيْراً.

*May God give you health.* أعْطاك (أعطى لك) اللهُ العافية.

*May God guide you.* هَداكَ اللهُ.

*They fear an evil day.* يخافون يوماً كان شرُّه مُستَطيراً.

*Long live the president.* عاشَ الرئيس.

صلّى اللهُ عَلَيْه وسلَّم.

*May God bless him and grant him salvation.*

*May God be pleased with him.* رَضِيَ اللهُ عَنّه.

b. It follows a conditional particle, e.g.

إذا طَلَعَت الشَمْسُ ذابَ الثَلجُ/يَذوبُ الثَلجُ.

*If the sun shines (in the future), the snow will melt.*

*If you write to him, he'll write to you.* إنْ كَتَبْتِ لَهُ يَكْتُبْ لَك.

### 3.3.13.2 Imperfect tense المُضارِع

This denotes an action or state of affairs obtaining at the <u>present</u> time, e.g.

| | |
|---|---|
| *He works in the foreign service.* | يَعْمَلُ في السِّلْكِ الخارجيّ. |
| *They live in Damascus.* | يَسْكُنونَ بِدِمَشْقَ. |
| *He speaks three languages fluently.* | يَتَكَلَّمُ ثَلاثَ لُغاتٍ بِطَلاقة. |

As can be seen in the conjugation table in section 3.3.12, the dual and plural forms (except the first person plural) have a final ن suffix and the singular and first person plural have *dammas* on their ends.

The imperfect signifies <u>future</u> time or potential future when:

a. The future prefix (سـ) or particle (سَوْفَ) are used, e.g.

| | |
|---|---|
| *He will take care of the baby.* | سَيَعْتَني بالطِّفْلِ. |
| *We shall return.* | سَوْفَ نَعود. |

b. The verb involves an invocation, e.g.

| | |
|---|---|
| *May God bless us all.* | يَرْحَمُنا ويَرْحَمُكُمُ الله.[4] |

c. It follows the particle قَدْ, giving the sense of 'may' or 'might', e.g.

| | |
|---|---|
| *She might visit Tunis.* | قَدْ تَزورُ تونِس. |

d. It follows the conditional particle إِنْ, e.g.

| | |
|---|---|
| | إِنْ تَتَّصِلْ بِهِ صَباحاً تَجِدْه. |

*If you call him in the morning, you'll find him.*

e. It follows the particle أَنْ, e.g.

| | |
|---|---|
| *She wants to graduate in June.* | تُريدُ أَنْ تَتَخَرَّجَ في حَزيران. |

---

[4] A response to يَرْحَمُكَ الله, which is said after someone sneezes.

لا بُدَّ أَنْ يَنتَصِرَ الحَقُّ.

*The truth must prevail.*

f. If the statement implies a future date, e.g.

*When is she expecting?* مَتى تَلِد؟

*She will deliver in May.* تَضَعُ في أيّار.

An imperfect verb acquires <u>past</u> significance when:

a. It is used after the conditional particle لَوْ, e.g.

لَوْ يَعمَلُ مَعَ أبيه لَتَعَلَّمَ الصَّنْعةَ.

*If he had worked with his father, he would have learned the trade.*

b. It is modified by the negative particles لَمْ or لَمّا, e.g.

*Jihad has never worked here.* لَمْ يَعمَلْ جِهادٌ هُنا قَطُّ.

*It has not snowed yet.* (rare usage) لَمّا يَهْطُلِ الثَلجُ.

c. The verb in the main clause has past reference, e.g.

عَلِمنا أنها تعمل في مصرف وتسكن مع خالتها. *We learned that she worked at a bank and lived with her aunt.*

تخَيّلتهم يدرسون بالمدارس ويتمتّعون بطفولتهم. *I imagined them studying at school and enjoying their childhood.*

### 3.3.13.2.1 The three moods of the imperfect verb

i. **The indicative** (الرفع): This is the default mood, that is, it is used when the imperfect verb is not governed by either subjunctive or jussive particles. It is marked by a *damma* on singular forms and the first person plural (تكتبُ) or by a ن suffix in the dual and plural forms (يكتبون), e.g.

*Do you know my address?* أتَعرفُ عُنواني.

*They work in farming.* يعملان بالزراعة.

ii. **The subjunctive** (النَصب): This is the mood when the imperfect verb is preceded by one of the subjunctive governing particles (see below). It is marked by either a *fatha* on the end of singular forms (تكتبَ) and the first person plural (نكتبَ) or by the deletion of the final ن in the dual and plural forms (يكتبوا) except the feminine plural, e.g.

أوَدُّ أنْ أشربَ فنجانَ قهوة معك. (*fatha*)

*I'd like to drink a cup of coffee with you.*

لَن يجدا ما يبحثان عنه في هذه الدُّكان. (deletion of *nūn*)

*They won't find what they are looking for in this store.*

## Subjunctive particles and their meanings:

أنْ    It governs an imperfect verb, resulting in a phrase that is equivalent in meaning to the verbal noun, e.g.

*I'd like to visit you.* (أودُّ زيارتَكم = ) أودُّ أنْ أزوركم

لَنْ    It negates verbs with future time, e.g.

*I won't talk to him any more.* لن أكلّمَه بعد اليوم.

كَيْ    It is used to express purpose ('in order to'), e.g.

اضغط هذا الزر كي تشغِّلَ الحاسوب.

*Push this button in order to turn on the computer.*

لِكَيْ    It is used to express purpose (same as كَيْ).

إذَنْ    It is used in response to a condition with the meaning 'then' (rarely used in MSA).

حَتّى    It has several meanings: 'in order to, till, until, up to'.

عامِله بلُطفٍ حَتّى يستجيبَ لك.

*Treat him kindly so that he may respond to you.*

اترُكْها على الشجرة حَتّى تَنضُجَ.

*Leave it on the tree till ti's ripe.*

سأمشي حَتّى أتعبَ. *I'll walk until I'm tired.*

Subjunctive particles in combination with other particles and/or prepositions:

ألاَّ    أنْ+لا    *not to*

221

in order to   لأَنْ   ل+أَنْ

in order not to   لِئَلاّ   ل+أَنْ+لا

in order to   لِكَيْ   ل+كَيْ

in order not to   كَيْلا   كَيْ+لا

in order not to   لِكَيْلا   ل+كَيْ+لا

Sometimes one may encounter an imperative subjunctive governed by ل (e.g. لِيَكْتُبَ). In this case, there is said to be an elided أَنْ (i.e. لأَن يكتب).

Less frequent are the following:

فَ   *Don't speed! [if you do] you'll regret it.* لا تُسرعْ فَتَنَدَمَ.

*I hope he comes so that I can meet him.* لَيْتَه يأتي فأُقابِله.

ل   It is used for emphasis after negated *kāna*.

*He wouldn't break the law.* ما كان لِيُخالِفَ القانون.

*I would not break my promise.* لم أكُنْ لأَخلفَ وعدي.

أو   سأعملُ جاهداً أو أدركَ غايتي.

*I'll work hard until I reach my goal.*

امنعْ عنه المساعدةَ أو يستقيمَ.

*Withhold support from him unless he straightens up.*

وَ   It is used after an interrogative or negative.

*[Do you expect me to] maintain contact* أتتَجاهلُني وأصلَك؟

*with you [at a time] when you ignore me?*

*I don't visit him, yet he remembers me.* لا أزورُه ويذكُرَني.

iii. **The jussive** (الجَزْمِ): The imperfect has this mood when preceded by a jussive particle. It is marked by *sukūn* on the singular forms (يكتبْ) and the first person plural or by the deletion of the final ن in the dual and plural forms (يكتبــ) except the feminine plural.

**Jussive particles**: These are of two types, those which govern one verb only (1), and those which govern two verbs (2, 3). The latter are subdivided into conditional particles, adverbs of time, and adverbs of place with a conditional sense.

1. The following jussive particles (حروف الجزم) govern one verb:

    لم is used to negate perfect verbs. Although it is followed by an imperfect form, it signifies the past.

    لمّا negates actions stretching from the past to the present. It is rather rare in Modern Standard Arabic.

    Imperative ل allows for an equivalent of the imperative in the first and third persons.

    Prohibitive لا negates imperative verbs.

    | | | |
    |---|---|---|
    | لَمْ | *He got only respect from them.* | لم يَلْقَ منهم إلاّ الاحترامَ. |
    | لمّا | *She has not finished her work yet.* | لمّا تُكمِلْ عملَها. |
    | ل | *Let's go shopping.* | لنَذهبْ إلى السوق. |
    | لا | *Don't neglect your work.* | لا تُهمِلْ عملَك. |

2. Conditional particles أدوات الشرط: These modify two verbs and make them jussive, one in the conditional clause and the other in the 'answer' to the condition (the main clause).

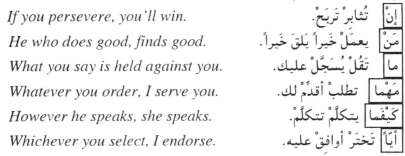

| | |
|---|---|
| *If you persevere, you'll win.* | إِنْ تُثابِرْ تَربَحْ. |
| *He who does good, finds good.* | مَنْ يعمَلْ خَيراً يَلقَ خَيراً. |
| *What you say is held against you.* | ما تَقُلْ يُسَجَّلْ عليك. |
| *Whatever you order, I serve you.* | مَهْما تطلبْ أقدِّمْ لك. |
| *However he speaks, she speaks.* | كَيْفَما يتكلَّمْ تتكلَّمْ. |
| *Whichever you select, I endorse.* | أيّاً تَختَرْ أوافِقْ عليه. |

3. Adverbs of time and place ظروف الزمان والمكان function just like conditional particles. They involve a conditional sense.

    مَتى تجتَمِعْ به أخبِرْهُ القصة.

*When you meet him tell him the news.*

أيَّانَ تَزُرْ بلادَنا تستَمتِعْ بجوِّها.

*Whenever you visit our country, you enjoy its weather.*

*Wherever she travels, he follows her.*   أينَما تسافِرْ يلحَقْ بها.

أنَّى تنظُري تري نباتاً أخضر.

*Wherever you look, you see lush vegetation.*

*Wherever he goes, he makes friends.*   حَيْثما يذهبْ يعقِدْ صداقاتٍ.

### 3.3.13.3 The imperative الأمْر

This form of the verb is used to request or command an action in the future. The regular imperative form is used with the second person only, e.g.

اكتبِ اسمَك بأعلى الصَفْحة.

*Write your name at the top of the page.*
(*kasra* on اكتب because a *hamzat waṣl* follows.)
*Get his address from the secretary.* خُذي عُنوانَهُ من أمين السرِّ.
*Listen to your mother's advice.*   استمِعا لنَصيحة أمِّكُما.
*Look out for the oncoming traffic.*   انتَبِهوا للسَيَّاراتِ المُقْبِلة.

The equivalent of the imperative can be produced for the first and third persons by using the particle (ل) (see 'Jussive Particles' above), e.g.

*Let's go to the theatre tonight.*   لنَذهَبْ إلى المَسْرَح مَساءَ اليوم.

A combination of (ف) and (ل) (pronounced *fal*) may be used.

فلأكتُبْ لأصدقائي/لأكتُبْ إلى أصدقائي.
*Let me (I should) write to my friends.*

A third person optative is made by using the particle ل preceded by ف or و and followed by the jussive, e.g.

فلتَسْتَجِبِ الحُكومةُ إلى طَلباتِهم ولْتُجري تَحْقيقاً بالأمْر.

224

*Let the government consider their demands and conduct an investigation in the matter.*

### 3.3.13.4 Compound tenses

<u>Use of</u> كان

The defective verb كـان may be used in combination with an imperfect verb to convey the sense of a progressive action in the past, e.g.

*She used to jog every morning.*  كانت تجري كل صباح.

*We were looking for a better price.*  كنّا نبحث عن سعر أفضل.

The progressive action may be related to another action in the past. e.g.

*I was reading when I heard the news.*  كنت أقرأ حين سمعت الخبر.

<u>Uses of</u> قَد

With a perfect verb following, قـد signifies completed action. It may be combined with لـ, و, or فـ with no change in meaning, though لقد is thought to be more emphatic than قـد, e.g.

*The guests have arrived.*  قد حضر الضيوف/لقد حضر الضيوف.

*If you think I have forgotten,*  إذا ظننتَ أنّي نسيتُ فقد أخطأت.

*you are mistaken.*

If used with the imperfect, it denotes possibility, e.g.

*I may/might return on Saturday.*  قد أرجع يوم السبت.

For a more detailed treatment, see Dickens and Watson, 1998 (pp. 449-460).

### 3.3.14 Indeclinable verbs الفعل الجامد

An indeclinable verb has a single, unchangeable form unrelated to time. It may take the same endings as a perfect verb such as

لَيْسَ (be/is not) or نِعْمَ (what an excellent...!), but without reference to a past action. It can also have an imperative form such as تَعالَ (come here!) and هَبْ (suppose!, lit. 'give'). Indeclinable verbs agree in gender with the noun they govern. They include:

### 3.3.14.1 Verbs of praise أفعال المَدح

| | |
|---|---|
| *What an excellent man our manager is!* | نِعْمَ الرَجُلُ مُديرُنا . |
| *It would be nice sending flowers.* | حَبَّذا إرسالُ أزهارٍ . |

Note that the noun which follows immediately after verbs of praise and blame is the agent (فــاعل) and is, therefore, in the nominative. The second noun is considered a postposed subject of the sentence (also nominative). You may encounter sentences with an accusative noun, e.g.

| | |
|---|---|
| *Lying is a bad trait.* | بِئْسَ خُلُقاً الكَذبُ . |

The accusative خُلُقاً here is an absolute object standing for an implied agent (الخُلُقُ), e.g.

| | |
|---|---|
| *Lying is a bad habit.* | بِئْسَ (الخُلُقُ) خُلُقاً الكَذبِ . |

### 3.3.14.2 Verbs of blame

| | |
|---|---|
| *His advice is bad.* | بِئْسَت النصيحةُ نصيحتُه . |
| *Boxing is a bad sport.* | ساءَت الرياضةُ المُلاكَمةُ . |

### 3.3.14.3 Verbs of wonder

| | |
|---|---|
| *What a beautiful garden!* | ما أجمَلَ هذه الحديقة! |
| *What a great man he is!* | أعظِمْ بهِ مِن رجلٍ! |

### 3.3.14.4 Other indeclinable verbs

| | |
|---|---|
| *I hope it will rain.* | عَسى المطرُ أن يهطلَ . |
| | طالَما انتظروا هذه الفُرصة . |

*They have long waited for this opportunity.*

قَلَّما يسكن الإنسانُ في المناطقِ المتَجَمِّدة .

*Man seldom lives in polar areas.*

| | |
|---|---|
| *Come to the grand opening!* | هَلُمّوا إلى الافتتاحِ الكبير. |
| *Say what you know/Give what you have!* | هاتِ ما عندَكَ! |
| *Suppose his heart is weak.* | هَبْ قَلبَهُ ضعيفاً. |

### 3.3.15 *Increased verb forms* الفِعْلُ المَزيد

The basic form of the triliteral verb consists of three original letters (e.g. ـــَـدَ/وَعَـ or و ع د 'to promise'), and that of the basic quadriliteral consists of four (e.g. ج ر دح/دَحْرَجَ 'to roll'). There are ten commonly used increased forms for the triliteral verb made by adding one or more letters to the basic form. Adding letters is not a haphazard process. There are fixed patterns according to which different verb forms are created.

The basic pattern (وَزْن) in Arabic grammars is represented by the three letters of the verb for 'to do' (ف ع ل). The ten increased forms have these three letters in addition to one or more others. In English grammars of Arabic, patterns (أوزان) are called forms, and they are numbered I to XV, the most common being patterns I to X. Both terms will be used in the chart below. The middle consonant in patterns II and V is doubled, this doubling being considered an added letter. The اِفـــعَلّ pattern (IX) has the third consonant doubled. Each pattern, or form, typically has a number of associated meanings in addition to that of the root although meanings of derived forms are not always predictable.

| Pattern | | Associated Meanings and Verb Meanings |
|---|---|---|
| I | فَعَل | Basic meaning of the verb only |
| II | فَعَّل | Causative (transitive from intransitive pattern I verbs; doubly transitive from transitive pattern I verbs): فَرّح '*to make happy*' |
| | | Intensive: كَسّر '*to smash to pieces*' |
| | | Multiplicity: غَلَّقتُ الأبوابَ '*I closed many doors*'. |

Relating s.o. to s.t.: كَفَّرَ 'to designate s.o. as كافِر'; فَسَّقَ 'to consider s.o. immoral, wanton'

Deprivation: سَلَخَ 'to strip, skin'; قَشَّرَ 'to peel'

Doing with s.t.: بَلَّطَ 'to cover with tiles'; شَجَّرَ 'to cover an area with trees'

Movement toward s.t.: شَرَّقَ 'to go east'

Transformation: عَجَّزَ الرجُل 'to become old'

Deriving a v. from a n.: خَيَّمَ 'to pitch a tent'

|     |       |
|-----|-------|
| III | فاعَل |

Reciprocity: كاتَبَ 'to correspond with'; صارَع 'to wrestle'; حادَث 'to converse with'

Multiplicity: ضاعَف 'to double'

Having the meaning of the basic root: سافَر 'to go on a trip'; عافى 'to become well'; داوَم 'to continue doing'

Causative (where the basic verb is intransitive):

غافَل 'to take s.o. by surprise'

Note that while Form II may involve reciprocity, the verb itself is transitive, with one of the reciprocal 'actors' appearing as agent and the other as object.

|    |       |
|----|-------|
| IV | أفعَل |

Causative: أكْرَمَ 'to give gratuity, honour'; أجلَسَ 'to seat'; أخْضَعَ 'to subjugate, vanquish'

Corresponding to the meaning of the v.: أهْدى 'to give s.t. as a gift'

Descriptive: أثمَرت الشجرةُ 'to bear fruit'; أمْطرت 'to rain'; أزهَر الحقلُ 'to bloom'; أورَق الشجرُ 'to put out leaves'; أفصَح 'to speak clearly'; أخطأ 'to make a mistake'; أبْطأ 'to be slow'; أسْرَعَ 'to be fast'

Transformation: أسلَمَ 'to convert to Islam'; أفْلسَ 'to become penniless, bankrupt'; أقفَرتِ المَدينةُ 'to be deserted'; أجْدَبَ 'to become dry;'

أَشْكَلَ الأَمْرُ 'to become problematic, confusing';
أَعْدَمَ ' to execute, reduce to nothing'

Movement toward a place: أَقْبَلَ 'to move forward'; أَدْبَرَ 'to move backward, retreat'; أَحْرَمَ 'to head toward a holy place'

Being at a time: أَصْبَحْنا في بَيْروتَ. ' to be in the morning'; أَمْسى ' to be in the evening'

Deprivation: أَعْذَرَ ' to deprive s.o. of an excuse'

| V | تَفَعَّل | Having a quality expressed in the root, a medio-passive of II with no agent necessary: تَأَدَّب 'to educate oneself'; تَجَمَّع 'to congregate'; تَأَلَّف 'to be composed of'; تَكَلَّم 'to speak'; تَعَرَّف 'to acquaint oneself'

Reflexive: تَعَلَّم ' to learn'; تَخَرَّب 'to be in ruins, damaged'

Affectation: تَجَلَّد 'to endure, tolerate suffering'; تَشَجَّع 'to be courageous'

Forming a v. from a n.: تَحَجَّر 'to become like a stone, petrify'; تَوَسَّدَ ذِراعَهُ 'to use s.t. as pillow'

Gradual occurrence: تَجَرَّعَ الدَّواءَ ' to take bit by bit'; تَحَسَّى 'to sip'; تَعَرَّق 'to perspire'

Intensity (medio-passive of II): تَفَرَّق ' to be dispersed into many groups' (as opposed to افتَرَقَ 'to go two ways')

Avoidance: تَجَنَّب 'to avoid'; تَحَرَّج 'to refrain from, avoid embarrassment'

Transformation: يَتَيَّم الطفلُ ' to become an orphan'; تَنَصَّر 'to become a Christian'; تَهَوَّد 'to become a Jew'; تَعَرَّب 'to become an Arab or be Arabized'; تَشَيَّع 'to adopt Shīʿa doctrine'

| VI | تَفاعَل | Reciprocal: تَضارَبَ الخَبَران 'to conflict with each other'; تَراسَل 'to correspond with'; تَنازَعَ 'to

dispute, quarrel'; تَماسَكَ 'to grab each other'

Reflexive of III: تَباعَدَ 'to draw apart'

Affectation: تَغافَلَ 'to feign illness'; تَمارَضَ 'to pretend to be careless'; تَظاهَرَ 'to pretend'; تَباكى 'to pretend not to see'; تَعامى 'to pretend to be sorry, shed crocodile tears'; تَجاهَلَ 'to feign ignorance;' تَناسى 'to pretend not to remember'

Gradual occurrence: تَوارَدَ المَدعوّون 'to come one by one'; تَتابَعَت الأخبارُ 'to follow one another'; تَساقَطَ المَطرُ 'to fall down gradually'

| | | |
|---|---|---|
| VII | انْفَعَلَ | Medio-passive form of I: انقَطَعَ 'to be or get severed or disconnected'; انكَسَرَ 'to be broken'; انعَدَمَ\ 'to become extinct'; انعَدَمَ 'to become non-existent'; انْهَزَمَ 'to be defeated' |

Medio-passive form of IV: انْغَلَقَ 'to get or be closed'; انْطَفَأَ 'to be extinguished'; انْصَلَحَ 'to get or be corrected, put right'; انطَلَقَ 'to dash forward, set out'; انْضافَ 'to be added;' انتَعْشَ 'to be revived'

| | | |
|---|---|---|
| VIII | افتَعَلَ | Medio-passive of I: اتَّصَفَ 'to be marked by, characterized;' |

Reflexive: اجتَمَعَ 'to get together, meet'; اكتَسَبَ 'to earn one's living'; اتَّشَحَ 'to don, put on, wear'; اتَّعَظَ 'to learn a lesson'; اتَّصَلَ 'to contact, call on the phone'

Reflexive of III (the v. needs a preposition): اعْتَرَضَ (على) 'to oppose'; 'to quarrel'; اختَلَفَ (عن، مع) 'to differ, disagree'

The meaning of the basic v.: اجْتَذَبَ 'to attract;' اتَّبَعَ 'to follow'; اختَطَفَ 'to snatch, abduct'; اتَّفَقَ 'to agree, happen, chance'

Reciprocal: (مع) اِخْتَصَمَ 'to quarrel;' اِقْتَتَلَ 'to fight one another;' اِشْتَبَكَ 'to clash, engage in battle'; اِسْتَبَقَ 'to race' (also non-reciprocal: 'to anticipate')

IX    اِفْعَلَّ    <u>Acquiring the attribute in the n.</u>: اِحْمَرَّ 'to become red'; اِحْوَلَّ 'to become cross-eyed'; اِعْوَجَّ 'to become crooked'

X    اِسْتَفْعَلَ    <u>Seeking the meaning in the basic v.</u>: اِسْتَغْفَرَ 'to ask forgiveness'; اِسْتَغَاثَ 'to ask for help'; اِسْتَأْذَنَ 'to ask permission'; اِسْتَسْلَمَ 'to give up oneself (lit. to seek peace'; اِسْتَعَدَّ 'to be prepared, ready'; اِسْتَجَابَ 'to answer prayer'; اِسْتَخْلَفَ 'to appoint as successor or caliph'; اِسْتَوْزَرَ 'to appoint as wazir or cabinet minister'; اِسْتَعْمَلَ 'to appoint as governor (عامل), use'; اِسْتَحْجَرَ 'to become like a stone'

The conjugation tables in Appendix 3 comprise verbs repre-senting different structures (sound, defective) and forms (I-X) conjugated in the perfect, imperfect, and imperative. The three moods of the imperfect are also included. The verbal noun and active and passive participles are provided at the top of every table next to the verb being conjugated.

### 3.3.16 *Verb structure*

Arabic verbs can be classified in terms of structure into sound (صَحِيح) and weak verbs (مُعْتَلّ). If a sound verb is made up of consonants, it is called strong (سَالِم) (not if *hamza* is part of it) (e.g., كتب). If, however, the second and third radicals are identical consonants, it is called doubled (مُضَعَّف). A *shadda* is used to mark the gemination of the two letters (e.g., مَرَّ). If *hamza* is one of the three radicals, it is called hamzated (مَهْموز).

| Sound Verbs | | | الفعل الصَحيح |
|---|---|---|---|
| hamzated مَهْموز | doubled مُضَعَّف | | strong سالِم |
| أكَلَ سألَ بَدَأ | مَدَّ | | عَلِمَ |

Weak verbs with an initial semi-vowel are called assimilated verbs because the و in وَصَفَ, for example, assimilates to the ت of افْتَعَلَ, thus becoming اتَّصَفَ rather than اوتَصَفَ (form VIII).

Hollow verbs are those weak verbs with a middle vowel (e.g., قال، نام، باع). The middle vowel changes to either *fatha, damma,* or *kasra* in the imperfect jussive and imperative.

Note the changes in the examples below when the weak verb is in the imperative or jussive, where the vowel either changes or disappears completely.

| Weak verbs | | | | الفعل المعتَلّ |
|---|---|---|---|---|
| لَفيف مَفروق | لَفيف مَقرون | ناقص | أجْوَف | مثال |
| Ass./def. | Hollow/def. | Defective | Hollow | Assimilated |
| وَفى | لَوى | دَعا/رَمى | قال/باعَ | وصَلَ/وَلَدَ/يَسُرُ |

Conjugation of weak verbs in the third person masculine singular, active and passive. The verbal noun, active participle, and passive participle are listed next to the verb.

وَجَدَ (وُجود، واجِد، مَوجود)

| | Perfect | Imperfect indicative | Imperfect subjunctive | Imperfect jussive | Imperative |
|---|---|---|---|---|---|
| Active | وَجَدَ | يَجِدُ | يَجِدَ | يَجِدْ | جِدْ/ أوجِدْ |
| Passive | وُجِدَ | يوجَدُ | يوجَدَ | يوجَدْ | -- |

قالَ (قَوْل، قائِل، مَقول)

|  | Perfect | Imperfect indicative | Imperfect subjunctive | Imperfect jussive | Imperative |
|---|---|---|---|---|---|
| Active | قالَ | يَقولُ | يَقولَ | يَقُلْ | قُلْ |
| Passive | قيلَ | يُقالُ | يُقالَ | يُقَلْ | -- |

باعَ (بَيْع، بائِع، مُباع)

|  | Perfect | Imperfect | Imperfect subjunctive | Imperfect jussive | Imperative |
|---|---|---|---|---|---|
| Active | باعَ | يَبيعُ | يَبيعَ | يَبِعْ | بِعْ |
| Passive | بيعَ | يُباعُ | يُباعَ | يُبَعْ | -- |

دَعا (دُعاء، داعٍ، مَدْعو)

|  | Perfect | Imperfect indicative | Imperfect subjunctive | Imperfect jussive | Imperative |
|---|---|---|---|---|---|
| Active | دَعا | يَدعو | يَدعُوَ | يَدْعُ | ادعُ |
| Passive | دُعِيَ | يُدْعى | يُدْعى | يُدْعَ | -- |

رَمى (رَمْيٌ، رامٍ، مَرْمِيٌّ)

|  | Perfect | Imperfect indicative | Imperfect subjunctive | Imperfect jussive | Imperative |
|---|---|---|---|---|---|
| Active | رَمى | يَرْمي | يَرْمِيَ | يَرْمِ | اِرْمِ |
| Passive | رُمِيَ | يُرْمى | يُرْمى | يُرْمَ | -- |

لَوى (لَوي/لَيّْ، لاوٍ، مَلويّ)

| | Perfect | Imperfect indicative | Imperfect subjunctive | Imperfect jussive | Imperative |
|---|---|---|---|---|---|
| Active | لَوى | يَلوي | يَلوِيَ | يَلوِ | اِلْوِ |
| Passive | لُوِيَ | يُلوى | يُلوى | يُلوَ | -- |

وَفى (وَفاءٍ، وافٍ، موفٍ)

| | Perfect | Imperfect indicative | Imperfect subjunctive | Imperfect jussive | Imperative |
|---|---|---|---|---|---|
| Active | وَفى | يَفي | يَفِيَ | يَفِ | فِ |
| Passive | وُفِيَ | يوفى | يوفى | يوفَ | -- |

Examples of weak verbs with negative and imperative forms.

| Imperative | Negative | Verb |
|---|---|---|
| *Give us twins!* أولِدي تَوأمَيْن. | لَم تَلِدْ .. | وَلَدَتْ زَوْجَتُهُ تَوأْمَيْن. |
| *Come at night!* صِلوا ليلاً. | لَمْ نَصِلْ .. | وصَلنا ليلةَ أمس. |
| *Be in Sudan..* كُنْ في السودان. .. | لَمْ يَكُنْ .. | كانَ أخي في السودان. |
| *Sell your car!* بِعْ سيّارَتَك. | لَم يَبِعْ .. | باعَ أخي سيّارتَهُ. |
| ادْعُنا قبلَ العيد. | لَم يَدْعُنا .. | دَعانا المُديرُ للعَشاء. |

*Invite us before the Eid!*

| *Throw your toy away!* ارمِ لُعبَتَك. | لَم يَرْمِ .. | رَمى الطفلُ لُعبَتَهُ. |
| اطْوِ صَفحةَ الخلافات. | لَم يَطْوِ .. | طَوى صَفحةَ الخلافات. |

*Open a new page!*

وقى اللقاحُ منَ المَرَضِ.   لَم يَقِ . .   قٍ منَ المَرَضِ باللقاح.

*Prevent sickness with vaccination!*

وَفى دَينَهُ كاملاً.   لَم يَفِ دَينَهُ.   ف دَيْنَكَ كاملاً.

*Pay off your debt completely!*

### 3.3.17 *Transitive and intransitive verbs*

The meaning of an intransitive verb (لازِم) is completed through the agent, e.g.

| | |
|---|---|
| *The man died.* | ماتَ الرجُلُ. |
| *The cold [weather] has come.* | جاءَ البَرْدُ. |

A transitive verb (مُتَعَدٍّ) takes an object in order to complete its meaning, e.g.

| | |
|---|---|
| *The young man brought a gift.* | أحضَرَ الشابُّ هديَّةً. |

Transitive verbs can take pronominal and nominal objects, e.g.

| | |
|---|---|
| *He made the audience wait.* | جَعَلَ الحاضرينَ ينتظرون. |
| *He told him the story.* | أخبَرَهُ القصَّةَ. |
| *He made you think.* | دَفَعَكَ للتَفكير. |

Intransitive verbs may take a preposition governing a noun or a pronoun, e.g.

| | |
|---|---|
| *He took him to jail.* | ذَهَبَ بهِ إلى السَجن. |
| *He needed her.* | احتاجَ إلَيْها. |
| *She told you all she knew.* | قالَت لَكُم كلَّ ما تعرفه. |
| *He approached me.* | دَنا مِنّي. |
| *He did not pay attention to you.* | غَفِلَ عَنكَ. |
| *He paid attention to us.* | اهتَمَّ بنا. |

An intransitive Form I verb can sometimes be given a transitive sense by adding a preposition as above or sometimes by changing

235

its pattern to فَعَّل or أفعَل (Forms II, IX), e.g.

| | |
|---|---|
| *Samer came.* | (intransitive). حَضَرَ سامِرٌ |
| *Samer prepared breakfast.* | (transitive). حَضَّرَ سامِرٌ الفَطورَ |
| *Samer brought his fiancée.* | (transitive). أحْضَرَ سامِرٌ خَطيبَتَهُ |

### 3.3.18 *Active and passive verbs*

A verb has an active voice if it has an agent (فاعِل). In terms of traditional English grammar, the object of the active sentence can be said to become the subject of the passive sentence, e.g.

*The woman has made a basket.* صَنَعَت المَرأةُ سلَّةً.

A passive verb has no agent. Instead, the object occupies the position of the agent and assumes its case and is called deputy agent (نائب فاعل), e.g.

*The basket has been made.* صُنِعَت السلَّةُ.

Verbs go through internal changes when changing from active to passive in the perfect and imperfect.

| | |
|---|---|
| Perfect | كَسَرَ ←•• كُسِرَ ◄─ ُ + ِ . |
| Imperfect | يَكْسِرُ ←•• يُكْسَرُ ◄─ ُ + َ . |

Note that in perfect verbs with a penultimate *alif* this changes to ي, e.g.

صامَ ←•• صيمَ – اصطادَ ←•• اصطيدَ – اقتادَ ←•• اقتيدَ

An *alif* and *alif maqsūra* at the end in perfect verbs change to ي in the passive:

بَنى ←•• بُنِيَ     رَمى ←•• رُمِيَ     دَعا ←•• دُعِيَ

The middle long vowel in imperfect verbs changes to *alif*, e.g.

يُريدُ ←•• يُرادُ     يَصيدُ ←•• يُصادُ     يَقولُ ←•• يُقالُ

### 3.3.19 *Verbs Used only in the passive*

Some verbs are used only in the passive. These include:

| | | | |
|---|---|---|---|
| *to be fond of* | أُولِعَ بالصَّيْد. | *to pass out* | أُغْمِيَ عَلَيْه. |
| *to have a fever* | حُمَّ المَريض. | *to become demented* | جُنَّ الرَجُل. |
| *to be taken care of* | عُنِيَ بِه. | *to be at a loss* | سُقِطَ في يَدِه. |
| | | *to be unconscious* | غُشِيَ عَلَيْه. |

## 3.4 Noun derivation الاسم المُشْتَق

Some grammarians consider the basic (unincreased) verbal noun (المَصْـدَر المُجَــرَّد) as the source of all derivations such as the basic (Form I) perfect verb (الماضي المُجَرَّد) and other derivations.

| | | |
|---|---|---|
| *collecting* جَمْع | Form I verbal noun | المَصْدَر المُجَرَّد |
| *to collect, add* جَمَعَ | Form I perfect verb | الماضي المُجَرَّد |
| *to collect, add* يَجْمَعُ | imperfect verb | المُضارِع |
| *meeting* (VIII) اجتماع | increased verbal noun | المصدر المُزيد |
| *academy, assembly* مَجْمَع | m-prefix noun | المصدر الميمي |
| *adventurer* مُغامِر, teacher مُدَرِّس | active participle | اسم الفاعل |
| *busy* مَشْغُول, *concise* مُخْتَصَر | passive participles | اسم المفعول |
| *file* مِبْرَد , *saw* مِنْشار, *iron* مِكْواة | noun of instrument | اسم الآلة |
| *cemetery* مَقْبَرة, *goal* مَرْمى , *office* مَكْتَب | noun of place | اسم المكان |
| *appointment* مَوْعِد, *sunset* مَغيب | noun of time | اسم الزمان |
| *humanity* إنْسانيّة | relative noun | المصدر الصناعي |
| *dance* رَقْصة, trip سَفْرة | noun of occasion | اسم المَرّة |
| *handsome* جَميل, *brave* شُجاع | assimilative adj. | الصفة المُشَبَّهة |
| *taller* أطْوَل | comparative noun | اسم التَفْضيل |
| *one* واحِد , *first* الأوَّل , *few* بِضْع , *over* نَيِّف | numerals | اسم العَدَد |

اسم الوَحدة singulative noun   سَمَكة *a fish* ، لَحمة *a piece of meat*
قَمحة *a grain of wheat*

اسم الفعل noun with a verbal force   (section 3.3.36) إلَيْك *here!*

اسم التصغير diminutive noun   (section 33.37) كُتَيِّب *booklet*

## 3.5 The nominal sentence الجملة الاسمية

A nominal sentence is made up of subject (مَبْتَـدَأ) and predicate
(خَبَر). Both constituents are normally nominative (مَرْفوع). The subject
is the topic of the sentence and the predicate informs about it.
The subject usually occupies the initial position, e.g.

الطقسُ صَحْوٌ.   *The weather is fine.*

صديقُ أخي مديرُ مصرفٍ تجاري.
*My brother's friend is manager of a commercial bank.*

### 3.5.1 *Forms of the subject*

The subject may be represented by several structures apart from
simple noun phrases. Some of these structures may not be
nominative themselves (e.g. items a and d), but they are considered
to be nominative because they occupy the position of a subject.

a. Phrase

أنْ تُسافرَ بالطائرة أحسنُ لك.   *To travel by plane is better for you.*

لَلْقراءةُ في المكتبة خَيرٌ منها في الدار. (low frequency)
*Reading at the library is better than reading at home.*

b. Relative clause

الَّذي يَسْعَدُ في عَمله وفي بيته قَلَّ مثالُهُ.
*Those who are happy at work and in their homes are few.*

c. Verbal noun

سفرُك بالطائرة أحسنُ لك.   *Travelling by plane is better for you.*

d. ما of exclamation (التعجُّبَّة)

*What a wonderful day!*    ما أجمَلَ هذا اليوم!

e. Declarative (الخَبَرية) كَم

*There are so many rooms in your house.*    كَم غُرفةٍ في بيتك!

f. Interrogative (الاستفهامية) كَم and other interrogative pronouns

*How many rooms are there in your house?*    كَم غُرفةً في بَيتِك؟

*who's at the door?*    مَنْ بالباب؟

g. Conditional pronoun

مَنْ يَزُرْ لندن يرَ جسرَها المشهور.

*Those who go to London see its famous bridge.*

h. Noun added to a conditional pronoun (مضاف إلى اسم الشرط)

*Whoever's novel you read I read.*    روايةُ مَنْ تقرأي أقرأ.

i. Noun added to an interrogative pronoun (مضاف إلى اسم الاستفهام)

*Whose car is in front of your house?*    سيّارةُ مَنْ أمامَ دارك؟

## 3.5.2 *Ellipted subject* حَذف المبتدأ

The subject is regarded as ellipted in the following conditions:
a. If there is evidence of it in the sentence.

*(This is) the first request.*    (هذا هو) المطلَبُ الأوَّل.

b. After an oath.

والله (قَسَمي) لأقاطعَنَّه.

*By God (my oath) I will stop associating with him.*

c. When its predicate is a verbal noun standing for it.

*A fair sentence.*    حُكْمٌ عادل.

This is elliptical for:

*(His sentence is) a fair sentence.*    (حُكمُه) حُكْمٌ عادل.

## 3.5.3 *Definiteness*

The subject is generally definite, but it may be indefinite if it occurs after a question or a negative word:

*Is there anybody at your house?*     هل أَحَدٌ في مَنزلك؟

*There are no clouds in the sky.*     لا غُيومَ في السَّماءِ.

a. As a representative of a class:

*One lira is better than nothing.*     لَيْرةٌ خَيرٌ مِن لا شَيءٍ.

b. After an adverb or a preposition:

*Rasha has good news.*     عند رَشا خَبَرٌ سعيدٌ.

c. As an invocation:

*Woe unto evil people.*     وَيْلٌ للمُفسِدين.

d. After إذا that introduces an unexpected event إذا الفُجائية:

نظرتُ فإذا حَوّامةٌ في السماءِ.

*I looked up and I suddenly saw a helicopter in the sky.*

e. When variation is intended:

*One day for you, one day against you (to*     يَومٌ لك ويومٌ عليك.

*express changing fortunes of life).*

### 3.5.4 *Forms of the predicate* أنواع الخَبَر

A predicate may be a single word, a clause, or a sentence. If a word, this must be a derived noun, that is, either active participle, passive participle, comparative form, or verbal adjective.

a. Noun or noun phrase (اسم)

*This man is a tailor.*     هذا الرجلُ خَيّاطٌ.

b. Active or passive participle (اسم فاعل ، اسم مفعول)

*The father is sitting.*     الأبُ جالسٌ.

*The children are happy.*     الأولادُ مَسرورون.

c. Comparative adjective (اسم تفضيل) (See 3.9)

*Ahmed is taller than his brother.*     أحمدُ أطولُ من أخيه.

d. Assimilative, or verbal adjective (صفة مَشبّهة)

*This man is generous.*     هذا الرجلُ كريمٌ.

e. A prepositional phrase

*My suitcase is in the car.* حقيبتي في السيارة.

f. *Idāfa* structure (مضاف ومضاف إليه), considering خلف an adverb.

*The sun is behind the clouds.* الشمسُ خلفَ الغُيوم.

g. A nominal or a verbal clause. A clause that functions as a predicate must have a pronoun which has reference to the subject. The reference may be an overt, covert, or ellipted pronoun.

*Travel has many advantages.* السَفَرُ مَنافعُه كثيرةٌ.

*Reading increases your information.* القراءةُ تُنَمّي معلوماتك.

*Milk is 20 liras per kilogram.* الحليبُ الكيلو (منه) بعشرين ليرة.

3.5.5 *Ellipsis of the predicate* (in parentheses) حَذف الخَبَر

a. In response to a question.

*Reem (is in the house).* – مَن في الدار؟ ‏↞‏ – ريم (في الدار).

*A new idea (I have).* – ماذا لدَيْك؟ ‏↞‏ – فكرةٌ جديدةٌ (لديّ)

b. There is evidence of it in the sentence.

هي لُبنانيةٌ وزوجُها (كذلك).

*She is Lebanese and (so is) her husband.*

c. Following unexpected إذا 'suddenly' (إذا الفجائية).

دخلتُ الحديقةَ فإذا الكلبُ (واقفٌ).

*I entered the garden and there was the dog (standing).*

d. After an oath.

*By God I shall serve my country.* عَهْدُ الله (عليّ) لأخدُمَنَّ وَطَني.

e. After a subject governed by *wāw* و of accompaniment.

المَرءُ وأعمالُه (مَحسوبةٌ عليه).

*Every man and his deeds (are counted against him).*

f. After a لولا clause in a conditional sentence if the predicate (response clause) indicates the existence of the subject.

*Had it not been for his*     لَوْلا مساعدتُه (متوفّرةٌ) لَفَشلتُ.
*assistance (being available), I would have failed.*

If the predicate does indicate a specific existence, it must then be explicit.

لَوْلا السيّارةُ مُتَعَطّلةٌ لَسافَرتُ بها.

*If it were not broken, I would have travelled by car.*

### 3.5.6 *Auxiliaries introducing nominal sentences* النَواسِخ

The verbs of the set of كان are called defective because the meaning is incomplete with the verb and the subject. A predicate is needed to complete the meaning, e.g.

*Marwan has become.* (incomplete meaning)     أصبحَ مَرْوانُ.

*Marwan has become a doctor.*     أصبحَ مَرْوانُ طبيباً.

Some defective verbs and particles (which may be called auxiliaries) are used to introduce nominal sentences. They change the subject and predicate in case and time signification. They may be classified in two categories based on the effect they have on the case of the subject and predicate. Set (A) comprising, كان، كاد and ما fall into one category. They keep the subject nominative (مَـرْفـوع) and make the predicate accusative (منصـوب). Set (B) comprising إنَّ and the particle لا used for class negation make the subject accusative and the predicate nominative.

### 3.5.6.1 The كان set

Defective verbs and particles keep the subject nominative and make the predicate accusative. If the predicate of defective verbs is a clause, its verb must be imperfect.

*Lana was walking along the street.*     كانت لانا تسير في الشارع.

The above sentence might be analysed as verb, subject, complement which comprises the second verb and a prepositional phrase. However, Arab grammarians view the sentence as nominal introduced by a defective verb which is followed by a subject (لانا) and a predicate (تسير في الشارع).

If the predicate is a verb, it may be perfect after six of the defective verbs, but it must be preceded by قَد (أصبح، أضحى، أمسى، بات، ظلّ، كان).

*The patient had recovered.*  أصبح المريضُ قد شُفِيَ.

### 3.5.6.1.1 Meanings of the members of the كان set

a. Description of the predicate (occurrence, event) (كان), e.g.,

*The weather was hot.*  كان الجَوُّ حاراً.

b. Co-occurrence of the predicate and the subject (ما، ما بَرح، ما زال، ما انفَكُّ، فَتِئَ).

*Reem is still the librarian.*  مازالت ريمُ أمينةَ المكتبة.

c. Negation (ليس)

*The wind is not strong.*  لَيْسَت الريحُ شديدةً.

d. Becoming (كان، صار، أمسى، أضحى، ظلّ، بات)

*The young woman has become a mother.*  صارت الفتاةُ أمّاً.

*Amer has become a doctor.*  أضحى عامرُ طبيباً.

e. Continuation of the predicate (ما دام)

*We walk so long as the weather is fine.*  نمشي مادام الجوُّ صحواً.

### 3.5.6.1.2 Conjugation of defective verbs (كان set)

a. Some are fully conjugated (perfect, imperfect, imperative): كان، كان، يكونُ، كُنْ. Example: أصبح، أضحى، أمسى، بات، ظلّ، صار

b. Some are partially conjugated (perfect, imperfect): ما انفَكُّ، ما ما زالَ، لا يَزالُ. Example: بَرحَ، ما زالَ، ما فَتِئَ

c. One conjugates in the perfect only: لَيْسَ

d. In one case, no conjugation possible: ما دامَ

Additional rules for كان

a. It may be ellipted after the conditional particles إنْ and لَوْ:

الرياضةُ تفيد وإنْ (كانت) مُتقطّعةً.

*Exercise is useful even though (it is) intermittent.*

*Help them even (this is) a little.*   ساعدوهم ولَوْ (كان ذلك) قليلاً.

b. It is inserted in a sentence to indicate past time:

*How nice the weather was!*   ما كانَ ألطفَ الجَوَّ!

c. If it is preceded by the negative ما, its predicate may take the preposition بـ as a prefix.

*His father was not stingy.*   ما كانَ أبوهُ بالبَخيلِ (أو: ببخيلٍ).

### 3.5.6.1.3 Verbs of approximation أفعال المقاربة (كادَ، أوشَك) (كَرَب rare)

The predicate of these verbs may be a clause (أنْ يفــعل) or an imperfect verb. If the latter, the predicate can precede the subject.

*The baby was about to sleep.*   كادَ الطفلُ ينامُ. /كادَ ينامُ الطفلُ.

*The day is about to be over.*   أوشكَ النهارُ أنْ ينقضيَ.

*The crisis is almost over.*   أوشكَت الأزمةُ تَنتَهي.

### 3.5.6.1.4 Verbs of hope أفعال الرجاء   (عَسى، حَرى، اخلَوْلَقَ)

Only عَســى is used in Modern Arabic, and it is conjugated in the perfect only. If the first-person pronoun is suffixed to عَسى, the word can either be pronounced عَسَيْتُ or عَسيتُ.

*I hope this experiment succeeds.*   عَسى هذه التجربةُ أنْ تنجحَ.

### 3.5.6.1.5 Verbs of beginning أفعال الشُروع: The most common include:

بدأ، أخَذ، أقبل، انبَرى، أنشأ، جَعَل شَرَع، طَفِق، قام، هَبَّ. These verbs function like كان, that is, they introduce a nominal sentence, where the subject is a noun and the predicate is a verbal clause with an imperfect verb (in some cases introduced by أنْ), e.g.

*She began inviting her friends*

*to the wedding.*　　　أخَذَتْ تَدعو صَديقاتها إلى زفافها .

*The assembly was about*　أوشَكَ المجلسُ أن يحجبَ الثقةَ عن الحكومة.

*to move for no confidence in the government.*

If these verbs are used in a sense other than beginning, they can be sound verbs followed by agent and direct object rather than an imperfect verb after them, e.g.,

*They have made their goal the*　　جَعَلوا هَدَفَهم مَحوَ الأُمِّية.

*eradication of illiteracy.*

*I took the letter to him.*　　　　　أخذتُ الرسالةَ إليه.

*The government began a new*　بدأتِ الحكومةُ خُطّةً خمسيةً جديدة.

*five-year plan.*

The verb in the last sentence would be a verb of beginning if the sentence read: بدأتِ الحكومة تنادي بخطةٍ خمسيةٍ جديدة.

## 3.5.6.1.6 The ما set (إنْ، ما، لا)

These are negative particles used with nominal sentences. They behave in a similar manner to ليس in keeping the subject nominative and making the predicate accusative.

The case-governing effect of these particles on the subject and predicate is rendered void if إلا precedes the predicate.

*Your brother is but a student.*　　　ما أخوكَ إلاّ طالبٌ.

*Don't worry; no harm will come to you.*　لا بأسٌ عليك.

## 3.5.6.2 The إنَّ set

These are particles that make the subject accusative (منصوب) and the predicate nominative (مرفوع).

إنَّ (for emphasis)

إنَّ الميناءَ مُزدَحمٌ.

*The port is congested.*

كَأنَّ *as though*

كَأنَّ لهجتَك مصريةٌ.

*Your accent sounds as though it is Egyptian.*

لكنَّ *but* (for contrast)

رنا طويلةٌ لكنَّ أختَها أطولُ منها.

*Rana is tall, but her sister is taller.*

لَيْتَ (for hope)

لَيْتَ أباك مسافرٌ معنا.

*I wish your father were travelling with us.*

لعَلَّ (for hope, request)

لعلَّ زياداً مُرتاحٌ في عملهِ.

*I hope Ziyad is happy with his job.*

The predicate of these particles may be a noun (adj.), a nominal clause, a verbal clause, a prepositional phrase, or an adverbial phrase (in this order below). Note that in the last two, the position of the subject and predicate is reversed. (See Word Order 3.8)

| | |
|---|---|
| *Summer is around the corner.* | إنَّ الصيفَ قريبٌ. |
| *Exercise has a great benefit.* | إنَّ الرياضةَ فائدتُها كبيرةٌ. |
| *I wish youth would come back.* | لَيْتَ الشبابَ يعودُ يَوماً. |
| *You are responsible for your family.* | إنَّ لأهلك حَقّاً عليك. |
| *There is an apartment over yours.* | إنَّ فوقَ شقّتك شقةٌ. |

- ما may be used after these particles, but in this case the subject is put in the nominative.

  *It seems as if our professor is tired.* كأنَّما أستاذُنا تعبانٌ.

- The *lām* of inception may be prefixed to the predicate without affecting the particles' government of the predicate.

*You have done a wonderful job.*  إنَّ عملَك هذا لَرائعٌ.

### 3.5.6.3 Class-negating لا (لا النافية للجنس)

- The subject and predicate of the class-negating لا must be indefinite, and its subject must follow it.

  *We have no problem.*  لا مَشكلةَ عندنا.

- The preposition بـ may be prefixed to it, but in this case it loses its case-governing effect on the subject (i.e., making it accusative).

  *Some plants are grown in no soil.*  تُزرع بعضُ النباتات بلا ماءٍ.

- The noun following لا may be a singular noun, the first term of an *idāfa*, or a plural.

  *No crime is greater than treason.*  لا جريمةَ أفظعُ من الخيانة.

  لا زعيمَ أمّةٍ أشهرُ من غاندي.

  *No national leader is more renowned than Gandhi.*

  *There are no female students in our class.*  لا طالباتَ في صفِّنا.

## 3.6 The verbal sentence الجملة الفعلية

A verbal sentence begins with a verb and has two main components when the sentence has an intransitive verb (لازِم): the verb and the agent (فاعل).

*The winter has come.*  جاءَ الشتاءُ.

If the verb is transitive (مُتَعَدٍّ), the sentence also has a direct object.

*The lawyer presented a piece of evidence.*  قدّم المُحامي دليلاً.

Some verbs take two and even three objects.

*The man gave his wife a gift.*  أعطى الرجلُ زوجتَه هديّةً.

In the following example, what is known as a second object in Arabic is called a direct object in English (i.e. *their deeds*), with the first object being the indirect object.

أرى اللهُ المُذنبينَ أعمالَهم حَسَرات.

*God showed the sinners (that the fruits of) their deeds as (nothing but) regrets.*

Passive sentences are derived from active ones and, therefore, may have one or more objects. A passive sentence in Arabic has a noun following the passive verb that corresponds to the direct object of the corresponding active sentence. In Arabic, the passive subject is termed 'deputy agent' (نائب فاعل), e.g.

| | |
|---|---|
| *The company imports cars.* | <div dir="rtl">تَستَوردُ الشركةُ السياراتِ.</div> |
| *The cars are imported.* | <div dir="rtl">تُستَوردُ السياراتُ.</div> |

If there is a second object in the corresponding active sentence, it is in the accusative (نصب) case in the passive sentence as in the sentences below.

أُلبِسَ الطفلُ زيَّ الجنود.

*The child was dressed in a soldier's uniform.*

### 3.6.1 *Components of a verbal sentence*

As indicated above, a verbal sentence principally comprises a verb and an agent and it can also have one or more objects. Passive sentences have a deputy agent (نائب فاعل) and in some cases also an object.

### 3.6.2 *Doubly transitive verbs (two objects)*

Some verbs modify two objects, e.g. (See sections 3.3.13-19.)

| | |
|---|---|
| *He sees life (as) work.* | <div dir="rtl">رأى: يرى الحياةَ عملاً.</div> |
| *She made her father her model.* | <div dir="rtl">جعَلَ: جعَلَتْ أباها قُدوةً.</div> |

| | |
|---|---|
| *I gave him my address.* | أَعْطى: أَعطيتُه عُنواني. |
| *He used his pen as a weapon.* | اتَّخَذَ: اتَّخَذَ قلمَه سلاحاً. |
| *She conveyed some happy news.* | بلَّغَ: بلَّغَتنا خَبَراً سعيداً. |
| *Suppose Seleem is your neighbour.* | هَبْ: هَبْ سليماً جارَكَ. |

Other doubly transitive verbs include the following:

| | | |
|---|---|---|
| *to make* صَيَّر | *to clothe* كَسا | *to inform* أبلغَ |
| *to dress* ألبَسَ | *to grant* مَنَحَ | *to leave* تَرَكَ |
| *to consider* اعتَبَرَ | *to donate* وَهَبَ | *to assume* ظنَّ |
| *to count* عَدَّ | *to claim* زَعَمَ | *to suppose* حَسبَ |
| *to detect* ألفى | *to find* وجَدَ | *to imagine* تخَيَّلَ |
| *to know* عَلِمَ | *to ask* سألَ | *to learn* تعلَّمْ |
| *to deem* خال | *to give* أهدى | *to reply* رَدَّ |

### 3.6.3 *Triply transitive verbs (three objects)*

These are verbs that modify three objects. Their use is rare in
Modern Standard Arabic.

أَعْلَمَ: أعلمتُ مُديرَ المكتب خالداً غائباً.

*I informed the manager that Khaled was absent.*

أخبَرَ: أخبَرَنا المُحاضِرُ الثقةَ أساسَ نَجاح العَمَل.

*The lecturer informed us that confidence was the basis of
business success.*

Other triply transitive verbs include the following.

| | | |
|---|---|---|
| *to report* نبَّأ | *to notify* أنبأَ | *to show* أرى |
| | *to narrate* حَدَّثَ | *to tell* خَبَّرَ |

### 3.6.4 *The five imperfect ن-verb forms* الأفعال الخمسة

The so-called five imperfect conjugations are imperfect second and third person conjugations with the following pronouns:

| | | |
|---|---|---|
| ن + ي + تفعل | | أنتِ تَفعَلينَ |
| ن + ا + تفعل | | أنتُما تَفعَلان |
| ن + و + تفعل | | أنتُم تَفعَلونَ |
| ن + ا + يفعل | | هُما يَفعَلان |
| ن + و + يفعل | | هُمْ يَفعَلونَ |

The attached nominative pronouns ا، و، ي are suffixed to these verb forms and they serve as agent with an active verb, deputy agent with a passive verb, and subject with a defective verb, e.g.

*They work.* (The *alif* is the agent.)      يَعمَلان.

*They are consulted.* (The *wāw* is the substitute.)    يُسْتَشارونَ.

*You will become.* (The *yā'* is the agent.)    سَتُصبحينَ.

The final ن marks the indicative mood (مضارع مرفوع) instead of *damma,* and its deletion marks the subjunctive (مضارع منصوب) and jussive (مـضـارع مـجـزوم) moods instead of *fatha* and *sukūn,* respectively (e.g. يفعلا، يفعلوا). (See sections 3.3.13.2.)

### 3.6.5 *Inflecting and non-inflecting verbs* إعراب الفعل وبناؤه

Inflection (إعراب) in general indicates a change in the function of a word. Words which undergo no change in their function, such as prepositions, do not show changes and are said to be uninflected (مَبني).

Table 1 shows non-inflecting verb forms (مبني) in the perfect, imperfect, and imperative and the markers used for each group.

Table 2 lists the inflecting forms (مُـعـرَب) of the imperfect indicative, subjunctive, and jussive and their markers.

Table 1  <u>NON-INFLECTING VERB FORMS</u>

| Marker | الماضي | المضارع | الأمر |
|---|---|---|---|
| ـَ | كَتَبَ، كتبت، أَكتبَنْ، أَكتبَنَّ | لأكتُبَنَّ، لنكتُبَنْ | |
| | كتبا، كتبَتا | | |
| ـُ | كتَبوا | | |
| ـْ | كتَبْنا، كتبْتُ يكتُبْنَ، تكتُبْنَ | اكتب، اكتُبْنَ، | |
| | كتبْتَ، كتبْت | | |
| | كتبتُما، كتبْتُم | | |
| | كتبتُنَّ، كتبْنَ | | |

deletion of ن      اكتبي، اكتبا، اكتبوا

deletion of long vowel      امْشِ، قُلْ، نَمْ

As can be seen in the two tables, the perfect and imperative forms are uninflected for mood (مـبني) and the imperfect is inflected for mood (مُعـرَب) except for the second and third person feminine plural. This applies to all its conjugations. An inflecting verb form (مُعـرَب) shows the mood markers on its end. A non-inflecting verb form has a marker that does not change. The table above illustrates which verb forms inflect, which ones do not, and what marking each type uses.

Table 2  <u>INFLECTING VERB FORMS (IMPERFECT)</u>

| | Marker | |
|---|---|---|
| أكتبُ، نكتبُ | ـُ | <u>Nom.</u> |
| تكتبُ، يكتبُ | | |
| تكتبان، تكتُبِينَ، تكتبونَ | ن | |
| يكتبان، يكتبونَ | | |
| أكتبَ، نكتبَ، يكتبَ، تكتبَ | ـَ | <u>Acc.</u> |
| تكتبي، يكتبا، تكتبا، يكتبوا، تكتبوا | deletion of ن | |

| | |
|---|---|
| أُكتبْ، نكتبْ، تكتبْ، يكتبْ، تكتبْنَ، تكتبْنَ | Juss. ـُ |
| تكتبي، يكتبا، يكتبوا، تكتبوا | deletion of ن |
| يَقُلْ، يصِل، يَمشِ، يغزُ | deletion of vowel |

### 3.6.6 *Agent* فاعل

According to Arabic grammatical analysis, the agent is nominative and must *follow* a sound, active verb; otherwise it is considered the subject of a nominal sentence. It may be (1) an overt inflected noun or noun phrase, (2) an overt non-inflected noun or noun phrase, or (3) a pronoun. With regard to its position, the agent may follow nouns that have a verbal force (اسم فــعل) and be a covert pronoun (see 4 below).

| | | |
|---|---|---|
| *The airplane has taken off.* | أقلعَت الطائرةُ. | ١. |
| *I like your work.* | يعجبُني عملُك | |
| *I like the novel, <u>Tale of Two Cities</u>.* | تعجبني "قصةُ مدينتين". | |
| *He has test-driven the new car.* | جرَّبَ (هو) السيارةَ الجديدة. | |
| *Someone to help you has come.* | جاءَ مَنْ يساعدُك. | ٢. |
| *She liked to travel by herself.* | أعْجَبَها أنْ تسافرَ وحدَها. | |
| *We sat in the sun.* | جَلَسْنا (نا) في الشَمس. | ٣. |
| *They took the evening flight.* | استقلّوا (و) طائرةَ المساء. | |
| *Quiet!* | صَهْ! (أنت) | ٤. |
| *Success is unlikely without work.* | هَيهاتَ النجاحُ بلا عمل. | |

### 3.6.7 *Deputy agent* نائب فاعل

In a passive sentence, the deputy agent is nominative and may be (1) an overt inflected noun, (2) a demonstrative, (3) a prepositional phrase, (4) an adverb, (5) a verbal noun, (6) a pronoun, and (7) a clause.

١- ضُرِبَتْ أوّلُ نقودٍ عربية بدمشق.

*The first Arab coins were minted in Damascus.*

٢- أخرِجَ هؤلاءِ من بيوتهم.

*Those were evicted from their homes.*

*Eating is allowed.* يُسمَحُ بالأكل. ٣-

*They fasted a month. (lit. A month was fasted.)* صِيمَ شهرٌ. ٤-

*Something good was done.* عُمِلَ عَمَلٌ نافعٌ. ٥-

*They were hurt in the accident.* أصيبوا (وِ) في الحادث. ٦-

*She was asked about her hobbies.* سُئِلَتْ (هي) عن هواياتها.

*It is not allowed to be late.* لا يُسْمَحُ أنْ تتأخَّرَ. ٧-

### 3.6.8 *Direct object* مفعول به

As the other two constituents of the sentence, the direct object may be (1) a noun, (2) a noun phrase, (3) an accusative attached pronoun, (4) an independent pronoun, and (5) a clause.

*We ask for forgiveness.* نرجو المغفرةَ. ١-

*I read that book.* قرأتُ ذلكَ الكتابَ. ٢-

*He heard us enter the house.* سمعَنا (نا) ندخلُ البيتَ. ٣-

*Thee we worship.* إيّاكَ نعبُدُ. ٤-

*I wish to visit you.* أودُّ أنْ أزورَك. ٥-

## 3.7 Gender number agreement between verb and agent

In a sentence beginning with a verb, the verb agrees in gender (but not number) with the following agent, e.g.

*Osama has arrived.* وصل أسامةُ. ١-

*The two ladies arrived.* وصلتْ السيّدتان. ٢-

*The scholars arrived.* وصل العُلماءُ. ٣-

*Marwan and Khaled arrived.* وصل مَروانُ وخالدٌ. ٤-

If the agent, however, is preceded by a particle of exception (إلا), the verb is always masculine even if the agent is feminine, e.g.

*Only Somaya arrived.*     ٥.   ما وصل إلاّ سُمَيَّةُ.

If the agent is separated from the verb by an intervening other word or phrase (e.g. prepositional phrase), either gender for the verb is permissible. That is, the verb may be in the masculine even if the agent is feminine, e.g.

*Layla has entered the house.*     دَخَلَتْ إلى البيت لَيلى.

or     دَخَلَ إلى البيتِ لَيلى.

## 3.8  Word order

In a sentence containing a verb, Arabic prefers verb-agent-object word order. (For a more detailed discussion, see Dickins and Watson, 1999, pp. 337-351, 377-382, 419-428, and Dickins, Hervey, and Higgins, 2002, pp. 116-119). One may also, however, use a subject-verb-object word order, e.g.

*Tariq works as a pilot.*     ١.   يعمَلُ طارقٌ طيّاراً.

*Tariq works as a pilot.*     ٢.   طارقٌ يعمَلُ طيّاراً.

It should be noted that while the meaning of 1 and 2 is practically the same, the agent in sentence 1 is rendered subject in sentence 2 and the clause يعمل طيارا serves as predicate.

There are certain grammatical constraints that determine the order in which words in a sentence are strung together. Some of these rules which apply to verbal sentences follow.

**Verb-object-agent** فعل – مفعول به – فاعل

This order is allowed in a verbal sentence if:
1.  The agent is modified by إلا, e.g.

ما جذب الزبائنَ إلاّ الأسعارُ المنخفضة.

*Nothing has attracted the customers but the low prices.*

254

2. The object is an attached pronoun and the agent is a noun (here the verb-object-agent order is the only possible one in a verbal sentence).

*We were appalled by her behaviour.*  راعَنا سُلوكُها .

3. An object pronoun is suffixed to the agent, e.g.

*The employee was married to her boss.*  تزوَّجَ الموظّفةَ رئيسُها .

4. The meaning is evident.

*Ali rode a horse.*  ركِبَ الحصانَ عليّ .

5. There is structural evidence of word roles (أخاك acc.).

*Your brother's coworkers blamed him.*  لامَ أخاك زُمَلاؤه .

## Object-verb-agent مفعول به – فعل – فاعل

This order is allowed if the following conditions obtain. The implied agent is in parentheses.

1. The object is in the initial position as a question word, e.g.

*Whom did you see?*  مَنْ رأيتَ (أنت) ؟

*Which food do you prefer?*  أيُّ طعامٍ تفضلون؟

2. The object is a separate pronoun.

*Thee we worship.*  إيّاكَ نعبُدُ (نَحنُ) .

In a nominal sentence, the basic word order is subject-predicate.

## Subject-predicate

The subject is in the initial position before the predicate if:

1. The subject is a particle which typically occupies the initial position such as a question word, conditional particle, or the exclamatory subject particle ما 'what', e.g.

*How many countries did you visit?*  كَم بلداً زرتَ؟

مَنْ يتأنّى يُدركْ ما تَمَنّى .

*He who moves cautiously will surely reach his goal.*

*How strange this story is!*  ما أغرَبَ هذه القصة!

Literally, *'What made this story strange!'*

2. The subject forms an *idāfa* structure with an interrogative.

255

*Whose car is in front of the house?* سَيَّارَةُ مَنْ أمامَ الدار؟

3. Both the subject and predicate are equivalent in definiteness with no evidence showing which one is intended as topic.

   *Your brother is my colleague.* أخوكَ زَميلي.

4. The subject is restricted to the predicate (modified by إلا or إنّما).

   *Life is but a dream.* ما الحياةُ إلاّ حُلْمٌ.

   *Salma is only a student.* إنَّما سَلمى طالبةٌ.

## Predicate-subject

The predicate is preposed if:

1. The predicate is an adverbial and the subject is indefinite.

   *We have company.* عندَنا ضُيوفٌ.

2. The predicate is a prepositional phrase and the subject is indefinite.

   *There is power in unity.* في الاتّحادِ قُوّةٌ.

3. The predicate is an interrogative word.

   *Where's your friend?* أينَ صديقُكَ؟

4. The subject is modified by إلا.

   *There is no God but Allah.* لا إلهَ إلاّ اللهُ.

5. The subject has a suffix that refers to the predicate.

   *The poor have their guardian.* للفُقَراءِ راعيهِم.

6. The predicate is an adverb of place.

   *This is Beirut. (You're listening to Radio Beirut.)* هُنا بَيْروتُ.

7. The predicate of كانَ is a clause.

   *Leila was cooking.* كانَتْ تطبُخُ لَيْلى.

8. The predicate is a prepositional phrase and the subject is indefinite.

   إنَّ في القصاصِ حياةً.

   *There is (preservation of) life in the penal code.*

   *Thanks are due to him who helps us.* إنَّما مَشكورٌ مَن يساعدُنا.

9. The predicate is restricted to the subject.

*No one but my brother-in-law is coming.*　ما قادمٌ إلاّ صِهْري.

## 3.9 Adverb of manner الحال

An adverb of manner (also termed 'circumstantial adverb') normally follows its referent. However, it must be preposed if:

1. A comparative noun is used to compare two states.

الدولارُ شراءً أغْلى مِنْهُ بَيْعاً.

*The dollar is more expensive, buying than selling.*

2. The referent is indefinite.

*Two cars passed us fast.*　تجاوَزَتْنا مُسرعةً سيَّارتان.

3. The referent is followed by إلاّ.

*Only your sister came back cheerful.*　ما رجع مُبتهِجاً إلاّ أختُك.

4. The adverb is a question word.

*How did you travel?*　كيفَ سافَرتِ؟

## 3.10 Attributive adjectives النَعْت

1. It is the norm that an adjective (or adjectives) follows the noun it modifies, e.g.

قرأت مقدِّمةَ ابن خَلدونٍ الطويلةَ.

*I have read Ibn Khaldoun's long Introduction.*

2. An adjectival can be a clause. In this case, if a noun is modified by two adjectivals, one being a single word and the other a clause, the single word should precede, e.g.

لَنا أستاذٌ مُملٌّ لا يصغي إليه أحَد.

*We have a boring professor to whom nobody listens.*

3. If a noun is indefinite, it may be separated from its adjective.

*We had a rainy day last week.*　أتانا يومٌ في الأسبوعِ الفائتِ مُمطِرٌ.

Sometimes the noun is modified by two adjectives that are separated from the noun by the particle لا or the particle إمّا. Separate particles must modify each one of the two adjectives:

Issam is neither tall nor short.     عِصامٌ لا قَصيرٌ ولا طويلٌ.

لِكَلِّ إنسانٍ نظرةٌ إمّا واقعيةٌ وإمّا خَيالِيةٌ.

*Everyone has a perspective, either realistic or fanciful.*

4. If two adjectives modify the same noun and one of them is a relative adjective (نِسبة), the *nisba* must come first.

*Modern Arabic literature.*     الأدَبُ العربيُّ المُعاصِرُ.

## 3.11 Prepositions حروف الجَرّ

Correct use of prepositions is one of the trickiest parts of Arabic. One of the greatest challenges for students of Arabic is knowing which preposition to use or whether to use a preposition at all. The main function of a preposition is to link one word to another. This may be a verb to a noun or a noun to another noun. In the former case, a preposition enables an intransitive verb to modify an object. There are nineteen proper prepositions. The glosses provided are approximate, since the exact meaning is determined by context.

| | | | |
|---|---|---|---|
| *except* حاشا | (with an oath) تَ | *with, in* بِ | *to* إلى |
| *except* عَدا | *many a* رُبَّ | *except* خَلا | *up to* حَتّى |
| *like* كَ | *in, on, at* في | *about* عَنْ | *on* عَلى |
| *of, from* مِنْ | *but for* لَوْلا | *to, for* لِ | *in order to* كَيْ |
| | *by* (for making an oath) وَ | | *since* مُذْ / مُنْذُ |

An additional group of words may also be included although they are considered by Arab grammarians as adverbs because these words denote time or place and form with the following noun an *idāfa* structure (see 3.3.7, items 4 and 5 under Accusative Nouns). They include the following.

| | | |
|---|---|---|
| *between* بَينَ | *after* بَعدَ | *in front of* أمامَ |
| *toward* جِهةَ | *south of* جَنوبَ | *under* تَحتَ |

| | | | | | |
|---|---|---|---|---|---|
| to the east شَرقَ | | below دونَ | | around حَولَ | |

at عِندَ  to the left of شِمالَ — to the north شِمالَ

before قَبلَ  over فَوقَ — to the west غَربَ

behind وَراءَ — in front of قُدّامَ

More so, even than other words, prepositions derive their meanings from context. This means that meaning cannot be assigned to a preposition out of context. For example, the preposition بـ may have these equivalences in English: zero in 1a below (under بـ), *by* in 1b, *with* in 2, *of* in 3, *for* in 4, *by* in 5, zero in 6, and so forth. Therefore, one should not expect a one-to-one correspondence between Arabic and English prepositions. The examples below illustrate the uses of prepositions and the categories of meaning associated with each one of them.

This preposition has three main uses.

إلى

1. Attaining destination in time and place.

   *He works from morning to evening.*  يعمل مِنَ الصباح إلى المساء.

   *She travelled from Beirut to Cairo.*  سافرَتْ من بيروتَ إلى القاهرة.

2. Accompaniment, in the sense also conveyed by مع.

   *Cents upon cents buy a house.*  الدراهمُ إلى الدراهمِ تشتري داراً.

3. Point of view, in the sense also conveyed by عند.

   القراءةُ أَحَبُّ إليَّ من مُشاهدة التلفاز.

   *Reading is preferable to me than watching television.*

بـ

This has 14 main uses.

1. Associative meaning, actual and figurative, respectively.

   a. *I have caught the bird.*  أمسَكْتُ بالطائر.

   b. *We passed by your father's village.*  مَرَرْنا بقَرية أبيك.

2. Instrumental: *I wrote with a pen.*  كتبتُ بالقلَمِ.

3. Explanatory: *He died of fever.*  ماتَ بالحُمّى.

4. Value: *I bought it for 50 liras.* اشتريتُها بخَمسينَ لَيْرة.

5. Oath: *I swear by God.* أُقسمُ بالله.

6. Causative: *Crying has made her blind.* ذهب البُكاءُ بِبَصَرها.

7. Substitutive: *I chose friendship over dispute.*

اخترتُ الصداقةَ بالخُصومة

8. Locative: *He lived in Baghdad.* عاش بِبَغداد.

9. Inclusive: *I bought the house with its furniture.*

اشتريتُ البيتَ بِأثاثه.

10. Accompaniment:

*So long! (Go with God's protection.)* بأمانِ الله.

*He lived in the countryside in peace* عاش في الريفِ بِسَلام.

11. Partitive: له ثروةٌ يستفيد بها أبناؤه.

*He has wealth from which his children benefit.*

12. Concerning, in the sense also conveyed by عَن:

*Ask a knowledgeable person about it.* فاسأل به خَبيرا.

13. Concerning, in the sense also conveyed by على:

*She trusts him with her life.* تأمَنُه بِحَياتها.

14. Emphatic (but otherwise redundant):

*Don't you know this is prohibited?* ألا تعلم بأنَّ هذا مَمنوع؟

*He put himself in a dilemma.* ألقى بنفسِه في وَرطة.

تَ (التاء)    Oath: (I swear) *By God.* (Old usage) تَالله.

حاشا    Exception: أضرَبَ العُمّالُ حاشا رئيسهم.

*All the workers went on strike except their foreman.*

حتّى    Completion: *We stayed up till dawn.* سَهرْنا حتّى الفَجر.

Exhaustion: أنفق مالَهُ في الخير حتّى آخرِ لَيْرة.

*He spent all his wealth on charity.*

خَلا    Exception:

*I know all her family except her brother.* أعرف أُسرَتَها خَلا أخيها.

| | |
|---|---|
| رُبَّ | Used either to increase or decrease the modified noun, a process determined by context. |

*Many a baby has no father (i.e., Jesus).* رُبَّ مَولودٍ ليس له أبٌ.

*Many a friend is closer than a real brother.* رُبَّ أخٍ لم تَلِدْهُ أمُّك.

عَدا    Exception:

*I work all year round except in July.* أعمَلُ طَوالَ السنةِ عدا تَمّوز.

عَلى    Superiority: *I prefer this to that.* أفضِّلُ هذا على ذاك.

Time (also conveyed by في):

*They surprised us when we were inattentive.* أخَذونا على حينِ غِرَّةٍ.

Preference, in the sense also conveyed by عن:

*Is she pleased with you?* أرَضِيَتْ عَلَيْك؟

Causative: *I thanked him for his favour.* شَكَرْتُه على صَنيعه.

Adversative denoting concession, in the sense also conveyed by مع: *She liked him despite his short stature.* أعجبَها على قِصَرِه.

Instrumental: *He played the lute.* عَزَفَ على العودِ.

Repair: *He failed, but he did not give up.* لقد فشلَ على أنّه لم يَيأس.

عَن    Deviation: *He deviated from his goal.* حادَ عَن هَدَفِه.

Distancing: *She despised office work.* رَغِبَتْ عنِ العَملِ المكتبيِ.

Time, in the sense also conveyed by *after*:

*I'll see you after a while.* سأراكُم عَن قَريبٍ.

Reference, in the sense also conveyed by على:

*He scrimped.* بخِلَ عَن نَفسِه.

Causative: زرناه عَن رغبةٍ بصداقته.

*We visited him in order to develop friendship.*

Substitution:

*He made the pilgrimage on behalf of his father.* حجَّ عَن أبيه.

في    Adverbial of time: *He works at night.* يعملُ في الليلِ.

Adverbial of place: *She lives in Meknas.* تسكنُ في مِكناسٍ.

Figurative: *He is a good role model for us.* لنا فيه قُدْوَةٌ حسنة.

Causal: عوقِبَ في مالٍ اختَلَسَه.

*He was convicted because of money he had embezzled.*

Locative, in the sense also conveyed by على:

*The paintings were fixed on the walls.* ثُبِّتَت اللوحاتُ في الجُدران.

كَ (الكاف)    Comparison: *She is like an angel.* هي كَالملاك.

Comparison, in the sense also conveyed by على:

*He remained unchanged (as is).* بقيَ كَما هو.

لِ (اللام)    Possession: *That car is mine.* تلك السيارةُ لي.

Semi-possession: *This key is to that door.* هذا المفتاح لذلك الباب.

Purpose: *Thank him because he protected you.* اشكريه لحمايَته لك.

Attribution:

*Table manners are for the French.* آداب المائدة للفَرَنسيين.

Destination, in the sense also conveyed by على:

*He fell on his hands.* خَرَّ لليَدَيْن.

Temporal: *I wrote it at the end of July.* كتبتُه لغُرَّةِ شهرِ تَمّوز.

Destination, in the sense also conveyed by في:

*He went his way.* مَضى لسَبيله.

لَ    Appeal for help: *I call on the ruler for help.* (archaic) يا لَلحاكم.

Exclamation: *How terrible!* يا لَلهَوْل!

مُنْذُ (مُذْ)    Temporal, in the sense also conveyed by *from*:

*I haven't seen him since Friday.* ما رأيتُه مُنذُ يومِ الجمعة.

Duration: ما رأيتُكَ مُنذُ ثلاثة أيام.

*I haven't seen you for three days* (past, negative verb).

مِنْ    This has nine main uses.

1. Origination: *We walked from the park.* سِرْنا منَ الحَديقة.

2. Duration: لَمْ أرَها مِن يومِ السَّبت.

*I haven't seen her since Saturday.*

3. Partitive (some):   مِنَ النَّاسِ مَنْ يُجزِلُ العَطاءَ.

  *Some people give abundantly.*

  *We ate some of their food.*   أكلنا شيئاً من طعامهم.

4. Specifying kind: *My watch is made of gold.*   ساعَتي مِنْ ذَهَب.

  *When it comes to fruit, I like grapes.*   أحبُّ العِنَبَ مِنَ الفواكه.

5. Emphatic (مِنْ redundant): *Is there a volunteer?*   هَل مِنْ مُتَطَوِّعٍ؟

  *No one showed up for our party.*   ما حَضَرَ حفلتَنا من أحَد.

6. Replacement:   أرَضيتُم بالحياة الدُّنيا مِنَ الآخرة؟

  *Do you prefer Worldly life to the Hereafter?* (Qur'ān)

7. Adverbial: *They met on Friday.*  (rare، في =.)   التَقوا مِنْ يوم الجمعة.

8. Reason:   عَشِقَها مِن جَمالِها.

  *He fell in love with her because of her beauty.*

9. Reference,  in the sense also conveyed by عَن:

  *He was unaware of it.*   كان في غَفلةٍ مِن أمرِه.

## 3.12 Negation النَفي

Negation is achieved by the use of a variety of particles, the weak verb لَيْسَ, and the noun غَيْر. The different particles affect the nouns and phrases they govern variably as in the examples.

*3.12.1 Negating verbs in the past*: This is accomplished through three particles (ما، لَمّا، لَمْ). Whereas the use of لَمّا and لَم requires a change in the verb form from past to مُضارع مَجزوم (jussive), ما does not affect the verb form at all. Note that ما with a perfect verb is stylistically less acceptable in MSA than لَم (RII versus RIII).

  *It did not rain in June.*   لَمْ تُمطِرْ في حَزيران.

  *The plane hasn't arrived yet.*   (rare, archaic)   لَمّا تَصِل الطائرةُ.

  *He did not learn French.*   ما تعَلَّمَ الفرنسيةَ.

Another use of ما involves negating a nominal sentence. Here ما behaves like لَيْسَ.

*That's not a book.*  (rare, archaic) .ماً هذا كتاباً

However, if negation by مـــا is limited by إلاً, then the sentence reverts to the regular subject-predicate (مبتدأ خبر) form.

*This is only a book.*  .ماً هذا إلاً كتابٌ

3.12.2 *Negating verbs in the imperfect indicative*: The particle لا is used for this purpose. It has no effect on the verb form.

*I don't eat meat.*  .لا آكُلُ اللحْمَ

The particle لا may also be used as a conjunction, in which case the two nouns conjoined by لا must contrast.

*That is a boy, not a girl.*  .ذلكَ وَلَدٌ لا بنتٌ

*I want the book, not the magazine.*  .أرَيدُ الكتابَ لا المجلّةَ

The particle لا may be used in complex sentences to modify each of the two clauses. The clauses may consist of either a nominal sentence, a perfect verb, a predicate, an adjective, or an adverb of manner (حال). لا must be used in both clauses, as in the examples.

.لا العُمّالُ يقبَلون بالتَفاوضِ ولا إدارةُ الشركة تُوافقُ على الإضراب

*Neither the workers nor the company administrators agree to negotiate a strike.*

*He neither wrote nor called.*  .لا كتبَ ولا اتّصَل

.أستاذُنا لا كاتبٌ ولا شاعرٌ، لكنّه عالمٌ

*Our professor is neither a writer nor a poet, but he is a scholar.*

*My sister is neither tall nor short.*  .أختي لا طويلةٌ ولا قصيرة

.جاءَ سالمٌ لا مُنشرحاً ولا مَهْموماً

*Salem showed up neither cheerful nor anxious.*

لا may combine with the interrogative *hamza*:

*Don't you like my cooking?*  ؟ألا يعجِبُكم طبخي

It may also combine with أَنْ (أَنْ+لا) to give ألّا, making the verb subjunctive منصوب.

*She decided not to travel.* قَرَّرَتْ ألّا تسافرَ.

A combination of إِنْ and لا produces إلّا which functions as a conditional particle, making the following verb مضارع مجزوم.

*If you don't eat, you will starve.* (rare) إلّا تأكُلْ تَجوعْ.

3.12.3 *Prohibitive* لا. This particle is thus named because it is used with negative commands. It is followed by the jussive.

*Do not write on the walls.* لا تكتبوا على الجُدران.

3.12.4 *Negating future time*: لَنْ is used to negate future time. It changes the form of the verb from indicative مـــضـارع مـــرفـــوع to subjunctive مضارع منصوب.

*We won't tolerate this behaviour.* لَنْ نحتَمِلَ هذا التَصَرُّف.

3.12.5 *Negating an entire class of a noun*: This is accomplished by لا (النافية للجنس) followed by an accusative noun (منصوب).

*He is alright.* لا بَأسَ به.

*There are no teachers at the school.* لا مُعَلِّمِينَ في المدرسة.

*There is no doubt about it.* لا رَيْبَ في ذلك.

لا combines with the interrogative *hamza*, as in this example.

*Aren't there any limits to your patience?* ألا حُدودَ لِصَبرِك؟

3.12.6 *Other negative particles*: These include إِنْ, لَيْسَ, and غَيْر.

1. The particle إِنْ functions like (1) the negative مـا, and (2) the weak verb لَيْسَ. In the latter function, it modifies a nominal sentence the subject being nominative (مرفوع) and the predicate accusative (منصوب) as follows:

*Men are but grown-up children.* (rare) إن الرجالُ إلّا أطفالٌ كبار.

*No one is better than anyone.* (rare) إنْ أَحَدٌ خَيْراً مِن أَحَدٍ.

265

2. The weak verb لَيْسَ modifies a nominal sentence. It keeps the subject nominative مَرفـوع and makes the predicate accusative مَنصوب.

*The weather is not hot.*　　لَيْسَ الطَقسُ حاراً.

3. غَـيْـرُ forms an *idāfa* structure with the following noun and is considered a noun in Arabic grammar. The word it combines with may be an adjective:

*This water is not good for drinking.*　　هذا الماءُ غَيرُ صالحٍ للشُرْب.

Note that, being a noun, غــير acquires the inflection appropriate for its position in the sentence. For example, غير is nominative in the example above because صــالحٌ للشــرب is the predicate of the sentence. So, if غــير is to be used in a sentence where the word with which it combines to provide the opposite meaning is an adverb of manner, for instance, it must take the adverbial case (accusative):

*Marwan came by car.*　　جاءَ مروانُ راكباً.

*Marwan came on foot.*　　جاءَ مروانُ غيرَ راكبٍ.

Another use of غــير is for exception. In this case, it is in the accusative and the following noun is in the genitive because غــير forms an *idāfa* structure with it, e.g.

*All the students came except Reem.*　　جاءَت الطالباتُ غَيْرَ ريم.

It may also function as agent, direct object, or object of a preposition in a sentence introduced by negative ما, e.g.

*Only Marwan came.*　　ما جاءَ غَيرُ مَروانٍ.

*I met only Marwan.*　　ما قابلتُ غيرَ مروانٍ.

*I heard from Marwan only.*　　ما سمعتُ من غيرِ مروانٍ.

## 3.13 Demonstratives اسمُ الإشارة

These pronouns are used to indicate specific people, animals, objects, and concepts. The most commonly used pronouns are distinguished by proximity, gender, case, and number.

In addition to the demonstratives in the table, there are a few demonstratives which indicate place, and by extension carry the meaning 'there' or 'there is/are'. These are: هُنا، هُناكَ، هُنالكَ، ثَمَّ، ثَمَّةَ. The ل in هُنالكَ signifies distance.

Note that only the dual pronouns change for case and that أُولئك and هؤلاءِ are used with both masculine and feminine nouns.

| | | القريب | القريب | | |
|البعيد|البعيد| | | | |
| ذلكَ | ذلكَ | هذا | هذا | مُفرَد | مذكَّر |
| ذَيْنكَ | ذانكَ | هذَيْن | هذان | مُثَنّى | = |
| أُولئكَ | أُولئكَ | هؤلاءِ | هؤلاءِ | جَمْع | = |
| تلكَ | تلكَ | هذه | هذه | مُفرَد | مؤنث |
| تَيْنكَ | تانكَ | هاتَيْن | هاتان | مُثَنّى | = |
| أُولئكَ | أُولئكَ | هؤلاءِ | هؤلاءِ | جَمْع | = |
| نصب وجر | رفع | نصب وجر | رفع | | |

## 3.14 Relative pronouns الاسم الموصول

A relative pronoun, as indicated by definite ال with which it begins, is definite. It modifies a clause which makes its meaning complete. Most relative pronouns decline for number and gender, as in the table below. Note that only the dual pronouns decline for case as well.

In addition to the variations of الَّذِي, there are three other relative pronouns. مَنْ is used with rational nouns, مـــ with non-rational nouns, and أيّ (followed by a genitive noun, or by a pronoun suffix) with both. The pronouns in the table are also used with rational and non-rational nouns except the plural forms which are used exclusively with nouns referring to humans, e.g.

| | |
|---|---|
| *The book that I have read.* | الكِتابُ الَّذِي قرأتُه. |
| *The books that I have read.* | الكُتُبُ الَّتِي قرأتُها. |
| | دَعَوْتُ كُلَّ مَنْ يعملُ في مَكتبي. |

*I invited all who work in my office.*

| | |
|---|---|
| *I liked what I saw.* | أعجَبَني ما رأيت. |
| *He'd like to work with any company.* | يحبُّ أنْ يعملَ في أيِّ شركةٍ. |
| *I know who the best performers are.* | أعرفُ أيَّهُم أحسنُ عَمَلاً. |

| مُذَكَّر | مُفرَد | الَّذِي | الَّذِي |
|---|---|---|---|
| = | مُثَنَّى | اللذانِ | اللَذَيْنِ |
| = | جَمْع | الَّذِينَ | الَّذِينَ |
| مُؤَنَّث | مُفرَد | الَّتِي | الَّتِي |
| = | مُثَنَّى | اللتانِ | اللَتَيْنِ |
| = | جَمْع | اللَواتي/اللاتي | اللَواتي/اللاتي |
| | | مَرفوع | مَنصوب |

Note that only أيّ fully inflects for case and it forms an *iḍāfa* structure with the noun it modifies, e.g.

| | |
|---|---|
| *I like any book on this topic.* | يعجبني أيُّ كتابٍ في هذا الموضوع. |

*I'll read any book on this topic.* سأقرأ أيَّ كتابٍ في هذا الموضوع.

أوصي بأيِّ كتابٍ في هذا الموضوع.

*I recommend any book on this topic.*

The pronoun أيّ is generally used in the singular masculine, but singular feminine is also found, e.g.

*Which university did you go to?* في أيِّ/أيَّةِ جامعةٍ درست؟

When the relative pronoun refers to a noun that is an object in the relative clause, the verb of the relative clause must have an attached pronoun suffixed to it, referring to that object. A frequent error made by students of Arabic occurs when they fail to make this reference.

أتعرِفينَ الفتاةَ الَّتي كلَّمتُها (ها)؟

*Do you know the girl to whom I talked?*

Similarly, if the referent is the object of a preposition, it must be pointed out in the relative clause by the appropriate pronoun, e.g.

(Literally) *The man who I wrote to him.* الرجلُ الذي كتبتُ له.

It is important to note that the relative pronoun is dropped if the referent is indefinite although it is kept in English, e.g.

لي زميلٌ (X) يتكلم ستَّ لغاتٍ.

*I have a colleague <u>who</u> speaks six languages.*

أيّ combines with مَن or ما, forming أيُّمَن 'whoever' and أيُّما 'whatever'. These compounds are mostly used as conditionals, e.g.

*Whoever comes first feeds the dog.* أيُّمَن يصلْ أولاً يُطعمْ الكلبَ.

## 3.15  Interrogatives الاستِفهام

Interrogatives include pronouns and particles. All interrogative pronouns are indeclinable and occupy initial sentence position.

*Where have you been?* أينَ كُنْتَ؟

| *Which magazine do you read?* | أيُّ مجلّة تقرأ؟ |
| *Which students were late?* | أيُّ الطلابِ تأخَّر؟ |
| *How are you?* | كَيْفَ حالُك؟ |
| *How did you travel?* | كيفَ سافَرت؟ |
| *When do I see you?* | مَتى أراك؟ |
| *Who is at the door?* | مَنْ بالبابِ؟ |
| *What is globalization?* | ما العَوْلَمة؟ |
| *What did you eat?* | ماذا أكلت؟ |

Much less common interrogatives in MSA are the following:

| *Where did you get that?* | أنّى لكَ هذا؟ |
| *When do you come back?* | أيّانَ تَرجِع؟ |

There are two particles, أ and هَلْ. They invite yes/no answers and can be used with a variety of structures.

| Verbal sentence: | *Did your brother arrive?* هل وصَلَ أخوك؟ |
| Nominal sentence: | *Is your father at home?* أوالدُكَ في الدار؟ |
| Choice question: | *Do you walk or ride?* أتَمْشي أمْ تركب؟ |
| Yes/no question: | *Did you read this book?* هل قرأتَ هذا الكتاب؟ |
| Modifying a preposition: | أفي داركُم مَسْبَح؟ |
| | *Is there a swimming pool in your house?* |

## 3.16 Conditional forms الشَرْط

Conditional forms, which include nouns and particles, modify sentences with two clauses; the subordinate clause is called الشَرْط (the condition clause, or protasis), and the main clause, the answer-clause (الجَـواب or apodosis). Some of these pronouns and particles make the mood of the imperfect verb jussive, others do not.

Compare the effect of أنّى, a pronoun, and إنْ, a particle, on the verbs following them. Both have the same effect.

| | أَنَّى تُسافِرْ أَتْبَعْكَ. |
|---|---|
| *Wherever you travel, I'll follow you.* | |
| *If you travel, I'll follow you.* | إِنْ تُسافِرْ أَتْبَعْكَ. |

Those nouns and particles in the table below marked جازِم induce the jussive mood. They allow only prepositions or the head of a genitive phrase مُضاف to precede them and yet keep their conditional sense and ability to make the following verbs jussive.

| *He who studies succeeds.* | مَنْ يَدرُسْ يَنجَحْ. |
|---|---|
| *To whomever you write, I write.* | لِمَنْ تكتُبْ أَكتُبْ. |
| *Not all who like you like me.* | لَيسَ كلُّ مَنْ يحبُّكَ يحبُّني. |

| حَرْف شَرْط | | اسِم شَرْط | |
|---|---|---|---|
| غير جازم | جازم | غير جازم | جازم |
| أمّا | إذْما | إذا | أيّانَ – مَتى |
| إمّا | إنْ | كُلَّما | أنَّى – أيْنَ |
| لَوْ | | حَيثُما لَمّا | أيْنَما |
| لَوْلا | | | أيّ – كَيفَما |
| لَوْما | | | مَنْ – مَهْما |
| | | | ما |

Two types of condition exist, the likely condition and the unlikely condition. إذا and إنْ are generally associated with likely conditions as in the examples below.

| *If you visit me, I visit you.* | إذا زُرتَني زُرتُك (أزورُك). |
|---|---|
| *If you visit me, I visit you.* | إنْ تَزُرُني (زُرتَني) أزورُك (زُرتُك). |

إذا must be followed by a perfect verb, and the answer-clause can be either past or present. On the other hand, إنْ can have up to four combinations of tenses with no evident change in meaning:

| | |
|---|---|
| Perfect-Perfect | *If you visit me, I visit you.* إنْ زرتَني زرتُك. |
| Imperfect-Perfect | إنْ تَزُرْني زرتُك. |
| Perfect-Imperfect | إنْ زرتَني أزورُك. |
| Imperfect-Imperfect | إنْ تَزُرْني أزورُك. |

The answer-clause in an إنْ-sentence is often introduced by فَ whether this answer-clause is positive or negative, e.g.

إنْ زُرتَ مصرَ فزُرِ الأهرامات.

*If you go to Egypt, visit the pyramids.*

إنْ زُرتَ مصرَ فلا تنسَ زيارةَ الأهرامات.

*If you go to Egypt, don't forget to visit the pyramids.*

Unlikely conditions are expressed with لَوْ and لَوْلا. لَوْ requires a perfect verb following it and the particle لَ prefixed to the verb of the answer-clause. لَوْلا is followed by a noun.

لَوْ أعطاني سيارتَه لَما أخَذتُها.

*If he had given me his car, I wouldn't have taken it.*

لَوْلا المَطرُ لَماتَ الزَرْعُ.

*Had it not been for the rain, the plants would have died.*

## 3.17 Transition words أدَوات الرَبط

Transition words, or connectors, are powerful devices which help students at almost all levels to produce cohesive discourse in speaking and writing. These words are used to bind words, phrases, and sentences together while expressing a particular function at the same time, such as contrasting ideas and expressing reason. They may be classified into six major groups. Each item is followed by an example and its translation. These translations are not meant to be the only possible renditions. Other translations may be more appropriate in different contexts. (See Al-Batal, Mahmoud, 1985 and Al-Warraki and Hassanein, 1994 for more detailed information and treatment.)

It is worth noting that و and ف are perhaps the most ubiquitous in MSA. Beside functioning as additive items (see the sections below), they may function as contrastive items, introduce circumstantial clauses and clauses in apposition, or have no English equivalent at all. Examine the uses of و and ف in the following passage:

صعدتُ إلى الحافلة ووضعت حقيبتي على الرف فوق مقعدي وجلست إلى جانب الشباك وأخذت أنظر إلى الركاب الآخرين عسى أن أعرف واحدا منهم. ولما حضر الجابي ناولته تذكرتي وابتسمت له شاكرا.

*I got on board the bus, (X) put my bag in the overhead compartment, (X) sat in a window seat, and started looking at the other passengers, hoping to recognize one of them. (X) When the conductor showed up, I handed him my ticket and smiled to him in appreciation.*

There are five instances of و, two of them may be translated as 'and'. Two serve almost the same function as that of the comma in English, and one may not be translated at all.

a. Additive items

| | | |
|---|---|---|
| الشُهرةُ والمالُ حديثُ الناس. | | وَ |
| *Fame and fortune are on everybody's lips.* | | *and* |
| وصل هاني فَأخوه. | | فَ |
| *Hani arrived, then his brother.* | | *then* |
| أعطني رقْمَ هاتفك فَأتَّصلَ بك. | | فَ |
| *Give me your phone number so that I can call you.* | | *so that* |

273

| | |
|---|---|
| صِلِ الحاسوبَ بالكَهرَباء. ثُمَّ افتَحْه. | ثُمَّ |
| Connect the computer to power, then turn it on. | then |
| أُحِبُّ الفواكِهَ وأيْضاً الخُضَرَ. | أيْضاً |
| I like fruits and vegetables, too. | too |
| سأشربُ القهوةَ أو الشايَ بعد العَشاء. | أوْ |
| I'll drink coffee or tea after dinner. | or |
| أتُفَضِّلُ القَهْوةَ أم الشاي؟ | أمْ |
| Do you prefer coffee or tea? | or |
| اخْتَلَفَ النُحاةُ في الإعْرابِ كَما اختَلفوا في أثرِه على المَعْنى. | كَما |
| Grammarians have disagreed about the syntactic functions of words and they have also disagreed about their semantic significance. | also |
| نَسِيَ سالم تَثبيتَ الحَجزِ بالطائرة، بالإضافةِ إلى ذلكَ لَمْ يحصُلْ على تأشيرةِ دُخولٍ إلى النمْسا. | بِالإضافةِ إلى |
| Salem forgot to reconfirm his airline reservations. In addition, he did not obtain an entry visa for Austria. | in addition (to) |
| هي تعملُ إلى جانبِ العنايةِ بأُسرَتها. | إلى جانب |
| She works, in addition to looking after her family. | in addition |
| لم يُحْضِرْ بحثَه علاوةً على تأخُّرِه. | علاوةً على |
| He didn't bring his paper, in addition to being late. | in addition |
| يُتقِنُ لُؤَيّ ثلاثَ لغاتٍ أوروبية فَضْلاً عن لُغَته الأم. | فَضْلاً عَن |
| Louai is proficient in three languages in addition to his own. | in addition to |

| | |
|---|---|
| **ناهيكَ** | راتِبي قَليلٌ ناهيكَ عَن غَلاء المَعيشة. |
| *let alone* | *My salary is low, let alone the high cost of living.* |
| **كَذلِكَ** | أبوه عالي الثَقافة وأمُّه كذلك. |
| *so, too* | *His father is highly educated and so is his mother.* |
| **بَل** | لَم يكنِ الجوّ حاراً بل لطيفا. |
| *rather* | *The weather wasn't hot, rather it was quite nice.* |
| **إمّا ... أو** | إمّا أنْ تَلتَزِمَ بقَوانينِ البِلاد أوْ تَرحَلَ عَنْها. |
| *either... or* | *Either abide by the laws of the land or leave it.* |
| **مِن جانِبٍ آخَرَ** | أساتِذَتُنا عُلَماءُ حَقّاً. مِن جانِبٍ آخَرَ إنَّهُم لا يُتقِنونَ فَنَّ التَدريس. |
| *on the other hand* | *Our professors are scholars indeed. On the other hand, they are not good teachers.* |
| **مِن جِهةٍ أخرى** | مِن جِهةٍ فشِل سليمٌ بالدِراسةِ لكِنْ مِن جِهةٍ أخرى نجح بالتِجارة. |
| *on the other hand* | *On the one hand, Seleem failed in his study; on the other hand, he succeeded in business.* |
| **مِثْل** | ثَمَّةَ مَعاجِمُ عَرَبِيَّةٌ قديمة مثلُ القاموسِ المُحيط. |
| *such as* | *There are old Arabic dictionaries such as Al-Qāmūs.* |
| **كَ** | أُصِبتُ بالتَسَمُّمِ البارحةَ مِن حَلْوى كَالّتي تأكُلينَها. |
| *like* | *I had poisoning yesterday from dessert like the one you're eating.* |
| **على سَبيلِ المِثال** | اقترح طبيبي عدّة فحوصاتٍ طبية كتحليلِ الدم على سَبيلِ المِثال. |
| *for example* | *My doctor suggested several tests such as a blood test, for example.* |

| | |
|---|---|
| امتَعَضَ الحاضرونَ مِن كلامِ المُحاضِرِ عَن دَوْرِ المَرأةِ في العملِ ولاسيَّما النساءُ مِنْهُم. | ولاسيَّما |
| *The audience was offended by the lecturer's talk about women's role in the labour force, particularly the women (in the audience).* | *particularly* |
| تفقَّدْتُ كُلَّ أوراقي قُبَيْلَ سَفَري وبخاصّةٍ جَوازَ سَفَري. | وبخاصّةٍ |
| *I checked all my documents before my trip, particularly my passport.* | *particularly* |
| أعجَبَ والدتي الحَرَمُ الجامعيّ خُصوصاً سَكَنَ الطالبات. | خُصوصاً |
| *My mother liked the campus, especially the dormitories.* | *especially* |
| نَقَلَ غَسّانُ أمْتِعَتَهُ إلى الطابَقِ العُلْويّ بما في ذلكَ كُتُبَه. | بما في ذلكَ |
| *Ghassan moved all his belongings upstairs, including his books.* | *including* |
| بالإشارةِ إلى كِتابِكُم المُؤرَّخِ في ١٠ تشْرينَ الأوَّلِ يُسعدُني أنْ أبلغَكُم مُوافَقَةَ المُديرِ على طلبِكُم. | بالإشارةِ إلى |
| *With regard to your letter dated October 10th, I am glad to inform you that the manager has approved your request.* | *with regard to* |
| سَتُكَلِّفُني هذه الرحْلةُ ثَلاثةَ أضْعافِ راتبي الشَهْريّ أيْ أكْثَرَ مِنْ ستّينَ ألْفِ لَيْرة. | أيْ |
| *This trip will cost me more than three times my monthly salary, that is, more than sixty-thousand lira.* | *that is* |
| يَنْبَغي عَلَيْنا السَيْطرةُ على التَلَوُّثِ. بِعبارةٍ أُخْرى يَجبُ مُواجَهَةُ أرْبابَ الصناعاتِ الثَقيلة. | بِعبارةٍ أُخْرى |
| *We should control pollution. In other words, we must take on the tycoons of heavy industries.* | *in other words* |

### b. Contrastive items

| | | |
|---|---|---|
| لكنْ/ولكن | انتَـــشَـــرَت الهَـــواتِفُ الخَلَويّة في المُدُنِ لكنْ لَيْسَ في الأرْياف. | |
| but | *Cellular phones have become common in towns, but not in the countryside.* | |
| لكنَّ | دعَوْتُه إلى حَفْلِ عَقْدِ قِران أخي لكنَّه اعتَذَر. | |
| but | *I invited him to my brother's wedding, but he declined.* | |
| و | قلتُ لها إني قابلت الرئيس ولم تصدقني. | |
| but | *I told her that I met the President, but she didn't believe me.* | |
| إلاَّ أنَّ | الكُوَيْتُ مِن أغنى البِلاد العربية بالنفْطِ إلاَّ أنَّه يَفْتَقِرُ إلى الأراضي الزراعية. | |
| however | *Kuwait is one of the richest Arab countries in oil. However, it lacks agricultural lands.* | |
| أمّا | طارِقٌ تونسيٌّ أمّا أحمَد فعِراقيٌّ. | |
| but | *Tareq is Tunisian, but Ahmed is Iraqi.* | |
| مُقارنةً بـ | هذا عَمَلٌ مُريح بالمُقارنةً بعَمَلي السابِق. | |
| compared to | *This is a comfortable job compared to my previous one.* | |
| مَعَ ذلك | باعَتْ دارَها وسيّارَتَها وحُليَّها ومَعَ ذلكَ لَم تَسْتَطِعْ إيفاءَ دَيْنها. | |
| despite | *She sold her house, car, and jewellery. Despite that, she could not pay off her debt.* | |
| مَعَ أنَّ | هو لاعِبُ كُرَةِ سَلَّةٍ ناجِح مَعَ أنَّه لَيْسَ طويلاً. | |
| although | *He is a successful basketball player, although he is not tall.* | |

| | |
|---|---|
| تَستَخدِمُ السُعوديَّةُ الريالَ كَنَقدٍ لَها بَيْنَما تستَخدِمُ الكُوَيتُ الدينار. | بَيْنَما |

*Saudi Arabia uses the riyal as its currency, whereas Kuwait uses the dinar.* — whereas

| | |
|---|---|
| سلسلةُ جبال لُبْنانَ الغَربية مُغَطَّاةٌ تَقريباً بالغابات. على عَكْسِها سلسلةُ جبال لُبْنانَ الشَرقية فَهيَ شِبْهُ عارية. | على عَكْس |

*The western Mount Lebanon is almost completely covered with woods. By contrast, the eastern range is almost barren.* — by contrast

| | |
|---|---|
| سَيَستَمِرُ عامِر بِمُمارَسة رياضَته اليَوْمِيَة حَتى وَلَوْ اضْطُرَّ للاستغناءِ عَنْ قَيْلولَته. | حَتَّى وَلَوْ |

*Amer will continue to exercise daily even though he has to give up his siesta.* — even though

| | |
|---|---|
| تَسْتَصلِحُ سوريةُ مِساحاتٍ واسعةً من الأراضي سَنوِيّاً على الرَغْمِ مِنْ نَقْصٍ حادٍّ في المِياه. | على الرَغْمِ مِن |

*Syria is reclaiming vast areas of land annually in spite of a severe shortage of water.* — in spite of

| | |
|---|---|
| يَتَمَنَّى أحمدُ أنْ يُتابِعَ دراسَتَهُ في أوروبا بَيْدَ أنَّ أسْرَته لا تَستَطيعُ تَحَمُّلَ نَفَقات دِراسَته. | بَيْدَ أنَّ |

*Ahmed wishes to continue his education in Europe. However, his family cannot afford the cost of his education.* — however

| | |
|---|---|
| لقد فَقَدتْ أملاكَها وقاطَعَتْها أسرتُها وانْقَطَعَ دَخْلُها. مَهْما يَكُنْ مِنْ أمرٍ فهيَ لا تَزالُ مُتَفائلةً. | مَهْما يَكُنْ مِنْ أمرٍ |

*She has lost her property, is shunned by her family, and lost her income. Nonetheless, she is still optimistic.* — nonetheless

| | |
|---|---|
| على أيِّ حال | إنِّي مَشْغولٌ اليومَ وبقيّةَ الأسبوعِ. على أيِّ حال سنَلتَقي في حَفلِ تَخَرُّجِ هبة في الشهرِ المُقبِل. |
| *however* | *I am busy today and for the rest of the week. We will meet, however, at Heba's graduation party next month.* |
| بَلْ | هذه المَضْغوطات قَليلَةُ الفائدة، بَلْ إنَّها قَد تَضُرُّ صحّتَك. |
| *rather* | *These pills have little benefit; rather they might do your health harm.* |
| بَلْ (مع النَفي) | لا يَتَخَصَّصُ هُمامُ بأمْراضِ القَلبِ فَحَسْب بَلْ بِجِراحَتِه أيْضاً. |
| *not only... but also* | *Homam specializes not only in cardiology, but also in heart surgery.* |
| عِوَضاً عَن | ما رأيُكُم بإهداءِ نَسيبٍ وعَروسِه رِحلةً إلى قُبْرُص عِوَضاً عَن أدَوات المَطبَخ؟ |
| *instead of* | *What do you think about giving Naseeb and his bride a vacation in Cyprus instead of kitchen utensils?* |
| بَدَلاً مِن | سَبَحْتُ أربَعينَ دَقيقةً بَدَلاً مِنَ الجَري حَوْلَ المَلعَبِ في هذا الحَرِّ. |
| *instead of* | *I swam for forty minutes instead of jogging in this heat.* |
| مِن ناحية أُخْرى | سَمِعْتُ الكَثيرَ عَن لُطْفِها وجَمالِها وسُمْعة عائِلتِها. مِن ناحية أُخْرى هي لَم تَحْصُلْ على شَهادةٍ جامعيّةٍ ولم تَعمَلْ أبَداً. |
| *on the other hand* | *I've heard a great deal about her nice manners, beauty, and good family. On the other hand, she didn't get a degree and she never worked.* |

c. Causative items

| | |
|---|---|
| إذْ | اضْطُرَّت هُدى إلى مُرافَقة أبيها المُسافِر إلى أمريكا إذْ أنَّه لا يَتَكَلَّمُ أيَّةَ لُغةٍ أجنبية. |
| *because* | *Houda had to escort her father to America because he speaks no foreign languages.* |
| بِما أنَّ | لِمَ لا تأخُذينَ إجازةً أطْوَلَ بِما أنَّكِ سَتُسافِرينَ خارِجَ البَلد؟ |
| *since* | *Why don't you take a longer vacation, since you will be travelling out of town?* |
| مِنْ هُنا | مِنْ هُنا يَتَبَيَّنُ لنا ضَعْفَ حُجَّة مُؤَيِّدي الأسواق الحُرّة. |
| *this* | *This indicates the weak argument of those advocating free markets.* |
| لأنَّ | أحبُّ المَشْيَ لأنَّهُ يساعدُني على التَفكير. |
| *because* | *I like walking because it helps me to think.* |
| بِسَبَب | رَحَلَ مَرْوانُ عَن قَطر بِسَبَب رُطوبة جَوِّها. |
| *because of* | *Marwan left Qatar because of its humid weather.* |
| نَظراً لـ | هي لا تأكلُ الحَلْوى أبَداً نَظراً لإصابَتِها بالسُكَّريّ. |
| *because* | *She never eats dessert because she is a diabetic.* |
| إذْ أنَّ | لا أظُنُّهُ قادراً على شِراءِ دارٍ جديدةٍ إذْ أنَّه بِلا عَمَلٍ الآن. |
| *because* | *I don't think he will be able to purchase a new house because he is unemployed now.* |
| بِفَضْلِ | وَصَلَتْ سِنْغافورة إلى هذا المُستَوى مِنَ المعيشة بِفَضْلِ سِياسة حُكومَتِها. |
| *thanks to* | *Singapore has attained this standard of living thanks to the policies of its government.* |

| | |
|---|---|
| يجبُ أَنْ نَنْتَظِرَ ساعتَيْنِ أُخرَيَيْنِ حَيْثُ أَنَّ مَوْعِدَ إقلاعِ طائِرَتِنا قَدْ تأَخَّرَ. | حَيْثُ أَنَّ |
| *We have to wait for two more hours because our flight has been delayed.* | *because* |
| اتَّصِلي مِنْ فَضْلِك بِوَفاء لِتَدْعيها إلى العَشاءِ. | لِ |
| *Please call Wafā' to invite her to dinner.* | *in order to* |
| خُذي الحافِلةَ كَيْلا تَبْتَلّي بالمَطَر. | كَيْلا |
| *Take the bus in order not to get wet.* | *in order not to* |
| جاؤونا في الأسْبوعِ الأخيرِ مِن رَمَضانَ لكَيْ يقْضوا العيدَ مَعَنا. | لِكَيْ |
| *They came to us in the last week of Ramadan in order to spend the Eid with us.* | *in order to* |
| لا آكُلُ قَبْلَ النَوْمِ لئَلا أُصابَ بالتُخْمة. | لئَلا |
| *I don't eat right before going to bed in order not to get indigestion.* | *in order not to* |
| تَسْتَيْقظُ رَشا في الرابِعةِ صَباحاً حَتّى تَدْرُسَ قَبْلَ الذَهابِ إلى المَدْرَسة. | حَتّى |
| *Rasha gets up at four in the morning in order to study before going to school.* | *in order to* |
| لقَدْ اشتَروا كُتُباً عَن تَدمُرَ وقرَؤوها لذلكَ لا حاجةَ لَهُم بِدَليلٍ سِياحيّ. | لِذلكَ |
| *They have bought books on Palmyra and read them. Therefore, they have no need for a tourist guide.* | *therefore* |
| كانَ الطَقْسُ ماطِراً والطُرُقاتُ غَيْرُ جَيِّدة والليلُ قَريب؛ وهكَذا فَضَّلْنا أَنْ نَنامَ في فُنْدُقٍ على الطَريق. | وهكَذا |
| *It was raining, the roads were bad, and it was getting dark. Therefore, we preferred to spend the night at a hotel on the road.* | *therefore* |

بِغَرَض

رَكِبْتُ القِطارَ إلى لَنْدَن بِغَرَضِ زِيارةِ المُتْحَف البِريطاني.

for the purpose of

*I took the train to London for the purpose of visiting the British Museum.*

بِهَدَف أَنْ

فَتَحَتِ الحُكومةُ أَبْوابَ الاستيراد والتَصْدير بِهَدَف أَنْ تُنَشِّطَ الاقتصاد.

for the purpose of

*The government relaxed the restrictions on imports and exports for the purpose of revitalizing the economy.*

مِن هُنا

لَقَد دَرَسَ كُتُبَ النَحْو وقرأ الأَدَبَ وحَفِظَ القُرآن. مِنْ هُنا أتى أسلوبُه السَلِسُ المُؤَثِّر.

hence

*He studied grammar books, read the literature, and memorized the Qur'ān; hence his flowing, effective style.*

مِن أَجْلِ

ذَهَبْتُ إلى الطَبيب مِن أجلِ فَحصٍ جِسْمِيٍّ عام.

for

*I went to the doctor for a general physical check-up.*

لِهذا السَبَب

هيَ مِن عُشّاقِ الموسيقا الأَندَلُسِيَّة، ولِهذا السَبَب تَخَصَّصَتْ بالشِعْرِ الأَنْدَلُسيّ.

for this reason

*She is a fan of Andalusian music. For this reason, she specialized in Andalusian poetry.*

لِئَلّا

أَحْمِلُ هذه المُفَكِّرةَ دائماً لِئَلّا أَنْسى مَواعيدي.

lest

*I always carry my pocket calendar lest I forget my appointments.*

نَتيجةً لِذلك

قَضى طَوالَ النَهارِ في المَسْبَح دون وَضعِ مَرْهَمٍ واقٍ مِنَ الشَمْس فأُصيبَ نَتيجةً لِذلك بحُروقٍ شَديدة.

as a result

*He spent the whole day at the pool without applying any sunscreen lotion. As a result, he suffered severe sunburn.*

### d. Sequential items

| | |
|---|---|
| أوَّلاً، ضَعي المَقاديرَ في الخَلَّاط. ثانياً، اخلطيها لِمُدّة دقيقة. | أوَّلاً، ثانياً |

*First, put the ingredients in the mixer. Second,*    *first, second*
*mix them for one minute.*

| | |
|---|---|
| أخيراً لَمْ يَسْتَطِعْ حُسامُ مُقاوَمةَ الحَنينِ لِوَطَنِه فتَرَكَ عَمَلَه وعاد. | أخيراً |

*Finally, Hussam could no longer stand his home-*    *finally*
*sickness, so he quit his job and went back.*

| | |
|---|---|
| بادئَ ذي بَدْء يجبُ ألاّ نَنسى أهميَّةَ هذه المُبادَرة. | بادئَ ذي بَدْء |

*First of all, we should not forget the*    *first of all*
*importance of this initiative.*

| | |
|---|---|
| يَلي هذه النُّقطةَ مَفهومُ وَعيِ الناس لحاضرِهم. | يَلي هذا |

*Next comes the notion of the people's aware-*    *next*
*ness of their current situation.*

| | |
|---|---|
| في النِهاية يُستَحسَنُ تَلخيصُ النقاط التي بُحثَت. | في النِهاية |

*Finally, here is a summary of the points discussed.*    *finally*

| | |
|---|---|
| خِتاماً أتوَجَّهُ بالشُكرِ لِكُلِّ مَنْ ساهَمَ في تَنفيذِ هذاالمشْروع. | خِتاماً |

*Finally, I'd like to thank all who contributed*    *finally*
*to the completion of this project.*

### e. Conditional items

| | |
|---|---|
| سَتَجدينَهُ في مَكتَبِه إذا اتَّصَلت به بَعدَ العاشرة. | إذا |

*You will find him in his office if you call him at ten.*    *if*

| | |
|---|---|
| لَنْ تَلحَقَ بالقطارِ وَإنْ رَكَضتَ إلى المَحَطّة. | وَإنْ |

*You won't catch the train even if you run to*    *even if*
*the station.*

| | |
|---|---|
| في حال | في حالِ نُزولِكَ في بَلَدِنا أرجو أنْ تَتَّصِلَ بِنا. |
| in case | *In case you are in our town, please give us a call.* |
| ما لَمْ | ضَعِ الكُتُبَ هُنا ما لَمْ يُطْلَبْ مِنْكَ وَضْعُها في مَكانٍ آخَرَ. |
| unless | *Put the books here unless you're asked to put them somewhere else.* |
| إنْ لَمْ | سَوفَ تُسْرَقُ سيّارَتُك إنْ لَمْ تَقفِلْها. |
| if not | *Your car will be stolen if you do not lock it.* |
| بِشَرْطِ | سَأتناولُ الغَداءَ مَعَك بِشَرطِ أنْ تَقبَلَ دَعوَتي إلى العَشاء. |
| provided | *I'll have lunch with you provided you accept my invitation to dinner.* |
| طالَما | لَنْ تُحَقِّقَ غايَتَك طالَما أنَّكَ تُؤَجِّلُ البَدْءَ في العَمَل. |
| so long as | *You won't realize your goal so long as you put off beginning it.* |
| وإلاّ | يَحْسُنُ أنْ تَنطلِقَ صَباحاً باكراً وإلاّ فَلَنْ تَسْتَطيعَ العَوْدةَ في ذاتِ اليَوْم. |
| otherwise | *You had better set out early in the morning. Otherwise, you won't be able to return on the same day.* |
| عَلى أنْ | خُذْ هذا المَبْلَغَ على أنْ تَرُدَّهُ في الشَهْرِ المُقْبِل. |
| on the condition | *Take this amount on the condition that you pay it back the next month.* |
| لَوْ | لَوْ كُنْتُ مَكانَك لَما تَرَدَّدْتُ في شِراء تلكَ الأسْهُم. |
| if | *If I were you, I would not have hesitated in buying those shares.* |
| إلاّ إذا | لَنْ أتابِعَ السَفَرَ إلاّ إذا تَحَسَّنَ الجَوّ. |
| unless | *I will not resume travelling unless the weather improves.* |

| | |
|---|---|
| ما كانَ باستطاعَتي إنجازُ هذه المَهمّة لَوْلا مُساعَدَتها. | لَوْلا |
| *I would not have been able to accomplish this* *mission had it not been for her assistance.* | *had it not* |
| ما كُنتُ لأَنْجحَ لَوْ لَمْ أَتلقَّ مُساعدةً منه. | لَوْلَمْ |
| *I wouldn't have succeeded if I had not received* *assistance from him.* | *if not* |
| سَوْفَ تُلغي رَنْدة سَفَرَها مالَم تتحَسَّنْ صحّةُ ابنها. | مالَمْ |
| *Randa will cancel her trip unless her son gets better.* | *unless* |

## f. Summative and other items

| | |
|---|---|
| باختصار إنَّ مَنافعَ هذا المَشروعِ تَزيد بكثيرٍ عَن مَآخذِه. | باختصار |
| *In short, the advantages of this project far* *outweigh its disadvantages.* | *in short* |
| لَقَـد أُلغِيَتْ الرحْلةُ إلى الدار البَيْضاء، وقد أَشْعَرَتْنا الشَركةُ بالإلغاءِ على الأَقَل قبلَ خُروجنا إلى المَطارِّ. | عَلى الأَقَلّ |
| *The flight to Casa Blanca was cancelled, and* *the airline notified us at least before leaving* *for the airport.* | *at least* |
| كَما نَوَّهْت/أَشَرْت  وكما نَوَّهْتُ مِن قَبْلُ لا بُدَّ مِن تَحسينِ شَبَكَةِ الاتِّصالات لاجتذابِ الاستثمارات. | كَما نَوَّهْت/أَشَرْت |
| *As noted before, the communications network* *must be improved to attract investments.* | *as noted* |
| بِصـورةٍ عـامّـة سَـتَظَلُّ هذه النقـاطُ مَـوْضِعَ بَحْثٍ في المُستَقبَلِ المَنظور. | بِصورةٍ عامّة |
| *In general, these points will continue to be* *studied for the foreseeable future.* | *in general* |
| يحُقُّ للمُقيم امتلاكُ العَقار سَواءَ كانَ مُواطناً أَمْ وافداً. | سَواءَ... أَمْ |
| *Residents (of the country) must have the right* *to own real estate whether they are citizens or aliens.* | *whether... or* |

في هذه الحال عَلَيْنا أنْ نَكونَ أكثَرَ حَذَراً. | في هذه الحال

*In this case, we must be more cautious.* | *in this case*

لا بُدَّ لِكُلِّ مَنْ يُريدُ تَسَلُّقَ الجِبال أنْ يكونَ لائِقاً جِسْمِياً. | لا بُدَّ

*Anyone who wants to climb mountains must* | *must*
*be physically fit.*

كُلَّما تَحَسَّسَ العامِلُ مَسْؤوليّتَه زادَ إنْتاجُه. | كُلَّما

*The more a worker is aware of his* | *the more.. the more..*
*responsibilities, the greater his productivity.*

راقب الوالدان طفلهما وهو يمشي خطواته الأولى. | و

*The two parents watched their toddler* | *(circumstantial)*
*take his first steps.*

راقبنا المرّيخ، وهو الكوكب الرابع بالمجموعة الشمسية، | و
بمنظار فلكي.

*We observed Mars, which is the fourth* | *which/who*
*planet in the solar system, through a telescope.*

ما إنْ أقلَعَتِ الطائِرَةُ حَتّى أعلَنَتِ المُضيفةُ عَنْ تَقديمِ | ما إنْ.. حَتّى
المُرَطِّبات.

*No sooner did the plane take off than the* | *no sooner than..*
*flight attendant announced the serving of refreshments.*

فَتَحْتُ بابَ شَقَّتي وإذا بالهاتِف والتِلفازِ وجهازِ | وإذا بِـ
التَسْجيلِ على الأرض.

*I opened the door of my apartment and there* | *s.t. unexpected*
*were the telephone, the TV, and the stereo*
*lying on the floor.*

ما كادَتْ أمّي تَضَعُ رِجلَها على الدَرَجةِ حَتّى سَقَطَتْ | ما كادَ.. حَتّى
على الأرض.

*My mother had hardly put her foot on the* | *hardly.. when*
*step when she fell down.*

إِنْ.. فَإِنَّما..        إِنْ دَلَّ هذا التَـفكيـرُ على شَيْءٍ، فَـإِنَّـما يَدُلُّ على عَـدَمِ
قَناعَةٍ بِجَدْوى تَعليمِ اللُغاتِ الأَجْنَبِيّة.

*This mentality indicates lack of conviction*     *if it v./ it v.*
*in the usefulness of teaching foreign languages.*
*(more lit.) If this thinking indicates anything, it is the lack*
*of conviction in the utility of teaching foreign languages.*

مِنْ نافلةِ القَوْل        ومِنْ نافلةِ القَوْلِ أَنَّ مُساعدةَ المُتَضَرِّرين بالزَلازِل إِنَّما
يندرِجُ تحتَ رُكنِ الزكاة.

*Needless to say, helping the victims of the*     *needless to say*
*earthquake is part of a Muslim's obligation.*

غَنِيٌّ عَنِ البَيان        وغَنيٌّ عَنِ البَيانِ أَنّ ادِّعاءَه لا أَساسَ له مِنَ الصحة.

*Needless to say, his claim is groundless.*     *needless to say*

## 3.18 Numbers اسم العَدَد

Numbers with nouns are a complex area for learners of Arabic. The complexity is due to the need to apply several rules simultaneously. For example, to express the meaning 'five records' خَمسةُ سجلّات, you have to be aware of the following facts in order to apply the appropriate rules:

- whether the noun is masculine or feminine
- whether the noun is singular or plural
- whether the number is between three and ten
- whether to 'add' the noun to the number
- whether the number is declinable or whether it is a compound number

3.18.1 *Cardinal numbers*: These denote quantity. The chart below illustrates the relationship among the components of a phrase expressing number. The two cases the counted noun assumes are genitive (gen.) with numbers 3-10, 100, and 1000, and accusative (acc.) with 11-99, including the tens (20, 30, etc.).

287

| NOUN FORM تركيب الاسم | | NUMBER AND COUNTED NOUN العدد والاسم المعدود | | |
|---|---|---|---|---|
| Case | Number | Feminine | Masculine | |
| variable | s. | سَيَّارةٌ | كِتابٌ | ١ |
| variable | d. | سَيَّارَتان | كِتابان | ٢ |
| gen. | pl. | خَمْسُ سَيَّارات | خَمسةُ كُتُبٍ | ١٠-٣ |
| acc. | s. | إحْدى عَشْرةَ سيارةً | أحَدَ عَشَرَ كِتاباً | ١١ |
| acc. | s. | إثْنَتا عَشْرةَ سيارةً | إثْنا عَشَرَ كِتاباً | ١٢ |
| acc. | s. | ثَلاثَ عَشْرةَ سَيَّارةً | ثَلاثةَ عَشَرَ كِتاباً | ١٩-١٣ |
| acc. | s. | عِشْرونَ سَيَّارةً | عِشْرونَ كِتاباً | ٩٠-٢٠ |
| acc. | s. | إحْدى وعشْرونَ سَيَّارةً | واحدٌ وعشْرونَ كِتاباً | ٢١ |
| acc. | s. | إثْنَتان وعشْرونَ سَيَّارةً | إثْنان وعشْرونَ كِتاباً | ٢٢ |
| acc. | s. | ثَلاثٌ وعشْرونَ سَيَّارةً | ثَلاثةَ وعشْرونَ كِتاباً | ٢٣ |
| gen. | s. | مئَةُ سَيَّارةٍ | مئَةُ كِتابٍ | ١٠٠ |
| gen. | s. | ألْفُ سَيَّارةٍ | ألْفُ كِتابٍ | ١٠٠٠ |
| gen. | s. | مِليونُ سَيَّارةٍ | مِليونُ كِتابٍ | ١٠٠٠٠٠٠ |

Summary:
- 1 and 2: The case of the counted noun varies according to its grammatical status in the sentence.
- 3-10: The counted noun is plural indefinite genitive.
- Compound numbers (13-19) are invariable, that is, they maintain the same indefinite accusative inflection regardless of their position.

*I have thirteen books.* عندي ثلاثةَ عَشَرَ كِتاباً.

288

اشتريتُ ثلاثةَ عَشَرَ كتاباً. *I bought thirteen books.*

قرأتُها في ثلاثةَ عَشَرَ كتاباً. *I read this in thirteen books.*

- 11 to 99: The counted noun is singular indefinite accusative.
- 100, 1000, 1,000,000: The counted noun (m. or f.) is singular indefinite genitive.

3.18.2 *Ordinal numbers*: These are used to rank order entities. There is total agreement in definiteness, number, case, and gender between the noun and the ordinal number. In definite phrases (see below), the article may be used with the noun and the number. Indefinite phrases obviously are without the article (e.g. كتابٌ ثانٍ). The ordinal numbers are:

أوّل، ثاني، ثالث، رابع، خامس، سادس، سابع، ثامن، تاسع، عاشر، عشرون، مئة، ألف

| | | |
|---|---|---|
| ١ | الكتابُ الأوّلُ | الصَفْحَةُ الأولى |
| ٢ | الكتابُ الثاني | الصَفْحَةُ الثانية |
| ٣-١٠ | الكتابُ الثالثُ | الصَفْحَةُ الثالثةُ |
| ١١ | الكتابُ الحادي عَشَرَ | الصَفْحَةُ الحاديةَ عَشْرَةَ |
| ١٢ | الكتابُ الثاني عَشَرَ | الصَفْحَةُ الثانيةَ عَشْرَةَ |
| ١٣-١٩ | الكتابُ الثالثَ عَشَرَ | الصَفْحَةُ الثالثةَ عَشْرَةَ |
| ٢٠ | الكتابُ العشْرونَ | الصَفْحَةُ العشْرونَ |
| ٢١ | الكتاب الواحدُ والعشْرونَ | الصَفْحَةُ الحاديةُ والعشْرونَ |
| ٢٢ | الكتاب الثاني والعشْرونَ | الصَفْحَةُ الثانيةُ والعشْرونَ |
| ٢٣ | الكتاب الثالثُ والعشْرونَ | الصَفْحَةُ الثالثةُ والعشْرونَ |
| ١٠١ | الكتابُ المئةُ والواحدُ | الصَفْحَةُ المئةُ والواحدةُ |
| ١٠٢ [5] | الكتابُ المئةُ والثاني | الصَفْحَةُ المئةُ والثانيةُ |

[5] العبارة: " الكتابُ الثاني بَعْدَ المئة" مستخدمة أيضاً.

الكتابُ المئةُ والخامسُ     الصَفْحَةُ المئةُ والخامسةُ     ١٠٥

الكتابُ المئةُ والحادي عَشَر     الصَفْحَةُ المئةُ والحاديةَ عَشْرَةَ     ١١١

الكتابُ المئتان والثاني عَشَر   الصَفْحَةُ المئتان والثانيةَ عَشْرَةَ    ٢١٢

الكتابُ الألفُ والحادي عَشَر   الصفحةُ الألفُ والحاديةَ عَشْرَةَ    ١٠١١

The case of ordinal numbers is determined by the grammatical status of the noun in the sentence, as in these examples.

قرأتُ الكتابَ المئةَ والثالثَ.        في الصفحةَ المئة والثالثة.

### 3.18.3 *Number noun agreement*

If the number is between 3 and 10, there is reverse agreement between the number and the noun it governs. That is to say, if the counted noun is masculine, the number may be apparently feminine (i.e. with the *tā' marbūṭa*) and if the counted noun is feminine, the number should be apparently masculine (i.e. without the *tā' marbūṭa*), e.g.

خمسُ سيارات *five cars*        *four books* أربعةُ كتب

Note that كــتب is masculine, and therefore the number أربعــة is apparently feminine. Similarly, the number خـمس is apparently masculine and the noun سيارات is feminine. Thus, masculine forms of the number look like they are feminine (e.g. أربعــة), while feminine forms look like they are masculine (e.g. ثلاث).

## 3.19 Partitives

Partitive items refer to either part, some, or all of an entity. These are nouns which form *idāfa* structures with the noun or pronoun they govern.

كلا، كلتا    (*both*) If these precede the noun they modify, they form with it an *idāfa* structure. In this case, they are invariable for case.

جاءَ كِلا الرجُلَيْن.  –  قابَلتُ كِلا الرجُلَيْن.  –  كتبتُ إلى كِلا الرجُلَيْن.

جاءَت كِلْتا المرأتين.  –  قابلت كِلْتا المرأتين.  –  كتبتُ إلى كِلْتا المرأتين.

However, if they form an *idāfa* with a pronoun, they decline just like a dual noun. Thus, the *alif* in كِلا is preserved in the nominative and it changes to ي in the accusative and genitive.

كتبتُ إلى الرجُلَيْن كِلَيْهِما – جاءَ الرجُلان كِلاهُما – قابَلتُ الرجُلَيْن كِلَيْهِما

كتبتُ للفتاتين كِلْتَيْهِما – أتت الفتاتان كِلْتاهُما – قابَلتُ الفتاتين كِلْتَيْهِما

Note: With a pronoun, كِلا and كِلْتا are used for emphasis as in the examples above.

| | |
|---|---|
| بِضْع | (*a few*) This indicates number agreement 3-9. All rules that apply to number-noun agreement apply to بِضْع. That is to say, the noun modified by بِضْع must be feminine and vice versa, e.g. |

بِضعةُ كُتُبٍ، بِضعُ سيّاراتٍ

| | |
|---|---|
| رُبْع | (*one quarter*) This functions as a head of a genitive phrase (i.e. *mudāf*), e.g. |

*He waited for a quarter of an hour.*  انتَظَرَ رُبْعَ ساعةٍ.

| | |
|---|---|
| ثُلْث | (*one-third*) This functions as a head of a genitive phrase (i.e. *mudāf*), e.g. |

أعطاها ثُلُثَ مالِه.

*He gave her one-third of his wealth.*

| | |
|---|---|
| نِصْف | (*one-half*) This functions as a head of a genitive phrase (i.e. *mudāf*), e.g. |

*I ate half the apple.*  أكلتُ نِصفَ التُفّاحة.

| | |
|---|---|
| نَيِّف | (*excess, some*) This has the same form for both masculine and feminine nouns and signifies numbers 3-9 (see section 3.13.1). |

291

One thousand and some books.    ألفُ كتابٍ ونَيِّفٌ

بَعْض    (*some*) This functions as a head of a genitive phrase (i.e. *muḍāf*), e.g.    قرأتُ بعضَ الصُحُف.

Sometimes the noun may occur without a following noun when the reference is clear from context, e.g.

*I prefer certain fruits.*    أفضِّلُ بعضَ الفواكه على بعضٍ.

The last بعض stands for بعضها where ها refers back to فواكه.

*They wrote to one another.*    كتَب بعضُهم إلى بعض.

جُلّ    (*most*) This functions as a head of a genitive phrase:

*Most of my friends are not here.*    جُلُّ أصدقائي غائبون.

مُعْظَم    (*most*) This functions as a head of a genitive phrase:

*most frequently*    في مُعْظَمِ الأحيان.

كُلّ    (*all*) This functions as a head of a genitive phrase:

كُلُّ شَخْصٍ مَسْؤُولٌ عن نَفسِه.

*Everyone is responsible for him- or herself.*

جَميع    (*all*) This functions as a head of a genitive phrase:

*All of them are from Lebanon.*    جَميعُهُم مِن لُبنان.

And it functions as *ḥāl* (حال adv. of manner), e.g.

*They arrived together/they all arrived.*    وَصَلوا جَميعاً.

عامّة    (*all*) This functions as a head of a genitive phrase:

كتابُهُ يناسبُ عامّةَ القُرّاء.

*His book is suitable for a general readership.*

سائِر    (*all*) Similar to جميع in connecting to a noun.

*in all countries*    في سائرِ البُلدان.

كافّة    (*all*) This can function as a head of a genitive phrase (i.e. *muḍāf*) as well as an adverbial (e.g. كافّةً).

*I wrote to all my friends.*

كتبتُ إلى كافّةِ أصدقائي/كتبتُ إلى أصدقائي كافّةً.

## 3.20 Nominal forms with a verbal force اسم الفعل

These words and phrases, some of them quite common, are considered nouns with the sense of a verb, but they do not have verb inflections. Some are interjections (آه), some prepositional phrases (إلَيْكَ), and others sound like verbs (صَـه). They may be grouped according to the verb form they signify, that is, perfect, imperfect, and imperative. The following items are among the most common.

Perfect الماضي:

| | |
|---|---|
| *to be quick* | سُـرْعانَ (ما) اتَّصَلنا بالشُّرطة وسَرعانَ ما حَضَروا. |
| *We called the police and they arrived in no time.* | |
| *to be different* | شَتّانَ (ما) |
| *How different the two men are!* شَتّانَ الرجلان/شَتّانَ ما بين الرجلين. | |
| *to be far, unlikely* | هَيْهاتَ هَيْهاتَ أنْ يصلَ إلى الحُكم. |
| *His getting to power is unlikely/a remote possibility.* | |

Imperfect المضارع:

| | |
|---|---|
| expression of pain, discomfort | آه |
| complaining about the heat | آهِ من هذا الحَرّ. |
| expression of boredom, disgust | أفَّ |
| Say not to them a word of contempt.[6] | فلا تَقُلْ لهُما أفَّ |

---

[6] *Holy Qur'ān*, chapter 17, verse 23. أف occurs three times in the *Qur'ān*.

Imperative الأَمْر:

| | |
|---|---|
| *beware* | حَذَارِ |
| *beware involvement in politics.* | حَذَارِ التَوَرُّطَ بالسياسةِ. |
| *quiet!, shut up!* | صَهْ! |
| *take, here you are* | إلَيْكَ/إلَيْكُم ... |
| *here is the news.* | إليكمُ الأخبارَ. |
| *take, here you are* | دونَكَ |
| *here's the book!* | دونَكَ الكتابَ! |
| *Amen, listen* (said after prayer or supplication) | آمين |
| *go on!* | إيه |
| *don't move!* | مَكانَكَ! |
| *leave me alone!* | إلَيْكَ عَنّي! |
| *take it easy, slowly* | رُوَيْدَكَ! |
| said to a child, meaning, '*dirty, don't touch!*' | كَخٍ! |
| *come! come on!* | هَلُمَّ، هَلُمّي، هَلُمّوا |
| *come on! let's go! hurry up!* | هَيّا (بنا) |

## 3.21 The diminutive الاسم المصغَّر

This noun can be derived from almost all nouns for the purpose of expressing belittling (e.g. جُبَيْل 'small mountain'), endearment (e.g. بُنَيّ 'little son'), ridicule (e.g. شُوَيْعِر 'petty poet'). Derivation is done according to three patterns, each one for a specific noun form. The pattern فُعَيْل is used with the triliteral noun (e.g. نَهْر/نُهَيْر 'stream'), فُعَيْعِل with quadriliteral nouns (e.g. كتاب/كُتَيِّب 'booklet'), and فُعَيْعِيل for the quinquiliteral (e.g. مِفتاح/مُفَيْتِيح 'small key'). Nouns with greater than five letters have the last one dropped (e.g. عَنْدَليب/عُنَيْدِل 'nightingale'). Note the following additional rules:
1.  Feminine nouns that are not marked for gender (e.g. شَـمـس

'sun'), acquire *tā' marbūṭa* in the diminutive (e.g. شُمَيْسَة).

2. Nouns containing a vowel are made diminutive by using the vowel in the root. For example, the root for باب 'door' is بوب. Therefore, the diminutive is بُوَيْب.

3. Compound nouns have the first item transformed, e.g.

$$\text{عَبْدُ الله} \ll \text{عُبَيْدُ الله}$$

Here are some of the most commonly used diminutives whose meanings have become lexicalized. Some of these words are adverbs which are basically considered nouns in Arabic.

| | | | |
|---|---|---|---|
| بُعَيْدَ | *a little after* | قُبَيْلَ | *a little before* |
| كُتَيِّب | *booklet* | شُجَيْرة | *a bush* |
| دُوَيْلة | *mini-state, statelet* | عُصَيّة | *a tiny stick* |

## 3.22 The vocative المُنادى

There are two main particles, which are used like the formal or archaic English 'Oh', to call the attention of an addressee: يا and أيُّهـا (and its feminine form أيّتُهـا). The particle يا is used with indefinite nouns and personal names, whereas أيُّها is used with nouns that have the definite article prefixed to them.

| | |
|---|---|
| *Hey, man! / Hey, Ahmed!* | يا رجُلُ! / يا أحمدُ! |
| *Ladies and gentlemen!* | أيُّها السَّيِّداتُ والسادةُ! |

If the addressee is a female or group of females, أيّتُها is used.

| | |
|---|---|
| *Sisters!* | أيّتُها الأخَواتُ! |

The nouns following the above particles are nominative. However, if the addressee is an *idāfa* phrase, the مُضاف, or the head of the genitive structure, is accusative.

| | |
|---|---|
| *School students!* | يا طُلّابَ المدرسة! |
| *Dearest ones!* | يا أعزّاءَنا! |
| *Hey, Abdalla!* | يا عَبْدَ الله! |

There are other, rarely used particles. They may be encountered especially in poetry and literary passages.

| | | |
|---|---|---|
| أ | أَسُعادُ! | *Hey, Su<sup>c</sup>ād!* |
| أَيْ | أَيْ بُنَيَّ! | *Little son!* |
| أَيا | أَيا جارَنا! | *Hey, neighbour!* |

## 3.23 Relative adjectives اسمُ النسبة

A *nisba* functions as both an adjective and a noun. It shows affiliation with a geographical region, profession, group of people, town, school of thought, and the like. It is related to the noun in one way or another. Most nouns are made *nisba* (i.e. relative adjective) by suffixing يّ to them. If the noun has the feminine marker ة, the definite article, or a final *alif*, it is dropped.

| | *Nisba* | | <u>Noun</u> |
|---|---|---|---|
| *Damascene* | دِمَشْقيّ | *Damascus* | دِمَشْق |
| *cultural* | ثَقافيّ | *culture* | ثَقافة |
| *Iraqi* | عِراقيّ | *Iraq* | العِراق |
| *French* | فَرَنسيّ | *France* | فَرَنسا |

In some nouns, internal long vowels are dropped.

| | | | |
|---|---|---|---|
| *civilian* | مَدَنيّ | *city, town* | مَدينة |
| *journalist* | صَحَفيّ | *newspaper* | صَحيفة |

If a long vowel in the root is deleted, it is restored when forming a *nisba*.

| | | | |
|---|---|---|---|
| *paternal* | أَبَويّ | *father* | أَبٌ |
| *brotherly* | أَخَويّ | *brother* | أَخٌ |
| *filial, of a son* | بَنَويّ | *son* | ابنٌ |
| *prophetic* | نَبَويّ | *prophet* | نَبِيّ |

| | | | |
|---|---|---|---|
| *secondary* | ثانَوِيّ | *second* | ثانٍ |

The endings ة، ى، ا، ء change into a و.

| | | | |
|---|---|---|---|
| *heavenly, divine* | سَماوِيّ | *heaven* | سَماء |
| *worldly* | دُنْيَوِيّ | *world* | دُنْيا |
| *abstract* | مَعْنَوِيّ | *meaning* | مَعنىً |
| *of a village, villager* | قَرَوِيّ | *village* | قَرْيَة |

However, in certain forms, an additional و simply appears:

| | | | |
|---|---|---|---|
| *of family, familial* | أسرَوِيّ | *family* | أسرة |
| *unionist, of unity* | وَحدَوِيّ | *unity* | وَحدة |

Most *nisba* nouns have sound plurals (e.g. سُورِيّ – سُورِيّون). There are a few exceptions, as in the following.

| | | | |
|---|---|---|---|
| *Arabs* | عَرَب | *Arab* | عَرَبِيّ |
| *Jews* | يَهود | *Jew* | يَهودِيّ |
| *gypsies* | نَوَر | *gypsy* | نَوَرِيّ |
| *natives of Baghdad* | بَغاددة | *native of Baghdad* | بَغدادِيّ |

## 3.24 Emphasis التَوكيد

Emphasis can be achieved in two ways: through duplication and the use of certain words. Duplication involves the repetition of the word to be emphasized twice or the use of an equivalent word. In the first example below, the verb is repeated, while in the second one the attached pronoun كَ ('you', genitive) is followed by its independent equivalent أنتَ ('you', nominative).

| | |
|---|---|
| *Ayman **has** arrived.* | وصل وصل أَيمَنٌ. |
| *I wrote to **you**.* | كتبتُ لكَ أنتَ. |

More frequently, emphasis is achieved by the use of نَفس، عَيْن، ذات and the partitives كِلا، كِلتا، كُلّ، أجمَع، جَميع، عامّة، كافّة. For the uses of the latter group, see Partitives 3.19.

| | |
|---|---|
| *We returned on the plane itself.* | رجَعنا بالطائرة نَفسِها . |
| Another less acceptable usage is: | رجَعنا بنفس الطائرة. |
| *The officials themselves talked to us.* | حَدَّثَنا المَسؤولونَ أنفُسُهُم. |
| *We discussed the problem itself.* | ناقَشْنا المُشكلةَ عَيْنَها . |
| *I want the book itself.* | أريدُ الكتابَ ذاتَه. |

Emphasis is also achieved by repetition of a word to express intense execution of an action, sequence of performance.

(a) intensification of the action, e.g.

| | |
|---|---|
| *to tear s.t. into pieces or shreds* | قَطَّعَها إرْباً إرْباً. |

(b) sequence of occurrence, e.g.

| | |
|---|---|
| *He read the word letter by letter.* | قرأ الكلمةَ حَرْفاً حَرْفاً. |
| *They entered the room one by one.* | دَخَلوا الغُرفةَ فَرْداً فَرْداً. |

(c) emphasis, e.g.

| | |
|---|---|
| *Arabic remained the same, unchanged.* | ظلَّت العَربيّةُ هيَ هيَ. |

## 3.25 The permutative البَدَل

The permutative is a word, phrase, or clause that substitutes for another. The substitution may be total, that is, one word stands for another one completely, as in:

زُرْتُ عَمّانَ عاصمةَ الأردُنّ.

*I visited Amman, the capital of Jordan.*

In the above example عَمّان and عاصمة الأردنّ refer to the same thing, and the use of either one can suffice to convey the meaning. In traditional English grammatical terminology, this is known as apposition. Note that both words have the same case. However, a part of an entity may also substitute for it as in the following.

قرأتُ الكتابَ أوّلَه.　　*I have read the beginning of the book.*

زُرنا إرلاندة شمالَها وجَنوبَها.　　*We visited Ireland, north and south.*

Another type of بَدَل is called بَدَل التَفصيل ) of elaboration).

اتَّصل أصدقاؤكَ سالم وهشام وماهر.

*Your friends Salem, Hisham, and Maher called.*

أسُسُ النجاحِ ثلاثةٌ: علمٌ وعَمَلٌ وأخلاق.　　*The fundamentals of*

*success are three: knowledge, work, and ethics.*

## 3.26 Conjunctions حروف العَطْف

Conjunctions are particles used to link two or more nouns, verbs, adjectives, or sentences. In this sense, they are a subset of, not all, connectors (see Transition Words 3.12), e.g.

| | | |
|---|---|---|
| وَ | *Marwan <u>and</u> his brother came by.* جاءَ مروانُ وأخوه.. | ١. |

٢. دَخَلَ الأستاذُ وجلسَ أمامَنا.

*The professor came in <u>and</u> sat in front of us.*

*We admired him <u>and</u> his expertise.* أعْجِبْنا به وبخبرته.　٣.

فَ　٤. سألَني إنْ كنتُ من هُنا فقُلتُ لا.

*He asked if I was from around here <u>and</u> I said no.*

ثُمَّ　٥. استَحَمَّ ثُمَّ دخل غُرفةَ نَوْمِه.

*He bathed <u>then</u> he entered his bedroom.*

أوْ　*I walk <u>or</u> jog in the morning.* أمشي أوْ أعدو صَباحاً.　٦.

أم　*Do you like grapes <u>or</u> cherries?* أتُحبُّ العنَبَ أم الكَرَز؟　٧.

Note that أوْ is used in affirmative sentences and أم in yes/no questions.

بَلْ　٨. لَم يحضُرْ هُوَ بَلْ أخوه.

*He didn't show up, <u>but</u> his brother did.*

لكِنْ　٩. أتكلّمُ الفرنسيةَ لكِنْ ليسَ الإسبانية.

*I speak French, <u>but</u> not Spanish.*

١٠. خُذِ القطارَ لا الحافلةَ. *Take the train, <u>not</u> the bus.*   لا

١١. أَعمَلُ كُلَّ يومٍ حتَّى في العُطلة.   حتَّى

*I work every day, <u>even</u> on a holiday.*

Note these two rules in using conjunctions:

(1) If the part before the conjunction has an attached or implied pronoun, it must be emphasized with a separate pronoun, then followed by the conjunction, e.g.

لم تحبَّه. أحبّت ماله.   >>    لم تحبَّه هو بَل مالَه.

(2) If the conjunction is used after a pronoun modified by a preposition, the same preposition must be repeated immediately after the conjunction, e.g.

كتبتُ لها. وكتبتُ لأخيها.   >>    كتبتُ لها ولأخيها.

## 3.27 Exception الاستثناء

There are three types of exception. These all involve an exceptive particle, عدا، إلاّ، سِوى and so forth. In the homogeneous type, the excepted noun and the noun from which exception is made are of the same category. The excepted noun following إلاّ is in the accusative (منصوب).

حَضَرَ الطلّابُ إلاّ خالداً.

*All the students have come except Khalid.*

In the second heterogeneous type, the excepted noun and the noun from which exception is made are of two different kinds. The excepted noun following إلاّ is also in the accusative (منصوب).

*I read the book except for one page.*   قرأتُ الكتابَ إلاّ صفحةً.

The third type is called 'dedicated'. Here the noun from which exception is made is deleted, and the sentence before إلاّ is dedicated to the excepted noun. This type occurs only in the negative and

the excepted noun takes on the case appropriate for its position,
إلاّ having no effect on case.

| | |
|---|---|
| *Only Khalid came.* | ما حَضَرَ إلاّ خالدٌ. |
| *I saw Khalid only.* | ما رأيتُ إلاّ خالداً. |
| *I wrote only to Khalid.* | ما كتبتُ إلاّ لخالدٍ. |

There are additional particles of exception that are considered
members of the إلاّ-set. They are much less frequently used. The
first two, خَـلا and عَـدا, may be treated as verbs, the following
object noun accordingly being accusative (منصـوب). (See also
Prepositions 3.11.)

| | |
|---|---|
| *All the students came except one.* حَضَرَ الطُّلاّبُ خَلا واحداً. | خَلا |
| حَضَرَ الطُّلاّبُ عَدا واحداً. | عَدا |

However, خَلا and عَدا may also be treated as particles. In this case,
they function as prepositions and the following nouns are put in
the genitive.

| | |
|---|---|
| حَضَرَ الطُّلاّبُ خَلا واحدٍ. | خَلا |
| حَضَرَ الطُّلاّبُ عَدا واحدٍ. | عَدا |

The so-called infinitive ما may be used before these two words,
thus confirming their verbal status.

| | |
|---|---|
| حَضَرَ الطُّلاّبُ ما خَلا واحداً. | خَلا |
| حَضَرَ الطُّلاّبُ ما عَدا واحداً. | عَدا |

The verb حاشا is a member of the set that does not allow ما.

| | |
|---|---|
| أضْرَبَ العُمّالُ حاشا المُديرينَ. | حاشا |

The last two members of the set are غَـيْـر and سِـوى. These are
considered nouns. The following noun is thus part of an *iḍāfa*
and is, therefore, genitive (مجرور). (See item 9 under Cases of the
Noun, 3.3.7.)

| | |
|---|---|
| لا أعْرِفُ غَيْرَ الطريقِ الرئيسيّة. | غَيْر |

سِوى لا أعرفُ سِوى الطريقِ الرئيسيّة.

## 3.28 The *iḍāfa* structure الإضافة

This is a structure that relates one noun to another, giving a meaning that typically corresponds to English 'of' phrases and genitive phrases. The first noun is called مُضاف ('added', which is the head of the genitive phrase) and the second مُضاف إليْه (literally, 'added to', which is the modifier), e.g.

كتابُ الطالبِ.    head = كتاب    الطالب = modifier

The structural characteristics of an *iḍāfa* phrase are the following:

1. The head, المُضاف, never takes ال, cannot have تَنوين; loses the final ن if it is dual or sound plural; and it has the case appropriate for its grammatical status, e.g.

   | | |
   |---|---|
   | *He is the teacher of the class.* | هو مُدَرِّسُ الصفِّ. |
   | *They are the two teachers of the class.* | هما مُدَرِّسا الصفِّ. |
   | *They are the teachers of the class.* | هم مُدَرِّسو الصفِّ. |
   | *That's the mountain top.* | تلك قِمّةُ الـجَبَلِ. |
   | *I saw the mountain top.* | رأيتُ قِمّةَ الجَبَلِ. |
   | *He got to the mountain top.* | وصل إلى قِمّةِ الجَبَلِ. |

2. The modifier (second word, third word, etc.) is in the genitive case (مجرور).

3. There may be multiple modifiers مُضاف إليْه:

   | | |
   |---|---|
   | *Reem's car* | سيّارةُ ريمٍ |
   | *the door of Reem's car* | بابُ سيّارةِ ريمٍ |
   | *the key to the door of Reem's car* | مفتاحُ بابِ سيّارةِ ريمٍ |

4. More than one مُضاف is not allowed by the rules of traditional Arabic grammar. However, this practice is on the rise in MSA, particularly in the press (e.g. سُورُ وأبوابُ المدينةِ). In more traditional, elegant writing, the second مُـضـاف is added after

the المُضاف إليه and an attached pronoun suffixed to it consistent with the مُضاف إليه (e.g. سورُ المدينةِ وأبوابُها).

In other words, it is not permissible to separate the two constituents of an *idāfa* structure (i.e. the head and modifier), even with another head مُضاف.

## 3.29 Elative adjectives التَفْضيل

The elative adjectives اسم التفضيل (i.e. comparative and superlative) are considered nouns in Arabic. They are fashioned from triliteral roots on the pattern أفْعَل. The root must be affirmative, declinable, active, with a derived adjective not patterned on أفعَل and it should allow comparison. To form a comparative adjective from an adjective, the long vowel, if any, is dropped and a *hamza* is prefixed to the root along the pattern أفعل, e.g.

*kinder* رَؤوف << أرأف          *farther* بَعيد << أبْعَد

If the adjective contains two identical consonants (e.g., جَـديد), they will be geminated in the comparative (e.g. أَجَـدّ). For the comparative degree, من is added to the أفعل pattern, e.g.

*Ahmed is taller than Samer.*          أحمَدُ أطوَلُ من سامرٍ.

The superlative is formed by relating the comparative to the noun being compared, forming an *idāfa* structure.

*Ahmed is the tallest student.*          أحمَدُ أطوَلُ طالبٍ.

The article الـ may be prefixed to the comparative to form the superlative. Note the insertion of the independent pronoun هو which functions as a copula (i.e. 'to be').

*Ahmed is the tallest.*          أحمَدُ هو (الطالبُ) الأطوَلُ.

A few nouns have feminine elatives as well, e.g.

دانٍ << أدني / دُنيا : (درجة الحرارة الدنيا *lowest temperature*)

عظيم << أعظم / عُظمى: (الحرارة العظمى *highest temperature*)

كبير >> أكبر / كُبرى (ابنتها الكبرى *her eldest daughter* )

صغير >> أصغر / صُغرى (البنت الصغرى *the youngest daughter* )

These masculine and feminine elatives can be plural as follows:

أكبر >> أكابر      كُبرى >> كُبرَيات

Some adjectives are not amenable to fit the pattern أفـعَل, such as colours and physical defects because they themselves are formed on the pattern أفعَل. In this case, comparative forms like أكثَر، أعظَم، أقَلّ، أخَفّ، أشَدّ are used along with the verbal noun of the adjective being compared in the accusative case, e.g.

*most interesting and exciting stories*      أجمَلُ القِصَصِ وأكثَرُها إثارةً

*more effective*      أشَدُّ تأثيراً

*less terrifying*      أقَلُّ رُعْباً

However, there are exceptions to the above rule with sentences like هي أبيضُ من أختها 'she has a fairer complexion than her sister'.

## 3.30 Defective nouns الاسم المنقوص

A defective noun ends with an ي that is part of its root. The final ي is deleted in indefinite active participles. For example, the active participle (اسم الفاعل) of the perfect (قَضى) is قاضٍ. The deleted ي, however, is restored by suffixing the article ال (القاضي) or relating قاضٍ to another noun in an *idāfa* structure (قاضي المحكمة *judge of the court*). The ي is also restored by adding the dual suffix ان (قاضيان). Note that the final ي shows only one inflection: the accusative, e.g.

subject, nom.      *The judge has arrived.* جاءَ القاضي.

object of prep., gen.      *I wrote to the judge.* كتبتُ إلى القاضي.

subject of *inna*, acc.      *The judge is fair.* إنّ القاضيَ عادلٌ.

## 3.31 Common errors أغلاط شائعة

Several types of errors are frequently found in the speech and writing of learners of Arabic. Although many of them are symptoms of developmental phases, some tend to persist. It is helpful to identify them in order for learners to be aware of them and subsequently correct them. Selected examples of the most common types of errors are listed below in order of highest frequency. The error is in the right-hand column, its intended equivalent to its left, and the meaning is in the left-hand column.[7]

### Defining the مُضاف

| | Correct form | Error |
|---|---|---|
| *at the Aleppo airport* | في المطار حَلَب / في مَطار حَلَب | |
| *in northern Japan* | في الشَمال اليابان / في شمال اليابان | |
| *stomach cancer* | السَرَطان مَعدة / سَرَطان المَعدة | |
| *my bedroom* | غُرفَتي نَوْم / غُرفَةُ نَوْمي | |
| *at the Palm Restaurant* | بالمَطعَم النَخلة / بمَطعَم النَخلة | |
| *my weight gain* | الزيادة وَزْني / زيادة وَزْني | |
| *Friday morning* | صَباح اليَوْم الجَمْعة / صَباح يَوم الجَمْعة | |

### Noun-adjective agreement

| | | |
|---|---|---|
| *last summer* | في صَيْف الماضي / في الصَيْف الماضي | |
| *Arab culture* | تُراث عَرَبيّة / تُراث عَرَبيّ | |
| *Arabs are wealthy* | العَرَب غَنيّ / العَرَبُ أغنياء | |
| *the plane is safe* | الطائرة مأمون / الطائرة مأمونة | |
| *I felt very nauseated.* | شَعَرتُ بالغَثَيان شَديد / بغَثَيان شَديد | |

---

[7] Most examples are taken from research done by Carmen Cross (1999).

### Wrong negative particle

| | |
|---|---|
| *I didn't do...* | لا فَعَلتُ / ما فَعَلتُ/لم أفعل |
| *I won't stay.* | لا سَأبْقى / لَنْ أبْقى |
| *He did not meet me.* | لَم قابَلَني / لَم يُقابِلْني |

### Doubly defined noun

| | |
|---|---|
| *his life* | الحَياتُه / حَياتُه |
| *her car* | السيّارتها / سيّارتها |
| *my apartment* | الشقّتي / شقّتي |
| *my studies* | الدِراساتي / دِراساتي |

### Failure to define a noun that should be definite

| | |
|---|---|
| *I called by telephone.* | اتَّصَلتُ بِهاتف / اتَّصَلتُ بالهاتف |
| *I went to school.* | ذَهَبْتُ إلى مَدرَسة / ذَهَبْتُ إلى المَدرَسة |
| *with family and friends* | مع عائلة وأصدقاء / مع العائلة والأصدقاء |
| *I'll swim in the sea.* | سَأسْبَح في بَحْرَ / سَأسْبَح في البَحْر |
| *I studied in the library.* | دَرَستُ في مَكتَبة / دَرَستُ في المَكتَبة |
| *I went shopping.* | ذهبْتُ إلى سوق / ذهبْتُ إلى السوق |

### Missing preposition

| | |
|---|---|
| *I apologized to him.* | اعتَذَرتُهُ / اعتَذَرتُ لَهُ (منه) |
| *He said to me.* | قالَني / قالَ لي |

### Number-noun agreement

| | |
|---|---|
| *seven or eight hours..* | سبعة أو ثمانية ساعات / سبع أو ثماني... |

### Missing verb

| | |
|---|---|
| *when I was in Syria* | حينَ في سورية / حينَ كنتُ في سورية |

### Wrong preposition

| | |
|---|---|
| *I went to the library.* | ذهبتُ في مكتبة / ذهبتُ إلى المكتبة |

| | |
|---|---|
| *at night* | على الليلة / في الليل |
| *fortunately* | بِحُسْن الخَظّ / لِحُسْن الخَظّ |
| *at a low price* | لِسعْر مُنْخَفِض / بِسعْر مُنْخَفِض |
| *I borrow from you.* | أَسْتَدِينُ مَعَك / أَسْتَدِينُ مِنْك |
| *I arrived in* | وَصَلتُ في / وَصَلتُ إلى |
| *I was finished with school.* | انْتَهَيْتُ مَعَ جامِعة / انْتَهَيْتُ مِنَ الجامِعة |

## Word order

| | |
|---|---|
| *because the weather was* | لأن كان الطقس / لأنَّ الطقسَ كانَ |
| *because his story includes* | لأن تَتَضَمَّن قِصّته / لأن قِصّته تَتَضَمَّن |
| *that a month passed by* | أن مَرَّ شَهراً / أنَّ شَهراً مَرَّ |

## Missing noun or pronoun

| | |
|---|---|
| *because she wanted to* | لأن كانَت تَريد / لأنَّها كانَت تَريد |
| *by Najeeb Mahfouz* | بِنجيب محفوظ / بِقلم نجيب محفوظ |

# Bibliography

Abboud, Peter F. and Ernest N. McCarus (eds.), *Elementary Modern Standard Arabic,* vols. I-II, Cambridge University Press, 1986.

Abdo, Dawood Atiyya, *Al-Mufradāt Ash-shā'i'a fil-Luġa al-'Arabiyya (Frequent Lexical Items in Arabic),* University of Riyadh, 1979.

Abu Sa'd, Aḥmad, *Mu'jam Faṣīḥ Al-'āmma (Dictionary of Standard Elements in Popular Speech),* Beirut: Dar al-'ilm lil-malayīn, 1990.

Al-Abed Al-Haq, Fawwaz, Language attitude and the promotion of standard Arabic and Arabization, *Al-'Arabiyya,* 31: 21-38, 1998.

Al-Batal, Mahmoud, The Cohesive Role of Connectives in a Modern Expository Arabic Text, unpublished doctoral dissertaion, the University of Michigan, 1985.

Al-Faḥḥām, Shaker, Speech at the Symposium on the Arabic Language and the Media, *Journal of the Arabic Language Academy in Damascus*, vol. 74, 3, 1998.

Al-Kahtany, Abdalla, the problem of diglossia in the Arab world, *Al-ᶜArabiyya*, 30: 1-30, 1997.

Alosh, Mahdi, *Implications of the Use of Modern Standard Arabic in the Arabic Adaptation of 'Sesame Street'*, unpublished master's thesis. Ohio University, 1984.

_____, Arabic diglossia and its impact on teaching Arabic as a foreign language, in *ACTFL Review of Foreign Language Education*, (ed.) Gerard Ervin, pp. 121-137, Lincolnwood, IL: National Textbook Company, 1991.

_____, *Learner, Text, and Context in Foreign Language Acquisition: An Arabic Perspective*, Columbus, the Ohio State University: National Foreign Language Resource Center, 1997.

Altoma, Saleh, *The Problem of Diglossia in Arabic: A Comparative Study of Classical and Iraqi Arabic*, Harvard Eastern Monograph Series, 1969.

Al-Warraki, Nariman Naili, and Ahmed Taher Hassanein, *The Connectors in Modern Standard Arabic*. The American University in Cairo Press, 1994.

Badawi, El-Said, *Mustawayāt al-ᶜArabiyya al-muᶜāṣira fī Miṣr (levels of contemporary Arabic in Egypt)*, Cairo: Dār el-maᶜārif, 1973.

Blanc, Haim, Stylistic Variations in Spoken Arabic: A Sample of Interdialectal Educated Conversation, in Charles Ferguson (ed.), Harvard Middle Eastern Monographs III, *Contributions to Arabic Linguistics*. Cambridge, Massachusetts: Harvard University Press, 1960.

Cross, Carmen, *A statistical study of the written errors committed by native English speakers learning Arabic as a foreign language*, unpublished MA thesis, Columbus: The Ohio State University, 1999.

Dickins, James and Janet C. E. Watson, *Standard Arabic: An Advanced Course*, Cambridge University Press, 1999.

El-Hassan, S. A., Educated Spoken Arabic in Egypt and the Levant: A Critical Review of Diglossia and Related Matters, in *Archivum Linguisticum* 8: 112-132, 1977.

Ellis, Nick C., What's in a word that makes it hard or easy: some intralexical factors that affect the learning of words, in Norbert Schmitt and Michael McCarthy (Eds.) *Vocabulary Description, Acquisition, and Pedagogy*, 140-155, Cambridge: Cambridge University Press, 1977.

Ferguson, Charles, Diglossia. *Word*, vol. XV, pp. 325-40, 1959.

Hussein, Taha, *Mustaqbalu al-Thaqāfati fī Miṣr (The Future of Intellectualism in Egypt)*, Cairo, 1944.

Kaye, Alan, Modern Standard Arabic and the colloquials, *Lingua*, 24: 374-391, 1970.

Masharqa, Zuheir, keynote address at the Symposium on the Arabic Language and the Media, *Journal of the Arabic Language Academy in Damascus*, vol. 74, 3, 1998.

Meiseles, Gustav, Educated Spoken Arabic and the Arabic Language Continuum, *Archivum Linguisticum*, vol. XI, 2, pp. 118-148, 1980.

Mitchell, T.F, *Dimension of Style in a Grammar of Educated Spoken Arabic*, 1980.

Mubarak, Mazen, *Nahwa Waᶜyin Luġawiyyin (Toward Linguistic Awareness)*, No publisher. Damascus, Syria, 1970.

Nasif, Ali, *Min Qaḍāyā Al-Luġati wa Al-Naḥw (Issues in Language and Syntax)*, Cairo, 1957.

Parkinson, Dilworth, Searching for Modern Fuṣḥā: Real Life Formal Arabic. *Al-ᶜArabiyya*, vol. 18, 1-2, 11-43, 1991.

Sabaḥ, Ḥusni, Foreword and Memories, *Arab Medical Journal*, vol. 90, 1986.

Salman, Mohamed, Speech at the Symposium on the Arabic Language and the Media, *Journal of the Arabic Language Academy in Damascus*, vol. 74, 3, 1998.

Sanqar, Salha, Speech at the Symposium on the Arabic Language and the Media, *Journal of the Arabic Language Academy in Damascus*, vol. 74, 3, 1998.

Sara, Qasim, *At-Taᶜrīb: Juhūd wa āfāq 'Arabization: Efforts and Possibilities'*, Damascus/Beirut: Dar al-Hijra 1989.

Sawaie, Mohammed, Sociolinguistic factors and historical linguistic change: The case of /q/ and its reflexes in Arabic, 1993.

Schmitt, Norbert and Michael McCarthy (Eds.),.*Vocabulary Description, Acquisition, and Pedagogy*, Cambridge: Cambridge University Press, 1997.

Schulz, Eckehard, Günther Krahl, and Wolfgang Reuschel, *Standard Arabic: An Elementary-Intermediate Course*, Cambridge University Press, 2000.

Sökmen, Anita J., Current trends in teaching second language vocabulary, in Norbert Schmitt and Michael McCarthy (Eds.), *Vocabulary Description, Acquisition, and Pedagogy*, 237-257, Cambridge: Cambridge Universty Press, 1997.

Shukri, Muhammad Fuad, Abdel-Maqsud al-Inani, and Sayed Muhammad Khalil, *Binā' Dawlat Miṣr Muḥammad ᶜAli: As-Siyāsa Ad-Dāḵiliyya 'The Construction of the State of Egypt of Muhammad Ali: Internal Policy'*. Cairo: Dar al-Fikr al-ᶜArabi, 1948.

فهرس

313

# Appendix 1

Voweled text

أُمَّةٌ وَحدَهُ

يا الله!! أفي لحظة عـابرة من صبـاح يوم الإثنين الماضي يلفظُ الرافعيُّ نَفَسَهُ في طَوايا الغَيْبِ كَومضة البَرقِ لفَّها الليلُ، وقَطْرَة النَدَى شربتها الشمسُ، وورقة الشَجَر أطاحَها الخَريفُ؛ ثمَّ لا يبقى من هذا القلب الجيَّـاش، وهذا الشُعـور المُرْهَف، وذلكَ الذهن الوَلود، إلاَّ كَما يبـقى مِنَ النور في العَـيْنِ، ومِنَ السُـرورِ في الحِسّ، ومِنَ الحُلْمِ في الذاكِرة!!

كان الرافعيُّ يكره مَوتَ العافيـة فمات به: أرسل إليَّ قبل موته المفاجئ يشكو فيه بعضَ الوَهْنِ في أعصابه، وأثَرَ الرُكود في قَريحتـه، ويقـترحُ عليَّ نظامـاً جديداً للعمل يجدُ فيـه الراحةَ حتَّى يخرجَ إلى المَعاش فيقصرَ جُهْدَهُ على الأدَب، ثم يسرُدُ في إيجاز عَزائمَه ونواياه، ويَعِدُ المستقبَلَ البعيدَ بالإنتاج الخَصب والثَمَر المختلف؛ ويقول: «إنَّ بُنَيَتي الوثيقة وقلبي القوي سيتغلَّبان على هذا الضعف الطارئ فأصمُدُ إلى حملة التطهير التي أريدُها.»

كتب الرافعيُّ إليَّ هذا الكتـاب في صباح الأحد، وتولَّى القَدَرُ عنّي الجوابَ في صبـاح الإثنين: قـضى الصديق العـامل الآمل الليلةَ الفاصلة بين ذَيْنكَ اليـومين على خيـر ما يقضيها الرَخيّ الآمنُ على صحتِّه وغبْطِته: صلَّى العشاءَ في عيادة وَلده الدكتور محمد؛ ثُمَّ أقبل على بعض أصحابه هُناك فجَلا عنهُم صَدَأَ الفُتور بحديثه الفَكه ومزْحه المُهَذَّب؛ ثم خرج فقضى واجبَ العَزاء لبعض الجِيرة؛ ثم ذهب وَحْدهُ إلى مُتَنَزَّه المدينة فاستَراضَ فيه طويلاً بالمشي والتأمُّل؛ ثم رجَع بعد مَوْهِنٍ مِنَ الليلِ إلى دارِه فأكَلَ بعضَ الأكلِ ثم أوى إلى مَضْجَعِه.

# Appendix 2
Answer key

## 2.4.3 Matching

The nouns that collocate are matched together.

| | |
|---|---|
| مُخْرِجُ / الفيلم | مَسيرَةُ / احتجاج |
| تَلُّ / الزَعْتَر | مَلابِسُ / عَسْكَرِيَّة |
| شاخِصُ / النَظَر | نَشيدٌ / وَطَنيّ |
| | مُكَبِّرُ / الصَوْت |

Verbs with the appropriate preposition.

| | |
|---|---|
| دارَ / حَوْلَ | راهَنَ / عَلى |
| قامَ / بـِ | اتَّجَهَ / إلى |
| انْقَسَمَ / إلى | اِعْتَدى / عَلى |
| | انْعَكَسَ / عَلى |

Nouns that go together.

| | |
|---|---|
| طالِب / مَدْرَسَة | أُمّ / أُسْرة |
| حِجاب / جامِع | صدامات / اشْتِباكات |
| شَرْقيّ / غَرْبيّ | شابّ / مُراهِق |
| | عَوَز / فاقَة |

## 2.4.5  Lexical ordering

Whole-part  دَرّاجَة: جنزير، سَرْج، مِقْوَد، مِصْباح، دَوّاسَة، دولاب

طَبْخة: مِلْح، بهارات، خُضَر، سَمْن، لَحْم، أرُز

Status  عَميد، وَكيل، أُسْتاذ، مُحاضِر، مُعيد، طالِب

رَئيس، قائد، ضابِط، جُندي

Degree of disagreement:

شِجار، تَنازُع، مُقاطَعة، اخْتِلاف، بَحْث، مُناقَشة، حِوار

Role in a process:

مُخْتَرِع، مُصَمِّم، صانِع، مُسْتَهْلِك

كاتِب، مُخْرِج، مُنتِج، مُمَثِّل، مُصَوِّر

Degree of responsibility:

رَئِيس الجُمْهوريَّة، وَزير الداخِليَّة، شُرْطيّ

مُدَقِّق حِسابات، مُحاسِب، بائِع

Analogy:

جَمَل : صَحْراء     سَفينَة : بَحْر

هَواء : إِنْسان     كَهْرَباء : آلة

General-specific:

تَعْليم، مَدْرَسَة، الرِياضيّات

Degree of liking:

مالَ إلى، أعْجَبَ، سَرَّ، أحَبَّ، عَشِقَ

Degree of dislike:

انْزَعَجَ مِنْ، أعْرَضَ عَنْ، نَفَرَ مِنْ، كَرِهَ، أبْغَضَ

# Appendix 3
## Verb Conjugations

At the top of each table, the verb is listed along with its verbal noun, active participle, and passive participle. On the next line, there is a listing of the forms commonly permissible for a particular verb. Contrary to what some grammar books imply, not all verb form slots are used with a particular verb. Each verb is conjugated in the perfect, the three moods of the imperfect, and the imperative. The tables are structured as follows:

Line 1: verb + verbal noun + active participle + passive participle
Line 2: Verb forms II-X
Line 3: Permissible forms
Line 4: Separate pronouns
Line 5: Verb conjugation in the perfect الماضي
Line 6: Verb conjugation in the imperfect indicative المضارع المرفوع
Line 7: Verb conjugation in the imperfect subjunctive المضارع المنصوب
Line 8: Verb conjugation in the imperfect jussive المضارع المجزوم
Line 9: Verb conjugation in the imperative الأمر

قالَ (قَوْلٌ، قائلٌ، مَقولٌ)

| X | XI | VIII | VII | VI | V | IV | III | II |
|---|----|------|-----|----|----|----|-----|-----|
| -- | -- | -- | تَقَوَّلَ | تقاوَلَ | -- | قاوَلَ | -- | قَوَّلَ |

| أنا | نَحْنُ | أنتَ | أنتِ | أنتُما | أنتُم | أنتُنَّ | هُوَ | هِيَ | هُما | هُما | هُم | هُنَّ |
|---|---|---|---|---|---|---|---|---|---|---|---|---|
| قُلْتُ | قُلْنا | قُلْتَ | قُلْتِ | قُلْتُما | قُلْتُم | قُلْتُنَّ | قالَ | قالَتْ | قالا | قالَتا | قالوا | قُلْنَ |
| أقولُ | نَقولُ | تَقولُ | تَقولينَ | تَقولانِ | تَقولونَ | تَقُلْنَ | يَقولُ | تَقولُ | يَقولانِ | تَقولانِ | يَقولونَ | يَقُلْنَ |
| أقولَ | نَقولَ | تَقولَ | تَقولي | تَقولا | تَقولوا | تَقُلْنَ | يَقولَ | تَقولَ | يَقولا | تَقولا | يَقولوا | يَقُلْنَ |
| أقُلْ | نَقُلْ | تَقُلْ | تَقولي | تَقولا | تَقولوا | تَقُلْنَ | يَقُلْ | تَقُلْ | يَقولا | تَقولا | يَقولوا | يَقُلْنَ |
|  |  | قُلْ | قولي | قولا | قولوا | قُلْنَ |  |  |  |  |  |  |

باعَ (بَيْعٌ، بائعٌ، مَبيعٌ)

| X | XI | VIII | VII | VI | V | IV | III | II |
|---|----|------|-----|----|----|----|-----|-----|
| -- | بايَعَ | ابتاعَ | -- | تَبايَعَ | -- | -- | بَيَّعَ |

| أنا | نَحْنُ | أنتَ | أنتِ | أنتُما | أنتُمْ | أنتُنَّ | هُوَ | هِيَ | هُما | هُما | هُمْ | هُنَّ |
|-----|--------|------|------|--------|--------|---------|------|------|------|------|------|-------|
| بِعْتُ | بِعْنا | بِعتَ | بِعتِ | بِعْتُما | بِعْتُم | بِعْتُنَّ | باعَ | باعَتْ | باعا | باعَتا | باعوا | بِعْنَ |
| أبِعُ | نَبيعُ | تَبيعُ | تَبيعينَ | تَبيعان | تَبيعونَ | تَبِعْنَ | يَبيعُ | تَبيعُ | يَبيعان | تَبيعان | يَبيعونَ | يَبِعْنَ |
| أبيعَ | نَبيعَ | تَبيعَ | تَبيعي | تَبيعا | تَبيعوا | تَبِعْنَ | يَبيعَ | تَبيعَ | يَبيعا | تَبيعا | يَبيعوا | يَبِعْنَ |
| أبِعْ | نَبِعْ | تَبِعْ | تَبيعي | تَبيعا | تَبيعوا | تَبِعْنَ | يَبِعْ | تَبِعْ | يَبيعا | تَبيعا | يَبيعوا | يَبِعْنَ |
| | | بِعْ | بيعي | بيعا | بيعوا | بِعْنَ | | | | | | |

نَمَّى (تَنمِيةٌ، مُنَمٍّ، مُنَمًّى)

| X | XI | VIII | VII | VI | V | IV | III | II |
|---|----|------|-----|----|----|----|-----|-----|
| -- | -- | انتَمى | -- | -- | -- | -- | -- | نَمَّى |

| أنا | نَحْنُ | أنتَ | أنتِ | أنتُما | أنتُمْ | أنتُنَّ | هُوَ | هِيَ | هُما | هُما | هُمْ | هُنَّ |
|-----|--------|------|------|--------|--------|---------|------|------|------|------|------|-------|
| نَمَّيْتُ | نَمَّيْنا | نَمَّيْتَ | نَمَّيْتِ | نَمَّيْتُما | نَمَّيْتُم | نَمَّيْتُنَّ | نَمَّى | نَمَّتْ | نَمَّيا | نَمَّتا | نَمَّوا | نَمَّيْنَ |
| أنَمّي | نُنَمّي | تُنَمّي | تُنَمّينَ | تُنَمِّيان | تُنَمّونَ | تُنَمِّيان | يُنَمّي | تُنَمّي | يُنَمِّيان | تُنَمِّيان | يُنَمّونَ | يُنَمِّينَ |
| أنَمِّيَ | نُنَمِّيَ | تُنَمِّيَ | تُنَمّي | تُنَمِّيا | تُنَمّوا | تُنَمِّينَ | يُنَمِّيَ | تُنَمِّيَ | يُنَمِّيا | تُنَمِّيا | يُنَمّوا | يُنَمِّينَ |
| أنَمِّ | نُنَمِّ | تُنَمِّ | تُنَمّي | تُنَمِّيا | تُنَمّوا | تُنَمِّينَ | يُنَمِّ | تُنَمِّ | يُنَمِّيا | تُنَمِّيا | يُنَمّوا | يُنَمِّينَ |
| | | نَمِّ | نَمّي | نَمِّيا | نَمّوا | نَمِّينَ | | | | | | |

## وفى (وَفَاءٌ، وافٍ، مَوفيٌّ)

| X | XI | VIII | VII | VI | V | IV | III | II |
|---|----|------|-----|----|---|----|-----|----|
| استَوْفى | -- | -- | -- | تَوافى | تَوَفّى | أوفى | وافى | -- |

| أنا | نَحْنُ | أنتَ | أنتِ | أنتُما | أنتُم | أنتُنَّ | هُوَ | هِيَ | هُما | هُما | هُم | هُنَّ |
|----|-------|------|------|--------|-------|---------|------|------|------|------|-----|-------|
| وَفَيْتُ | وَفَيْنا | وَفَيْتَ | وَفَيْتِ | وَفَيْتُما | وَفَيْتُم | وَفَيْتُنَّ | وَفى | وَفَتْ | وَفَيا | وَفَيَتا | وَفوا | وَفَيْنَ |
| أفي | نَفي | تَفي | تَفينَ | تَفِيان | تَفونَ | تَفينَ | يَفي | تَفي | يَفِيان | تَفِيان | يَفونَ | يَفينَ |
| أفيَ | نَفيَ | تَفيَ | تَفيِ | تَفِيا | تَفوا | تَفينَ | يَفيَ | تَفيَ | يَفِيا | تَفِيا | يَفوا | يَفينَ |
| أفِ | نَفِ | تَفِ | تَفي | تَفِيا | تَفوا | تَفينَ | يَفِ | تَفِ | يَفِيا | تَفِيا | يَفوا | يَفينَ |
| | | فِ | في | فِيا | فوا | فينَ | | | | | | |

## أكَلَ (أكلٌ، آكلٌ، مأكولٌ)

| X | XI | VIII | VII | VI | V | IV | III | II |
|---|----|------|-----|----|---|----|-----|----|
| استأكل | -- | -- | تَآكَلَ | -- | انأكَلَ | -- | آكَلَ | أكّلَ |

| أنا | نَحْنُ | أنتَ | أنتِ | أنتُما | أنتُم | أنتُنَّ | هُوَ | هِيَ | هُما | هُما | هُم | هُنَّ |
|----|-------|------|------|--------|-------|---------|------|------|------|------|-----|-------|
| أكَلْتُ | أكَلْنا | أكَلْتَ | أكَلْتِ | أكَلْتُما | أكَلْتُم | أكَلْتُنَّ | أكَلَ | أكَلَتْ | أكَلا | أكَلَتا | أكَلوا | أكَلْنَ |
| آكُلُ | نأكُلُ | تأكُلُ | تأكُلينَ | تأكُلان | تأكُلونَ | تأكُلْنَ | يأكُلُ | تأكُلُ | يأكُلان | تأكُلان | يأكُلونَ | يأكُلْنَ |
| آكُلَ | نأكُلَ | تأكُلَ | تأكُلي | تأكُلا | تأكُلوا | تأكُلْنَ | يأكُلَ | تأكُلَ | يأكُلا | تأكُلا | يأكُلوا | يأكُلْنَ |
| آكُلْ | نأكُلْ | تأكُلْ | تأكُلي | تأكُلا | تأكُلوا | تأكُلْنَ | يأكُلْ | تأكُلْ | يأكُلا | تأكُلا | يأكُلوا | يأكُلْنَ |
| | | كُلْ | كُلي | كُلا | كُلوا | كُلْنَ | | | | | | |

## سَأَلَ (سُؤالٌ، سائلٌ، مسؤولٌ)

| X | XI | VIII | VII | VI | V | IV | III | II |
|---|---|---|---|---|---|---|---|---|
| -- | -- | سا ءَلَ | -- | -- | تَسَوَّلَ | تَساءَلَ | انسأَلَ | -- | -- |

| أنا | نَحْنُ | أنتَ | أنتِ | أنتُما | أنتُنَّ | أنتُم | هُوَ | هِيَ | هُما | هُما | هُم | هُنَّ |
|---|---|---|---|---|---|---|---|---|---|---|---|---|
| سألتُ | سألنا | سألتَ | سألتِ | سألتُما | سألتُنَّ | سألتُم | سألَ | سألَتْ | سألا | سألَتا | سألوا | سألنَ |
| أسألَ | نسألَ | يسألَ | يسألَ | تسألان | تسألَ | تسألونَ | يسألَ | تسألَ | يسألان | تسألان | يسألونَ | يسألنَ |
| أسألَ | نسألَ | يسألَ | يسألَ | تسألا | تسألَ | تسألوا | يسألَ | تسألَ | يسألا | تسألا | يسألوا | يسألنَ |
| أسألْ | نسألْ | يسألْ | يسألْ | تسألا | تسألْ | تسألوا | يسألْ | تسألْ | يسألا | تسألا | يسألوا | يسألنَ |

| سَلْ | سَلي | سَلا | سَلوا | سَلنَ |
|---|---|---|---|---|

OR

| اسألْ | اسألي | اسألا | اسألوا | اسألنَ |
|---|---|---|---|---|

## بَدَأَ (بَدءٌ، بادئٌ، مَبْدوءٌ)

| X | XI | VIII | VII | VI | V | IV | III | II |
|---|---|---|---|---|---|---|---|---|
| -- | -- | ابتَدَأَ | -- | -- | -- | أبدَأَ | بادَأَ | -- |

| أنا | نَحْنُ | أنتَ | أنتِ | أنتُما | أنتُنَّ | أنتُم | هُوَ | هِيَ | هُما | هُما | هُم | هُنَّ |
|---|---|---|---|---|---|---|---|---|---|---|---|---|
| بَدَأتُ | بدأنا | بَدَأتَ | بَدَأتِ | بَدَأتُما | بَدَأتُنَّ | بَدَأتُم | بَدَأ | بَدَأتْ | بَدَأا | بَدَأتا | بَدَأوا | بَدَأنَ |
| أبدأ | نبدأ | يبدأ | يبدأ | تبدأان | تبدأنَ | تبدأونَ | يبدأ | تبدأ | يبدأان | تبدأان | يبدأونَ | يبدأنَ |
| أبدأ | نبدأ | يبدأ | يبدأ | تبدأا | تبدأنَ | تبدأوا | يبدأ | تبدأ | يبدأا | تبدأا | يبدأوا | يبدأنَ |
| أبدأ | نبدأ | يبدأ | يبدأ | تبدأا | تبدأنَ | تبدأوا | يبدأ | تبدأ | يبدأا | تبدأا | يبدأوا | يبدأنَ |

| ابدأ | ابدأي | ابدأا | ابدأوا | ابدأنَ |
|---|---|---|---|---|

## رأى (رُؤْيَةٌ، راءٍ، مَرْئِيٌّ)

| X | XI | VIII | VII | VI | V | IV | III | II |
|---|----|------|-----|----|----|----|-----|----|
| -- | -- | -- | -- | تَراءى | -- | أرى | راءى | -- |

| هُنَّ | هُم | هُما | هُما | هِيَ | هُوَ | أنْتُنَّ | أنْتُم | أنْتُما | أنتِ | أنْتَ | أنا | نَحْنُ | أنا |
|------|-----|------|------|------|------|---------|--------|---------|------|-------|------|--------|------|
| رَأَيْنَ | رَأوا | رَأَيْتا | رَأيا | رَأتْ | رأى | رَأيْتُنَّ | رَأيْتُم | رَأيْتُما | رَأيتِ | رَأيتَ | رَأيتُ | رَأينا | رَأيتُ |
| يَرَيْنَ | يَرَوْنَ | تَرَيان | يَرَيان | تَرى | يرى | تَرَيْنَ | تَرَوْنَ | تَرَيان | تَرين | تَرى | أرى | نرى | أرى |
| يَرَيْنَ | يَرَوْا | تَرَيا | يَرَيا | تَرى | يرى | تَرَيْنَ | تَرَوْا | تَرَيا | تَرَي | تَرى | أرى | نرى | أرى |
| يَرَيْنَ | يَرَوْا | تَرَيا | يَرَيا | تَرَ | يَرَ | تَرَيْنَ | تَرَوْا | تَرَيا | تَرَي | تَرَ | أرَ | نرَ | أرَ |

## جَرَّ (جَرٌّ، جارٌّ، مَجْرورٌ)

| X | XI | VIII | VII | VI | V | IV | III | II |
|---|----|------|-----|----|----|----|-----|----|
| -- | -- | اجْتَرَّ | انْجَرَّ | -- | -- | -- | -- | جَرَّ |

| هُنَّ | هُم | هُما | هُما | هِيَ | هُوَ | أنْتُنَّ | أنْتُم | أنْتُما | أنتِ | أنْتَ | أنا | نَحْنُ | أنا |
|------|-----|------|------|------|------|---------|--------|---------|------|-------|------|--------|------|
| جَرَرْنَ | جَرّوا | جَرَّتا | جَرّا | جَرَّتْ | جَرَّ | جَرَرْتُنَّ | جَرَرْتُم | جَرَرْتُما | جَرَرْتِ | جَرَرْتَ | جَرَرْتُ | جَرَرْنا | جَرَرْتُ |
| يَجْرُرْنَ | يَجْرُونَ | تَجُرّان | يَجُرّان | تَجُرُّ | يَجُرُّ | تَجْرُرْنَ | تَجُرّونَ | تَجُرّان | تَجُرّينَ | تَجُرُّ | أجُرُّ | نَجُرُّ | أجُرُّ |
| يَجْرُرْنَ | يَجُرّوا | تَجُرّا | يَجُرّا | تَجُرَّ | يَجُرَّ | تَجْرُرْنَ | تَجُرّوا | تَجُرّا | تَجُرّي | تَجُرَّ | أجُرَّ | نَجُرَّ | أجُرَّ |
| يَجْرُرْنَ | يَجُرّوا | تَجُرّا | يَجُرّا | تَجُرَّ | يَجُرَّ | تَجْرُرْنَ | تَجُرّوا | تَجُرّا | تَجُرّي | تَجُرَّ | أجُرَّ | نَجُرَّ | أجُرَّ |
| اجْرُرْنَ | جُرّوا | | جُرّا | | جُرَّ | جُرّي | | | | | | | |

دافَعَ (مُدافَعَةٌ، مُدافِعٌ، مُدافَعٌ)

| X | XI | VIII | VII | VI | V | IV | III | II |
|---|---|---|---|---|---|---|---|---|
| دُفِعَ | دافَعَ | -- | -- | تَدافَعَ | اندَفَعَ | -- | -- | -- |

| Imperative | Jussive | Subjunctive | Indicative | Perfect | Pronoun |
|---|---|---|---|---|---|
| | أُدافِعْ | أُدافِعَ | أُدافِعُ | دافَعْتُ | أنا |
| | نُدافِعْ | نُدافِعَ | نُدافِعُ | دافَعْنا | نَحْنُ |
| دافِعْ | تُدافِعْ | تُدافِعَ | تُدافِعُ | دافَعْتَ | أنتَ |
| دافِعي | تُدافِعي | تُدافِعي | تُدافِعينَ | دافَعْت | أنتِ |
| دافِعا | تُدافِعا | تُدافِعا | تُدافِعان | دافَعْتُما | أنتُما |
| دافِعوا | تُدافِعوا | تُدافِعوا | تُدافِعونَ | دافَعْتُم | أنتُم |
| دافِعْنَ | تُدافِعْنَ | تُدافِعْنَ | تُدافِعْنَ | دافَعْتُنَّ | أنتُنَّ |
| | يُدافِعْ | يُدافِعَ | يُدافِعُ | دافَعَ | هُوَ |
| | تُدافِعْ | تُدافِعَ | تُدافِعُ | دافَعَتْ | هِيَ |
| | يُدافِعا | يُدافِعا | يُدافِعان | دافَعا | هُما |
| | تُدافِعا | تُدافِعا | تُدافِعان | دافَعَتا | هُما |
| | يُدافِعوا | يُدافِعوا | يُدافِعونَ | دافَعوا | هُم |
| | يُدافِعْنَ | يُدافِعْنَ | يُدافِعْنَ | دافَعْنَ | هُنَّ |

أَخْرَجَ (إِخْرَاجٌ، مُخْرِجٌ، مُخْرَجٌ)

| X | XI | VIII | VII | VI | V | IV | III | II |
|---|----|------|-----|----|----|----|-----|-----|
| اسْتَخْرَجَ | -- | -- | انخَرَجَ | تَخَارَجَ | تَخَرَّجَ | أخْرَجَ | -- | خَرَّجَ |

| Imperative | Jussive | Subjunctive | Indicative | Perfect | Pronoun |
|------------|---------|-------------|------------|---------|---------|
| | أُخْرِجْ | أُخْرِجَ | أُخْرِجُ | أخْرَجْتُ | أنا |
| | نُخْرِجْ | نُخْرِجَ | نُخْرِجُ | أخْرَجْنا | نَحْنُ |
| أخْرِجْ | تُخْرِجْ | تُخْرِجَ | تُخْرِجُ | أخْرَجْتَ | أنتَ |
| أخْرِجي | تُخْرِجي | تُخْرِجي | تُخْرِجينَ | أخْرَجْتِ | أنتِ |
| أخْرِجا | تُخْرِجا | تُخْرِجا | تُخْرِجانِ | أخْرَجْتُما | أنتُما |
| أخْرِجوا | تُخْرِجوا | تُخْرِجوا | تُخْرِجونَ | أخْرَجْتُم | أنتُم |
| أخْرِجْنَ | تُخْرِجْنَ | تُخْرِجْنَ | تُخْرِجْنَ | أخْرَجْتُنَّ | أنتُنَّ |
| | يُخْرِجْ | يُخْرِجَ | يُخْرِجُ | أخْرَجَ | هُوَ |
| | تُخْرِجْ | تُخْرِجَ | تُخْرِجُ | أخْرَجَتْ | هِيَ |
| | يُخْرِجا | يُخْرِجا | يُخْرِجانِ | أخْرَجا | هُما |
| | تُخْرِجا | تُخْرِجا | تُخْرِجانِ | أخْرَجَتا | هُما |
| | يُخْرِجوا | يُخْرِجوا | يُخْرِجونَ | أخْرَجوا | هُم |
| | يُخْرِجْنَ | يُخْرِجْنَ | يُخْرِجْنَ | أخْرَجْنَ | هُنَّ |

تَزَوَّدَ (تَزَوُّدٌ، مُتَزَوِّدٌ، مُتَزَوَّدٌ)

| X | XI | VIII | VII | VI | V | IV | III | II |
|---|----|------|-----|-----|-----|-----|-----|-----|
| استَزوَدَ | -- | -- | -- | -- | تَزَوَّدَ | -- | زاوَدَ | زَوَّدَ |

| Imperative | Jussive | Subjunctive | Indicative | Perfect | Pronoun |
|-----------|---------|-------------|------------|---------|---------|
|  | أتَزَوَّدْ | أتَزَوَّدَ | أتَزَوَّدُ | تَزَوَّدْتُ | أنا |
|  | نتَزَوَّدْ | نتَزَوَّدَ | نتَزَوَّدُ | تَزَوَّدْنا | نَحْنُ |
| تَزَوَّدْ | تتَزَوَّدْ | تتَزَوَّدَ | تتَزَوَّدُ | تَزَوَّدْتَ | أنتَ |
| تتَزَوَّدي | تتَزَوَّدي | تتَزَوَّدي | تتَزَوَّدينَ | تَزَوَّدْتِ | أنتِ |
| تَزَوَّدا | تتَزَوَّدا | تتَزَوَّدا | تتَزَوَّدانِ | تَزَوَّدْتُما | أنتُما |
| تَزَوَّدوا | تتَزَوَّدوا | تتَزَوَّدوا | تتَزَوَّدونَ | تَزَوَّدْتُم | أنتُم |
| تَزَوَّدْنَ | تتَزَوَّدْنَ | تتَزَوَّدْنَ | تتَزَوَّدْنَ | تَزَوَّدْتُنَّ | أنتُنَّ |
|  | يتَزَوَّدْ | يتَزَوَّدَ | يتَزَوَّدُ | تَزَوَّدَ | هُوَ |
|  | تتَزَوَّدْ | تتَزَوَّدَ | تتَزَوَّدُ | تَزَوَّدْت | هِيَ |
|  | يتَزَوَّدا | يتَزَوَّدا | يتَزَوَّدانِ | تَزَوَّدا | هُما |
|  | تتَزَوَّدا | تتَزَوَّدا | تتَزَوَّدانِ | تَزَوَّدَتا | هُما |
|  | يتَزَوَّدوا | يتَزَوَّدوا | يتَزَوَّدونَ | تَزَوَّدوا | هُم |
|  | يتَزَوَّدْنَ | يتَزَوَّدْنَ | يتَزَوَّدْنَ | تَزَوَّدْنَ | هُنَّ |

تَصافَحَ (تَصافُحٌ، مُتَصافِحٌ، مُتَصافَحٌ)

X   XI   VIII   VII   VI   V   IV   III   II

صَفَحَ  صافَحَ  --تَصَفَّحَ  تَصافَحَ  --  --  اسْتَصْفَحَ

| Imperative | Jussive | Subjunctive | Indicative | Perfect | Pronoun |
|---|---|---|---|---|---|
| | أَتَصافَحْ | أَتَصافَحَ | أَتَصافَحُ | تَصافَحْتُ | أنا |
| | نَتَصافَحْ | نَتَصافَحَ | نَتَصافَحُ | تَصافَحْنا | نَحْنُ |
| تَصافَحْ | تَتَصافَحْ | تَتَصافَحَ | تَتَصافَحُ | تَصافَحْتَ | أنتَ |
| تَصافَحي | تَتَصافَحي | تَتَصافَحي | تَتَصافَحينَ | تَصافَحْتِ | أنتِ |
| تَصافَحا | تَتَصافَحا | تَتَصافَحا | تَتَصافَحانِ | تَصافَحْتُما | أنتُما |
| تَصافَحوا | تَتَصافَحوا | تَتَصافَحوا | تَتَصافَحونَ | تَصافَحْتُم | أنتُم |
| تَصافَحْنَ | تَتَصافَحْنَ | تَتَصافَحْنَ | تَتَصافَحْنَ | تَصافَحْتُنَّ | أنتُنَّ |
| | يَتَصافَحْ | يَتَصافَحَ | يَتَصافَحُ | تَصافَحَ | هُوَ |
| | تَتَصافَحْ | تَتَصافَحَ | تَتَصافَحُ | تَصافَحَتْ | هِيَ |
| | يَتَصافَحا | يَتَصافَحا | يَتَصافَحانِ | تَصافَحا | هُما |
| | تَتَصافَحا | تَتَصافَحا | تَتَصافَحانِ | تَصافَحَتا | هُما |
| | يَتَصافَحوا | يَتَصافَحوا | يَتَصافَحونَ | تَصافَحوا | هُم |
| | يَتَصافَحْنَ | يَتَصافَحْنَ | يَتَصافَحْنَ | تَصافَحْنَ | هُنَّ |

333

انْجَذَبَ (انْجِذابٌ، مُنْجَذِبٌ، مُنْجَذَبٌ)

X XI VIII VII VI V IV III II

-- جاذَبَ -- -- تَجاذَبَ انْجَذَبَ اجْتَذَبَ -- --

| Imperative | Jussive | Subjunctive | Indicative | Perfect | Pronoun |
|---|---|---|---|---|---|
| | أنْجَذِبْ | أنْجَذِبَ | أنْجَذِبُ | انْجَذَبْتُ | أنا |
| | نَنْجَذِبْ | نَنْجَذِبَ | نَنْجَذِبُ | انْجَذَبْنا | نَحْنُ |
| انْجَذِبْ | تَنْجَذِبْ | تَنْجَذِبَ | تَنْجَذِبُ | انْجَذَبْتَ | أنتَ |
| انْجَذِبي | تَنْجَذِبي | تَنْجَذِبي | تَنْجَذِبينَ | انْجَذَبْتِ | أنتِ |
| انْجَذِبا | تَنْجَذِبا | تَنْجَذِبا | تَنْجَذِبان | انْجَذَبْتُما | أنتُما |
| انْجَذِبوا | تَنْجَذِبوا | تَنْجَذِبوا | تَنْجَذِبونَ | انْجَذَبْتُم | أنْتُم |
| انْجَذِبْنَ | تَنْجَذِبْنَ | تَنْجَذِبْنَ | تَنْجَذِبْنَ | انْجَذَبْتُنَّ | أنْتُنَّ |
| | يَنْجَذِبْ | يَنْجَذِبَ | يَنْجَذِبُ | انْجَذَبَ | هُوَ |
| | تَنْجَذِبْ | تَنْجَذِبَ | تَنْجَذِبُ | انْجَذَبَتْ | هِيَ |
| | يَنْجَذِبا | يَنْجَذِبا | يَنْجَذِبان | انْجَذَبا | هُما |
| | تَنْجَذِبا | تَنْجَذِبا | تَنْجَذِبانَ | انْجَذَبَتا | هُما |
| | يَنْجَذِبوا | يَنْجَذِبوا | يَنْجَذِبونَ | انْجَذَبوا | هُم |
| | يَنْجَذِبْنَ | يَنْجَذِبْنَ | يَنْجَذِبْنَ | انْجَذَبْنَ | هُنَّ |

334

اشْتَرى (اشْتِراءُ، مُشْتَرٍ، مَشْتَرىً)

X XI VIII VII VI V IV III II

-- شَرَّى -- -- -- -- اشْتَرى -- استَشْرى

| Imperative | Jussive | Subjunctive | Indicative | Perfect | Pronoun |
|---|---|---|---|---|---|
| | أَشْتَرِ | أَشْتَرِيَ | أَشْتَري | اشْتَرَيْتُ | أنا |
| | نَشْتَرِ | نَشْتَرِيَ | نَشْتَري | اشْتَرَينا | نَحْنُ |
| اشْتَرِ | تَشْتَرِ | تَشْتَرِيَ | تَشْتَري | اشْتَرَيْتَ | أنتَ |
| اشْتَرِي | تَشْتَرِي | تَشْتَرِي | تَشْتَرِينَ | اشْتَرَيْت | أنتِ |
| اشْتَرِيا | تَشْتَرِيا | تَشْتَرِيا | تَشْتَرِيان | اشْتَرَيْتُما | أنتُما |
| اشْتَروا | تَشْتَروا | تَشْتَروا | تَشْتَرونَ | اشْتَرَيتُم | أنتُم |
| اشْتَرينَ | تَشْتَرينَ | تَشْتَرينَ | تَشْتَرينَ | اشْتَرَيتُنَّ | أنتُنَّ |
| | يَشْتَرِ | يَشْتَرِيَ | يَشْتَري | اشْتَرى | هُوَ |
| | تَشْتَرِ | تَشْتَرِيَ | تَشْتَري | اشْتَرَتْ | هِيَ |
| | يَشْتَرِيا | يَشْتَرِيا | يَشْتَرِيان | اشْتَرَيا | هُما |
| | تَشْتَرِيا | تَشْتَرِيا | تَشْتَرِيان | اشْتَرَيتا | هُما |
| | يَشْتَروا | يَشْتَروا | يَشْتَرونَ | اشْتَروا | هُم |
| | يَشْتَرينَ | يَشْتَرينَ | يَشْتَرينَ | اشْتَرينَ | هُنَّ |

احْمَرَّ (احْمِرار، مُحْمَرٌّ، --)

| X | XI | VIII | VII | VI | V | IV | III | II |
|---|----|------|-----|----|----|----|-----|----|
| حَمَّرَ | -- | -- | تَحَمَّرَ | -- | -- | احْمَرَّ | -- | |

| Imperative | Jussive | Subjunctive | Indicative | Perfect | Pronoun |
|---|---|---|---|---|---|
| | أحْمَرَّ | أحْمَرَّ | أحْمَرُّ | احْمَرَرْتُ | أنا |
| | نَحْمَرَّ | نَحْمَرَّ | نَحْمَرُّ | احْمَرَرْنا | نَحْنُ |
| احْمَرَّ | تَحْمَرَّ | تَحْمَرَّ | تَحْمَرُّ | احْمَرَرْتَ | أنتَ |
| احْمَرِّي | تَحْمَرِّي | تَحْمَرِّي | تَحْمَرِّينَ | احْمَرَرْتِ | أنتِ |
| احْمَرّا | تَحْمَرّا | تَحْمَرّا | تَحْمَرّانِ | احْمَرَرْتُما | أنتُما |
| احْمَرّوا | تَحْمَرّوا | تَحْمَرّوا | تَحْمَرّونَ | احْمَرَرْتُم | أنتُم |
| احْمَرِرْنَ | تَحْمَرِرْنَ | تَحْمَرِرْنَ | تَحْمَرِرْنَ | احْمَرَرْتُنَّ | أنتُنَّ |
| | يَحْمَرَّ | يَحْمَرَّ | يَحْمَرُّ | احْمَرَّ | هُوَ |
| | تَحْمَرَّ | تَحْمَرَّ | تَحْمَرُّ | احْمَرَّتْ | هِيَ |
| | يَحْمَرّا | يَحْمَرّا | يَحْمَرّانِ | احْمَرّا | هُما |
| | تَحْمَرّا | تَحْمَرّا | تَحْمَرّانِ | احْمَرَّتا | هُما |
| | يَحْمَرّوا | يَحْمَرّوا | يَحْمَرّونَ | احْمَرّوا | هُم |
| | يَحْمَرِرْنَ | يَحْمَرِرْنَ | يَحْمَرِرْنَ | احْمَرَرْنَ | هُنَّ |

استَوْلى (استيلاءً، مُسْتَوْلٍ، مُسْتَوْلىً)

X  XI  VIII  VII  VI  V  IV  III  II

ولّى  والى  أولى  تَوَلّى  تَوالى  --  --  استَوْلى

| Imperative | Jussive | Subjunctive | Indicative | Perfect | Pronoun |
|---|---|---|---|---|---|
|  | أسْتَوْلِ | أسْتَوْليَ | أسْتَوْلي | استَوْلَيْتُ | أنا |
|  | نَسْتَوْلِ | نَسْتَوْليَ | نَسْتَوْلي | استَوْلَيْنا | نَحْنُ |
| اسْتَوْلِ | تَسْتَوْلِ | تَسْتَوْليَ | تَسْتَوْلي | استَوْلَيْتَ | أنتَ |
| اسْتَوْلي | تَسْتَوْلي | تَسْتَوْلي | تَسْتَوْلينَ | استَوْلَيْتِ | أنتِ |
| اسْتَوْليا | تَسْتَوْليا | تَسْتَوْليا | تَسْتَوْليان | استَوْلَيْتُما | أنتُما |
| اسْتَوْلوا | تَسْتَوْلوا | تَسْتَوْلوا | تَسْتَوْلونَ | استَوْلَيْتُم | أنتُم |
| اسْتَوْلينَ | تَسْتَوْلينَ | تَسْتَوْلينَ | تَسْتَوْلينَ | استَوْلَيْتُنَّ | أنتُنَّ |
|  | يَسْتَوْلِ | يَسْتَوْليَ | يَسْتَوْلي | استَوْلى | هُوَ |
|  | تَسْتَوْلِ | تَسْتَوْليَ | تَسْتَوْلي | استَوْلَتْ | هِيَ |
|  | يَسْتَوْليا | يَسْتَوْليا | يَسْتَوْليان | استَوْليا | هُما |
|  | تَسْتَوْليا | تَسْتَوْليا | تَسْتَوْليان | استَوْلَيَتا | هُما |
|  | يَسْتَوْلوا | يَسْتَوْلوا | يَسْتَوْلونَ | استَوْلوا | هُم |
|  | يَسْتَوْلينَ | يَسْتَوْلينَ | يَسْتَوْلينَ | استَوْلَيْنَ | هُنَّ |

# Appendix 4

## Conjugations of Forms I-X with Derived Nouns

## تصريف الأوزان العشرة مع المشتقات من الأسماء

| Derived Nouns | | | | | Passive | | Active | | |
|---|---|---|---|---|---|---|---|---|---|
| TP | PP | AP | VN | Imp. | Imper. | Per. | Imper. | Per. | Form |
| زمان/مكان | المفعول | الفاعل | المصدر | الأمر | المضارع | الماضي | المضارع | الماضي | الوزن |
| مَفْعَل | مَفعول | فاعِل | فَعْل، فِعالة | اِفْعَلْ | يُفْعَل | فُعِلَ | يَفْعَلُ | فَعَلَ | I |
| -- | مُفَعَّل | مُفَعِّل | تَفعيل | فَعِّلْ | يُفَعَّل | فُعِّلَ | يُفَعِّلُ | فَعَّلَ | II |
| -- | مُفاعَل | مُفاعِل | مُفاعَلة، فِعال | فاعِلْ | يُفاعَل | فوعِلَ | يُفاعِلُ | فاعَلَ | III |
| -- | مُفْعَل | مُفْعِل | إفعال | أفْعِلْ | يُفْعَل | أفْعِلَ | يُفْعِلُ | أفْعَلَ | IV |
| -- | مُتَفَعَّل | مُتَفَعِّل | تَفَعُّل | تَفَعَّلْ | -- | -- | يَتَفَعَّلُ | تَفَعَّلَ | V |
| -- | مُتَفاعَل | مُتَفاعِل | تَفاعُل | تَفاعَلْ | يُتَفاعَل | تُفوعِلَ | يَتَفاعَلُ | تَفاعَلَ | VI |
| مُنْفَعَل | مُنْفَعَل | مُنْفَعِل | إنْفِعال | إنْفَعِلْ | -- | -- | يَنْفَعِلُ | إنْفَعَلَ | VII |
| مُفْتَعَل | مُفْتَعَل | مُفْتَعِل | إفْتِعال | إفْتَعِلْ | يُفْتَعَل | إفْتُعِلَ | يَفْتَعِلُ | إفْتَعَلَ | VIII |
| -- | -- | مُفْعَلّ | إفْعِلال | إفْعَلَّ | -- | -- | يَفْعَلُّ | إفْعَلَّ | IX |
| مُسْتَفْعَل | مُسْتَفْعَل | مُسْتَفْعِل | إسْتِفْعال | إسْتَفْعِلْ | يُسْتَفْعَل | إسْتُفْعِلَ | يَسْتَفْعِلُ | إسْتَفْعَلَ | X |

Legend: Per.=Perfect; Imper.=Imperfect; Imp.=Imparative; VN=Verbal Noun; AP=Active Participle; PP=Passive Participle; TP=Nouns of Time and Place